The Financial Times Guide to Business Coaching

FT Prentice Hall
FINANCIAL TIMES

In an increasingly competitive world, we believe it's quality of
thinking that gives you the edge – an idea that opens new
doors, a technique that solves a problem, or an insight that
simply makes sense of it all. The more you know, the smarter and
faster you can go.

That's why we work with the best minds in business and finance
to bring cutting-edge thinking and best learning practice to a
global market.

Under a range of leading imprints, including *Financial Times
Prentice Hall*, we create world-class print publications and
electronic products bringing our readers knowledge, skills and
understanding, which can be applied whether studying or at work.

To find out more about Pearson Education publications, or tell us
about the books you'd like to find, you can visit us at
www.pearsoned.co.uk

The Financial Times Guide to Business Coaching

Anne Scoular

**Financial Times
Prentice Hall
is an imprint of**

Harlow, England • London • New York • Boston • San Francisco • Toronto • Sydney • Singapore • Hong Kong
Tokyo • Seoul • Taipei • New Delhi • Cape Town • Madrid • Mexico City • Amsterdam • Munich • Paris • Milan

PEARSON EDUCATION LIMITED

Edinburgh Gate
Harlow CM20 2JE
Tel: +44 (0)1279 623623
Fax: +44 (0)1279 431059
Website: www.pearsoned.co.uk

First published in Great Britain in 2011

ISBN: 978-0-273-73444-4

® OPP is a registered trademark of OPP Ltd.
® MBTI, Myers–Briggs Type Indicator and Myers–Briggs are registered trademarks of the
Myers–Briggs Type Indicator Trust. OPP Ltd is licensed to use the trademarks in Europe.
® FIRO-B is a registered trademark of CPP, Inc. OPP Ltd is licensed to use the trademark
in Europe.

British Library Cataloguing-in-Publication Data
A catalogue record for this book is available from the British Library

Library of Congress Cataloging-in-Publication Data
Scoular, Anne.
    The Financial Times guide to business coaching / Anne Scoular. – – 1st
ed.
        p. cm
    Includes bibliographical references and index.
    ISBN 978–0–273–73444–4 (pbk.)
    1. Executive coaching. 2. Executives – – Training of. 3. Leadership– –
Study and teaching. I. Title. II. Title: Guide to business coaching.
III. Title: Business coaching.
    HD30.4.S426 2011
    658.4'07124 – – dc22
                                        2010046592

10 9 8 7 6 5 4 3 2 1
15 14 13 12 11

Typeset in 9pt Stone Serif by 30
Printed and bound in Great Britain by Ashford Colour Press Ltd, Gosport, Hampshire

For Pam and Denys, and
for Daniel

Contents

Publisher's acknowledgements

We are grateful to the following for permission to reproduce copyright material:

Figures

Figure 6.1 from Carol Kauffman; Figure 7.1 adapted from *Group Processes: An Introduction to Group Dynamics*, National Press Books (Luft, J. 1970); Figure 7.2 from Get Feedback, www.getfeedback.net; Figure 9.1 from Interpreting the Demographic Changes, *Philosophical Transaction of the Royal Society B*, 1805–09 (Laslett, P. 1997), The Royal Society; Figure 10.1 from An integrative model of work attitudes, motivation and performance, *Human Performance*, 3, 65–85 (Katzell, R. and Thompson, D. 1990), Lawrence Erlbaum Associated, Inc. (Taylor & Francis Group); Figure 10.2 from Self-determination Theory and the Facilitation of Intrinsic Motivation, Social Development and Well-being, *American Psychologist*, 55, 68–78 (Ryan, R.M. and Deci, E.L. 2000), APA, reprinted with permission; Figure 11.1 from *The Evidence-based Coaching Handbook*, John Wiley & Sons (Stober, D.R. and Grant, A.M. 2006) 369, John Wiley & Sons; Figures 12.1, 12.2, 12.3, 12.4, 12.5 from Meyler Campbell.

Tables

Tables 4.1, 4.2 from Meyler Campbell; Table 11.1 from Cultural variation of leadership prototypes across 22 European countries, *Journal of Occupational and Organisational Psychology*, 73, 1–29 (Brodbeck, F.C. *et al.*, 2000), The British Psychological Society, Reproduced with permission from the British Journal of Psychology, © The British Psychological Society.

Text

Page 92 adapted from *Working Identity*, Harvard Business School Press (Ibarra, H. 2004) 167–70; page 95 from Carol Kauffman; Quote on page 122 from Consulting at the top, *Consulting Psychology Journal*, 48, 61–66 (Keil, F., Rimmer, E., Williams, D. and Doyle, M 1996), APA, reprinted with permission; page 137 from *Time to Think: Listening to ignite the human mind*, Cassell (Kline, N. 1999).

In some instances we have been unable to trace the owners of copyright material, and we would appreciate any information that would enable us to do so.

1

Introduction: the business of coaching

Good business coaching is so powerful that if it was a drug, it would be illegal. A client walks into a coaching session stressed, overburdened, ready to give up – and an hour later emerges transformed: clear, focused, calmer, fit again to fight and win.

Coaching this good looks like magic – but it's actually about consistent and disciplined application of the right tools at the right time. This book is about how to become that almost-magician, whether as part of your 'day job' or as an external coach.

First, though, this chapter gives you an overview of the field. It describes the market, the players, the numbers, where people use coaching – and when they shouldn't. Then Chapter 2 describes the plethora of ways people earn a living with it. Or you might like to hop straight to Chapter 3, 'Do you have what it takes?'. Or even plunge right into Chapter 4, 'Developing your coaching: first steps'.

Market size and growth

Still here? Great!

In 2003 *The Economist* magazine estimated the coaching market was worth $1 billion worldwide, and in the fast-growth stage of doubling within 24 months.[1] It did indeed power ahead through the boom years. Then the credit crunch hit – but astonishingly, while organisations crashed and whole economies quaked, business coaching has been largely unaffected. While some external coaches' business plunged temporarily, most recovered quickly and many others reported it as their busiest time ever. Even where bulk programmes were cut, senior executives clung determinedly to their own coach, and found funding for it from ever more creative corners of the budget.

The data from the major surveys back this up. Meyler Campbell's Business of Coaching Surveys in 2008 and 2009; Sherpa Coaching's in 2005–09; *Harvard Business Review's* Special Report in January 2009; EFMD's in March 2009; and the biggest of them all, the Frank Bresser Consulting Survey 2008/09 covering 162 countries all around the world, all showed remarkably similar results.[2] Overall, business coaching has scarcely missed a beat, with coach earnings down overall by just 8% in the USA (Sherpa), but holding at the same level or even increasing in Europe. This doesn't mean coaching within organisations, and individual external coaches, haven't been cut back: many have, particularly programmes targeted at more junior staff, and many individual coaches have exited the market or suffered a setback. (For the difference between the coaches who flourished and those who didn't, see Chapter 12.) Where the long-predicted shake-out in the market does seem to have happened is in 'life coaching', which has experienced a 'precipitous' (Sherpa) drop in earnings of up to 40% in some sectors. The same survey found an equally brutal flight to quality in coach training courses: in four years, the number of coaches whose training was from telephone-only programmes, dropped from 38% of the market to only 5% (www.sherpacoaching.com).

As budgets have come under pressure, organisations may not have cut overall, but they have certainly been more selective about who gets coached, with 73% of coaching spend now directed at senior management to executive levels, up from 62% in 2007 (Sherpa). As coaching is focused on more senior clients, so senior coaches capable of working with them are actually in increased demand and the earnings of the elite coaches continue to hold up, and even rise. Both the Meyler Campbell and the Sherpa studies cited found top-level coach earnings holding or increasing.

Yet all this is happening while the supply of well-qualified business coaches also continues to go up. Note, both supply *and* price are rising: business coaching is for the moment defying basic economics.

And not just ordinary supply: a feature of the surge in business coaching that fascinates me is the extraordinary calibre of the business people retraining to become business coaches, whether to enhance their leadership capability in-house, or to add to their portfolio career externally. Within just our own Meyler Campbell alumni community, which is very small, there are two winners of the highest prize for human resources

(HR) in the United Kingdom; the International President of the Chartered Institute of Transport and Logistics; several London Business School Professors; the co-founder of Brazil's top coaching business; the entrepreneur behind Monster.com; senior leaders from all five of the law's 'Magic Circle' and all the leading global management consultancies...

Causes of market growth

What *is* driving all this?!

In economic terms, it can only mean demand continues to exceed supply – there remains in my view a vast unmet need. But there's more.

Let's zoom down to the individual human level. My Mother didn't need a coach. She lived in the same house from marriage to death, had a single clear role which she filled capably and confidently, and a strong network of the same friends and confidants all her life. News arrived via a solitary daily paper and the radio; over half her life was lived before there was a television in the house. I on the other hand am now on my third career, plus hiccups and byways en route. I have worked, counting brief business visits, in over 40 countries, and along with time zones, languages, retrainings and accreditations, new colleagues, new tasks, have always had multiple roles – team member, boss, subordinate, leader, finding something to thaw for dinner. And my world is crowded with emails, BlackBerries, people coming in from other time zones, the news, the bustle. It's exhausting but it's fun and stimulating.

That level of stimulation is the point. Compared with only one generation ago, the level of *cognitive load* (i.e. the amount of incoming data we need to process) has multiplied hugely. But my brain hasn't – so coaching is for me and many others, the equivalent of plugging in some extra processing capacity. With a great coach, it's like plugging into the National Grid – a surge of energy and clear focus that recharges the batteries and hauls me back up to peak form.

Back up at the system level, there are many other drivers, some of them cumulative over more than one generation. They include:

■ *Job leaps*. The fashion for stripping out layers of management has left surviving managers with much greater leaps between job levels. And when they arrive up there they're surrounded by people so pressed with their own targets they have little time to help.

■ *Time stretch*. The 40-hour working week may still be a reality elsewhere, but many in business have clocked those hours by Wednesday, and it doesn't end on Friday either.

■ *Space stretch.* To be up to date I need to be alert to what's happening in my field on three continents. I can't of course, but technology gives the illusion it's possible, so I need to struggle on trying.

■ *Time shrink.* Though our working days are longer, and work corrodes rest and holidays, the time horizons for delivery of results is much shorter. When asked his view on the French Revolution, Chinese Premier Zhou Enlai is alleged to have replied gravely, 'It's too early to tell'. Now firms' performance is measured in quarter-years, and average time in post for CEOs is shrinking fast.

■ *Fragmented support structures.* Few of the people working in the City of London, or any of the other great world intellectual, political or financial centres, were actually born there, so family, school and college friends can be far off. Increasing numbers have never or are no longer married.[3] Solo parenting is common, and the number of people living entirely alone is so high it's affecting the housing supply. Our increasing isolation is endemic, significant, and concerning policy-makers: see Robert Putnam's data-rich yet compelling book, *Bowling Alone.*[4]

■ *New pressures.* Senior executives need to juggle not just shareholder return, but now corporate social responsibility (CSR), political correctness, environmental awareness – while performing in a media spotlight of increasingly savage intensity; think BP's Tony Hayward and the 2010 oil spill. And after almost 600 years of business as we know it in Europe, bad luck, you're in just the first or second generation where there's no one at home to do the laundry: your partner's working too, so don't forget to pick up the dry cleaning on the way home.

Is this just whining? As Alex Linley points out[5] the last 50 years have been the most blessed that humankind has ever experienced in its whole history of this planet: no world war, several distressing diseases beaten for the first time, more people than ever before with enough to eat, and unparalleled profusion of consumer goods.

He's right, of course. But that very abundance means choice, so I come back to arguing: the single biggest reason for the explosion of coaching, is it helps us deal with cognitive (over)load.

What coaching tackles

If you haven't experienced coaching yourself, what might you expect? We'll say more shortly, but as a 'starter pack':

- The coach should quickly put you at your ease, then help you clarify what precisely you would like to get from the session.

- They then help you marshall ideas, solutions, and plans quite quickly, by serving as a sounding board for you to try out your thinking; providing space to reflect; and challenging where appropriate.

- Typical topics which people often sort out through business coaching include prioritising the use of time, managing key relationships, building the right team and using it well, building confidence, raising self-awareness, and understanding and improving one's impact.

- And it's often energising, thought-provoking, liberating, inspiring.

The limits of coaching

But before we all get too excited, coaching is not a panacea. Powerful, yes. The answer to everything, no. Circumstances where it cannot or should not be used include:

- *Where the coachee doesn't want to*. Rule no. 1: the coachee has to have free choice on whether or not to be coached. Because its essence is digging the answers out of a high-performing mind, if the mind doesn't want to cooperate, it won't work.

- *Or can't*. Coaching needs not only the coach but also the coachee to be sane. None of us is fit to be coached all the time. In the short term, personal issues such as relationship breakdown at home or sudden bereavement can send us enough 'out of our mind' for coaching not to be the answer. (The answer is a counsellor or therapist, trained, qualified and highly experienced in the specific issue. Why need they be highly experienced? Because immensely able senior businesspeople are perfectly capable of pulling the wool over the eyes of a gullible therapist and hence not get the help they really need, even though they seem on the outside to be ticking the right box: I've seen it happen. Specialist therapists accustomed to working with senior business folk and getting past their defences can be found through corporate wellness centres/ Employee Assistance Programmes (EAPs)/specialist GPs/word of mouth.) The prospective coachee might alternatively have a personality disorder which no amount of coaching can change (see Chapter 7).

- *Cultural difference*. It should not be assumed that coaching can be applied in every cultural context. In some cases where the culture of a global organisation is so powerful that it to some extent overrides local variation, at least while employees are in their 'work' mindset, it could be fine. Motorola Corporation, for example, has such a powerful, positive and pervasive organisational culture that coaching which works at global HQ in Schaumburg, Illinois, may well be equally productive for their people in Singapore and Beijing. But it might not. (For more on cultural difference see Chapter 11.)

■ *Hostile context.* Coaching is for more or less healthy people, and more or less healthy organisations. The coachee needs to trust the coach, if they are to open up and tell the truth. And both coach and coachee need to trust the organisation being open to reasonable individual and organisational change, if their plans are going to have any chance of succeeding. So coaching works fine in Microsoft, where it is deeply embedded and widely used. But I have seen toxic law firms where it doesn't work at all, backfiring on both coach and coachee.*

■ *Personality difference.* Some healthy high-functioning people just don't like the coaching approach. In Myers–Briggs terms (see Chapter 7), typically Ns take to coaching like a duck to water, while ISTJs can strongly prefer a more structured training or mentoring approach to development (see below for the difference). But not all Ns, and not all ISTJs – hence more reason, yet again, for the individual being given the choice.

Now we've got our feet back on the ground – this stuff is good, but it's not Superman – let's look at some basic definitions and distinctions.

Defining terms

As coaching has become a 'good thing', the word has been spread thinly over almost everything, like raspberry jam. At worst, I once heard a senior accountant say, 'We coached him out'. No, you didn't – you fired him.

---

* I don't single out law firms by accident: they are statistically among the most depressed of all occupations. See Seligman, M. (2003) *Authentic Happiness,* London: Nicholas Brealey, pp 177ff. A firm where more people are depressed than anywhere else, and some of the cheerful ones are psychopaths, isn't likely to be a healthy work environment. (Lawyers are exceptional in their incidence of depression, but they're not alone on psychopathy: its incidence is high compared with the general population in all the glittering pinnacles of global business: see Babiak, P. and Hare, R. (2006) *Snakes in Suits,* New York: Regan Books/Harper Collins: gripping and essential reading for anyone working in the high-stakes contexts that attract them.) There are of course law firms, investment banks, hedge funds, etc. with healthy cultures – many of our graduates are leaders in some fine examples – but coaches practising in global financial centres do need to be alert as to who is offering them work. See Chapter 7 for more.

If we're really going to help people, then the terms need to be crystal clear. Hence my basic definition of what coaching is:

> **traditional mentoring (or training or advising or consulting) _puts in_ advice, content, information. Coaching, by contrast, _pulls out_ the capacity people have within.**

So the essence of everything else is downloading – telling people what to do. But the essence of coaching is uploading: drawing out from within people's own ideas, hopes, dreams, plans. Already you'll see why it works so powerfully:

- People are much more likely to implement things they've thought up for themselves.
- Most people, even already successful ones, have very considerable untapped potential just waiting to be brought out – see for example the data from neuroscience scans in Chapter 11.
- And anyway, intelligent people often resent being told what to do and don't listen, so you might as well ask instead.

(For more on why coaching works, see Chapter 11, entitled, imaginatively, 'Why it works'.)

So mentoring, training, consulting, _put in_; coaching _pulls out_.

Of course, in practice they blend a little: a good mentor will coach some of the time, and coaches may lob things in occasionally to keep clients on their toes. But at the heart of coaching is this ability to pull out from people clear thinking, higher achievement, inspired vision, leadership, fee-earning, game-changing performance. (For how to do this, see Chapter 5: it's simple, but not easy!) Clients vaguely knew they had it within them, but the scale of what they actually leap up to achieving often astonishes them. A bit rubs off on us too: we learn to self-coach, and I observe coaches are a pretty clear-sighted, quick-thinking bunch: perhaps this is another reason why many have weathered the recession better than most.

Continuing on definitions and distinctions, let's now look at some of the different flavours coaching and its near-cousins come in.

Coaching _v_. mentoring

You know the mantra: mentoring puts in, coaching pulls out. Fifteen years ago some organisations weren't clear on this distinction, and indeed one famous organisation had it the wrong way round. But there is now widespread agreement, as there jolly well should be, for the distinction has the ultimate pedigree of Classical antiquity. In Greek myth, Odysseus was about to go off on a voyage. Concerned about his son Telemachus, he consigned the youngster to the care of Mentor, an older, wiser man – and according to some versions of the myth, actually Athena, the Goddess of Wisdom, in disguise. A good thing too, as what with one thing and another Odysseus ended up being away ten years. In the meantime, Mentor/Athena brought up the boy, and well – but there was no nonsense about asking questions, Goddesses tell mortals what to do.

Directive/non-directive

Because in modern practice each borrows a little from the other, in day-to-day reality coaching may not be entirely pull or mentoring entirely push. Instead two very useful terms define the difference more generically: 'directive' means telling (and variants), wherever it occurs, and 'non-directive' means drawing the answers out of the client, wherever it occurs. These terms will keep reappearing through the rest of the book.

Life coaching v. business coaching

Life coaching covers the whole of your life: diet, fitness, relationships, etc. Business coaching is about business, so the content differs. In terms of the *skills* used, there is some overlap, as both draw on the same basic skills, but there is one important difference: business coaching is generally a business-to-business sale, while life coaching is generally sold by the practitioner direct to the end user. This has significant implications for *contracting*. There's much more on this in Chapter 5; here I just note that business coaching, where there are several clients, sometimes with conflicting demands, and often across different cultures and time zones, involves considerably greater *complexity*.

Business coaching v. executive coaching

In the US, the two terms are very distinct, with executive coaching meaning working solely with the most senior executives in the organisation, and business coaching usually meaning working with those lower down the organisation chart. In the UK, however, the two terms are more interchangeable, with business coaching usually taken as a comprehensive term to cover both.

Business coaching v. leadership coaching

The word 'leadership' is getting spread around rather; everyone is now a leader. But leadership (or 'C-suite' – Chief Executive Officer/Chief Operating Officer, etc.) coaching has somehow avoided that, and still means coaching the toughest people in the firm: those right at the top, who whether their title happens to begin with a 'C' or not, have all the executive toys but in some sense the jobs from Hell.

Business, executive and leadership coaching differ little in the skill sets used, but a leadership coach needs to be able to work as an equal with perhaps a raging 'Alpha male/female' at full throttle or these days, a cerebral hedge fund squillionaire. Those who can, come from varied routes, but whatever else they have, they need a tough hide, personal gravitas and the ability to capture a leader's attention in split seconds.

Coaching v. counselling

Much simpler: the clients of a coach are presumed to be well, the clients of a counsellor – or therapist, or clinical psychologist, or psychiatrist – are not. There is also a subtle but important difference in the power relationships. The situation is changing, but within the 'medical model' there is still a slight power differential: practitioners, particularly the white-coated ones, have expertise and the people they work with are called 'patients'. Coaches by contrast work with clients, and the power relationship is absolutely that of equals. (For the difference between the various mental health practitioners, see the box.)

Mental health professionals

In approximately descending order of the severity of conditions they work with:

- *Psychiatrists* – trained in medicine, plus postgraduate specialist training in psychiatry; as medically qualified doctors, are certified to prescribe medication.
- *Clinical psychologists* – trained in psychology and then specialise in clinical psychology; work with more chronic conditions, typically employed in the National Health Service. Occasionally further licensed to use medication, but generally control symptoms with 'talking therapies'.
- *Psychotherapists* – intensive and lengthy training in one or more of the different forms of psychotherapy, typically undergoing personal therapy themselves.
- *Counsellors* – trained in counselling (courses typically half the length of psychotherapy training). Work with people facing life transitions, less severe forms of depression and anxiety, and personal growth issues, typically in private practice.

> ■ *General practitioners* (GP) – trained in medicine; may prescribe medication or refer on to other professionals. The proper first place for a coach to refer to if there is any question of any of the above professionals being required; the GP is the proper 'gatekeeper' and can diagnose/assess in order to make the right referral.

How coaching is used

Now let's look at who uses coaching and what they use it for.

Coaching tends to be bought for senior people. From the organisation's perspective, this is partly because it's expensive, whether provided internally or externally. From the supply side, you might think coaches like everyone else in business, 'follow the money' – senior levels are where you can earn most. True, but I also think coaching is naturally more useful in the later stages of a career. At the beginning, young professionals, like it or not, need to be told a great deal. Law, accountancy and medical students spend many years stuffing down technical information, then when they arrive in the workplace it begins all over again as they learn their profession in practice. MBAs structure the intensive learning bursts differently, but they're still typically in the first half of careers. And along the way there are regular periods of retraining.

But from about mid-career on, it is no longer just a matter of technical competence. The higher you climb, the less charted the waters and the more you have to make your own, often difficult, judgement calls. In addition, to be authentic and charismatic, leaders have to draw out their own genuine vision from within and convey it compellingly. Little of that can be taught, but a lot of it can be coached.

How else is coaching used? In essence, business leaders have coaches for the same reason that athletes do – it's a mind game. More specifically, typical tasks include:

- transition: for example, VP Latin America promoted to the global board;
- 'first 100 days', i.e. planning ahead of time how to land best in a new role;
- strategy, sales or marketing planning: digging out the fresh new ideas, and challenging stale or habitual thinking;
- decision-making under uncertainty: minimising downside risk and increasing the likelihood of success;
- managing exceptional load or its sometime consequence, stress;

- keeping a clear head through turbulence, e.g. mergers, acquisitions, downsizing;
- developing high-potentials;
- fixing whatever's holding someone back, e.g. improving inter-personal skills;
- ensuring an expensive new hire integrates well, and stays.

Who provides the coaching?

In this chapter we've talked about the pressures on us all in business and how coaching is a growing response to that. You might be beginning to see the lure coaching has for its clients.

But what motivates *coaches* to enter this fast-growing profession and what do they actually do?! In the next chapter we switch from the 'demand' to the 'supply' side and meet the coaches, in all their various manifestations: some may surprise you!

2

The coaches

So the market for coaching is roaring ahead, and we've seen something of the demand driving that. In this chapter we consider supply – the coaches themselves, in all their many guises.

If I say 'business coach', the first thing that might come into your mind is a full-time *external* coach, whizzing round in their fast car from one interesting corporate client to another. But in fact, these are only a tiny minority among the 'suppliers': the vast amount of business coaching is done by people *within* organisations – leaders, managers, HR and learning and development (L&D) professionals, line managers, lawyers, accountants, headhunters, etc., etc. Sometimes it's explicitly labelled coaching, but more often they're using their coaching skills to do their 'day job' even better.

Millions of people are coaching every day. To look in more detail at the many ways they do it, imagine if you would, a spectrum. At one end, people wholly internal to an organisation – those still entirely 'in captivity'; at the other end, the sole trader coach who operates entirely on his or her own – the 'lone ranger'; and all the permutations in between. In this chapter we journey from one end to the other of that spectrum – and along the way, to bring it to life, some real people have kindly shared their stories.

Specifically, we'll consider the following:

1 Within organisations:
   - leader as coach;
   - HR/L&D director;
   - line manager;
   - applied coaching: the headhunter, the Bishop ... ;
   - specialist coaching companies;
   - the foot-in-both-camps transition.

2 Outside organisations:

- the not-very-freelance;
- associations:
    - tight;
    - loose;
    - referral networks;
- specialist;
- professional freelance coach/'lone ranger';
- portfolio career.

1. Within organisations

Leader as coach

In an important *Harvard Business Review* article,[1] Daniel Goleman (2000) said there were six core leadership styles – coercive, authoritative, affiliative, democratic, pace-setting and coaching – and the more of them a leader has mastered, the better. He continued:

> '... of the six styles, our research found that the coaching style is used least often. Many leaders told us they don't have the time in this high-pressure economy for the slow and tedious work of teaching people and helping them grow. But after a first session, it takes little or no extra time. Leaders who ignore this style are passing up a powerful tool: its impact on climate and performance are markedly positive... coaching improves results.'

That article made famous the leadership style now widely called 'leader as coach'. As we saw in the rapacious arrogance of the credit crunch – and as Paul Babiak laid out in his chilling book *Snakes in Suits*[2] on psychopaths in the boardroom – this doesn't mean the leader as shark has gone away.* (Indeed, as coaching moves to centre stage as a leadership style, the risk increases that unscrupulous leaders will adopt its techniques to manipulate others.) But leaders who genuinely are decent human beings, and who are as strong on the sixth – coaching – style as on all the others, do seem

---

* I can't recommend this book highly enough: uncomfortable reading, but the scales will fall from your eyes and you'll realise, according to objective data by hard-nosed scientists in many fields including criminology and business, there are more of them around than you thought. Best be prepared.

to have exceptionally good results. Of course, this could just be correlation, not causation – it may be that the kind of person innovative enough to have learned to coach was going to have great results anyway.

But *pour encourager les autres*, see the box for what some leaders have said about having an ability to coach in their leadership armoury.

Leaders as coach

Simon Brown
formerly Vice President, Microsoft, now Managing Director, LeadEagle

For me the basics of coaching are the basics of inspiring leadership. The human asset in most organisations is amazing – creative (often beyond what others expect) and capable of change. And what is required to unlock this potential? In my view, it's not command-control or micro-managing. It is self-awareness, sincere belief in human potential, attentive listening and non-judgemental questioning. Does that sound like coaching?

In my experience, creating this environment energises people at all levels in the organisation and accelerates their growth. I have seen organisational change being embraced in a wholehearted way. I have seen the quality of decision-making improve as people say what is really on their mind and not what they think others want to hear. And as a leader following this path I have found work to be more energising and helping to fulfil my mission in life, which some years ago I realised was all about building meaningful relationships.

So what's the catch? Just as it's hard work to be a great coach, it's hard work (although very rewarding) to be a humanistic leader. But often the hardest thing is holding firm in the face of a prevailing wind of judgemental behaviour in business. Quick decisions and action give the perception of being in control – this is dangerous if activity is rewarded over meaningful long-term outcomes. I have learned the importance of defining the objective to win our people's hearts and minds as part of a change programme, and I have learned the importance of staying true to my principles.

Billy Norris
Managing Director, GAM Fund Management Ltd, Ireland

There's a quote I like relating to leadership transition. An important and often difficult task for aspiring/new CEOs is learning to get a handle on 'mastering the art of forming coalitions and winning the support of people who are competitors – the political side of a company, characterized by unspoken relationships, alliances and influence exerted by coalitions'.[3] Finding the appropriate leadership style to use in situations is a skill in itself and this is where I feel a non-directive coaching approach has aided my development. Developing more effective listening has helped me listen more attentively to my fellow colleagues and leads to more developed trust.

One of the nicest things that has happened to me since I started the coaching course is that over the last year, I feel both the communication channels and relationship with my boss have developed very positively. From my perspective, I really do listen better and try as best I can to be objective and understand his positional situation on matters (not mine). I think he appreciates this more than me simply telling him how I feel he should do things from my point of view! When asked straight out, I also think more about how I project my opinions/views.

My personal reason for developing my coaching skill set is driven by my interest in this area and because I care genuinely about helping people. You can develop a skill set in any walk of life but I want to coach inside/outside my organisation because I want to give something to people (my time) that will hopefully ultimately help them. Along the coaching path, I have also developed increased self-awareness about who I am and as a consequence, am a much happier person.

Dick Tyler
formerly Managing Partner, CMS Cameron McKenna LLP, now Executive Partner CMS Legal Services EEIG

I wanted to develop my coaching ability to make me better in my current job. We'd talked about adopting a coaching style of leadership both in Cameron McKenna and CMS, but we hadn't really been clear (in our own minds or with those who we hoped would benefit from it) about what it meant. What we understood by it was that it was about helping and supporting individuals to achieve their full potential, in the context of their specific jobs and their individual strengths and weaknesses.

The nature of law firms (in particular, the fact that partners are owner–producers and that management authority is delegated by them to those who manage, rather than inherent to those in management positions) is that a directive style of leadership simply does not work. Management is about establishing the principles ('this is the way we do things here') and communicating and applying them consistently. It's about providing a framework where people are clear about what's being measured and rewarded (or penalised) and an environment which encourages and promotes good behaviours and marginalises or separates from those who won't or can't demonstrate them. But in the words of the senior partner of another (very eminent) firm, 'the only real power that I have is the power of suggestion'.

The recipients of my management are generally high achievers, highly intelligent and full of insecurities. If my job is to provide the framework and the environment, then management is necessarily about letting the individuals set the agenda and letting him/her think (genuinely!) that they own the outcomes. I find that coaching helps me almost every day and in almost every conversation I have (i.e. all those where I don't have the need to be truly directive/coercive, which is a need that only arises when we have a crisis of some sort and a need for an immediate and clear response). If coaching isn't universally applicable, it's because I forget to do it or don't do it well. If one accepts the premise that many of the reasons for people under-performing at work have got nothing to do with work itself (e.g. they're to do with home life etc.), then a coaching style of management is hugely helpful in helping people improve their performance.

Specific examples:

■ A relatively recently-appointed partner with a young child and another one in contemplation who's juggling being a mother, wife, producer (in the office) and has an international practice involving lots of travel. With help from me as her coach, she's decided to focus her time in the office on her producer role rather than management tasks and has worked out that the best thing for her to do is to make her home and her family her number one priority for her children's early years.

■ A marketing professional who's been working too hard for her own good but can't let anything go who has been coached to devise her own solution to her work/life balance issues. So she's worked out what are the highest and best uses of her time and what more resources she needs, and has acknowledged that she has to be willing to delegate more and to take responsibility as a leader as well as a doer.

■ A marketing professional who has a justifiable sense of grievance about the way he's been treated by another part of the organisation. By being coached, he's been able to find a way of working with the people against whom he has the grievance, which hasn't resulted in any loss of his own self-respect, he's producing better work and is enjoying it more than he ever has before and he also has achieved a state of contentment and empowerment in how he manages his work/life balance.

Jayne Styles
Chief Investment Officer, Amlin plc, London

Coaching has been invaluable for my job ... and for me! I am able to use my coaching skills to develop my team and others in the company. Particularly where people are moving to new management roles, when confidence can be an issue. Also the ability to listen at 'Level 3' helps so much in the corridor conversations when somebody is going through a difficult time.

HR/L&D director

Goleman's leadership research obviously applies in general to HR/L&D directors as leaders in their business.* But they often also have an explicit strategic coaching brief; typically it is HR or L&D who spearhead the thinking on 'how coaching is done around here'. That is, they ensure it supports the organisation's goals, and seek to drive quality up, and costs down.

But the job might start more prosaically. An HR/L&DD who is newly arrived in an organisation, particularly if the business has deliberately recruited at a more strategic level than before, often starts by cleaning up a mess. Typically they find coaching all over the place, with even millions being spent but no one having central oversight or control over quality, provision or budget. A year or three later they have knocked it into shape: written a coaching strategy for the business; flushed most of it out into the open, brought the spending either under centralised control or, if devolved, ensured the centre is informed; campaigned to ensure the coaching delivers the strategic objectives of the organisation; and run an

---

* I am referring to L&D and HR together, although of course there are differences in their brief and expertise, because their areas can overlap, with some organisations seeing coaching falling primarily within the HR remit and others, especially where it is a separate function, seeing it as part of L&D.

initial screening of external and internal coaches against agreed organisational standards.

Clean-up done, the day-to-day coaching-related work might, depending on the organisation, role, and individual, then include:

▩ As an HR business partner working with line managers who say 'X needs a coach'. The HR director (HRD) tactfully explores what is *actually* needed – X might indeed genuinely need a coach, but they might instead need better managing, a mentor, disciplinary action, protection from concealed bullying or a thousand other things – the HRD's first step is triage/diagnosis.

▩ If a coach is genuinely needed, they consult their 'little black book' to decide who would be best and ascertain who is available, with the right background and qualifications, yet affordable. Best practice is then to offer the line manager and/or X two or three names from which to choose, give the chosen coach a confidential background briefing and keep an eye on the coaching as it proceeds. Sometimes these coaches will be internal to the organisation, sometimes external, but either way the HR leader knows who is around and has a knack for suggesting the right match.

▩ L&Ds are also drowned in applications from would-be external coaches – many get 20–50 unsolicited emails or letters a day. Most are in the bin within seconds unless something unusual catches their eye, or the prospective coach has been introduced by a trusted contact.

▩ If they have a global remit, the HRD is also seeking to ensure commonality of standards, quality service provision and budget compliance, across different sectors, national cultures and time zones.

▩ And then they have their own coaching portfolio. Informally, it's a constant part of the job ('Susan, could I just have a word?'). They're often also formally coaching a few senior members of the organisation, which in turn requires them to contract, coach and maintain up-to-date records, supervision, accreditation and continuing professional development (CPD) hours, like any other coach (see Chapter 5).

HR/L&D in professional services firms

In professional services firms (PSFs) – lawyers, accountants, management consultants, etc. – coaching is particularly crucial: the only thing in those organisations which makes money is people, and highly intelligent often highly-strung people at that. Improving their performance has a direct, immediate and potentially large impact on the bottom line. So the L&D/ HRDs are certainly doing all the above, but often they are also fighting another, tougher battle: getting the professionals, the lawyers, accountants, management consultants, etc., to coach well themselves.

This is because the official culture in most PSFs is that coaching and development of the next generation is a core part of the professional's task (though few firms recognise this by commensurately reducing billablehours targets). Some actively enjoy that part of the role, but others demur, seeing their role as doing only the actual legal, accounting or consultancy work they 'signed on for'. So the L&D director is frequently tactfully pushing the coaching responsibility back to the partner or manager who requested it, then equipping them to handle it, perhaps by running seminars and short training courses on coaching for partners, and mopping up pockets of resistance.

In advanced organisations, where all the above battles have been patiently fought and won, the next stage is to seek to develop a 'coaching culture'; for an example within the PSF world, see the box.

Building coaching culture

Nigel Spencer, Director of Learning and Development for law firm Simmons & Simmons, is particularly well equipped to work on developing a coaching culture in his firm because, as Nigel tells it:

'My PhD was on how change happens and the power of individuals to create it – even if I was examining these themes in the context of 3,000–5,000 years ago in Classics and Aegean archaeology! In our firm over the last five years we have definitely been able to be successful agents for change on much briefer and more individual timescales; through coaching we have undoubtedly helped individuals be resourceful, motivated them to stay within the firm and to move their careers in directions they would otherwise not have gone, manage more effectively upwards with their line managers, restructure their teams, and achieve business benefits with their internal clients, driving some measure of change in the business units.

We did it by applying some of the same principles as in my archaeology research, particularly the power of individuals to create change. One key to this was choosing the right people to influence through coaching; in other words, the leaders of particular business units, or the firm itself. It has taken us 4–5 years of patient work with this body to move to a place where coaching is now widespread in the firm internationally, where senior leaders now boast to their peers that they have a coach and everyone else should have one too, and where enough of the leaders have personally experienced the benefit of coaching that they will have no hesitation in recommending it to others – in short, to a position where there is significant 'pull energy' from the business unit leaders and different offices for coaching of their staff because it is known to be an effective development tool.

I would like to think that the development of some key individuals through coaching has made them more strategic, allowed them to make better decisions at crucial times and to see the bigger picture – thus, hopefully, leading to change in the trajectories of their group as a whole and perhaps even creating a higher quality of firm leadership. But it is difficult to claim honestly that coaching in isolation has led to specific change at this group or firm level. We have been one factor, no more, no less – although hopefully an important one and certainly one which would never have existed without us beginning the 'journey' towards a coaching culture in the firm 4–5 years ago.

Coaching in the 'day job'

In some sectors, being able to coach gives one a powerful advantage, even if it is not formally included in the job description. Many successful executive search consultants, for example, have undergone coach training, as making sales, drawing information and capability out of candidates, coaching them for job interviews and helping them build and sustain motivation are all part of the job.

Right across business, many people coach because it's useful, it works and it fits with either their personal style or the demands of their role, or both. See the box on the headhunter and the Bishop.

Coaching in the 'day job'

The headhunter

Anita Hoffmann, originally a chemical industry and professional services executive with a technical background, is the co-founder and co-leader of Heidrick & Struggles' Global Alternative & Renewable Energy and Sustainability Practice, the first such global practice in a top executive search firm. She added coach training to her qualifications in 2005. Anita comments:

'We work exclusively at the top of companies, and the positions we help fill are mission-critical to the companies' future. In my work, I speak with, interview and assess 1,000–2,000 executives per year, from all over the world, either as candidates for current searches, as potential future candidates or to build relationships with executives who become future clients.

I did not expect my coaching training to be as useful as it has turned out to be; in essence, every conversation a senior headhunter has with an executive is partly a coaching session. Helping them articulate what they really want from the next stage in their career is vital for both them and me: many executives mid career want to change tack and do something 'worthwhile' and are often attracted to the climate change/sustainability/renewable energy area, but don't know how to transition into this very fragmented industry or what kind of impact they would like to have on the climate change issue.

If you don't know if you want to be the CEO of a start-up company, become an adviser to a venture capital fund, influence public policy or what work–life balance you want, then it is very easy to accept a position that sounds exciting and then find it almost impossible to extricate yourself from it without serious reputational damage if you have picked the wrong opportunity. So to achieve really successful results (high-performing executives that create value for shareholders and are happy in their jobs), coaching is actually quite crucial.'

The Bishop

The Rt Rev. Jana Jeruma-Grinberga is Bishop of the Lutheran Church of Great Britain, a multicultural church worshipping in eight languages. As Bishop, she is both its pastoral leader in this country, and the equivalent of the 'CEO' of church business. As Jana puts it:

'I have been doing this job for a year and a half, it has bedded down and I'm a bit clearer on what I'm doing and why. I think I'm using coaching almost all of the time now. I do even have specific coaching sessions with Pastors about any issues they might have in their congregations. At other times I catch myself and have a little smile inwardly – at Synod, congregations, wherever, I use listening techniques to try and pick up what people are saying, and often stop the meeting to sum up what everyone is saying and check everyone is bought into the arguments and the solutions being discussed. So I use lots of coaching techniques, it's useful for listening in meetings, participating in meetings and problem solving as well.'

Specialist coaching companies

For those who get hooked on coaching, want to keep working at the same level of challenge and with bright high-performing people, yet still have the trappings of organisational life – smart offices, someone to fix the computer, colleagues down the corridor – working in a small elite organisation where they just coach might seem like a dream. And indeed, for those few who are selected into these organisations, the coaching side of work is indeed highly stimulating. Such companies also typically reinvest heavily in their coaches, with great attention paid to quality supervision and constant ongoing learning.

But upmarket coaching firms have upmarket overheads, and that means their coaches must, like any other professionals in high-performing consultancies and PSFs, balance their delivery work with constant business development and sales, to achieve tough sales targets. For an example of this approach, see the box on the next page.

Praesta

Praesta Partners (www.praesta.com) is a leading UK coaching firm. It is unusual in specialising only in business coaching, in being a fully fledged corporate entity (a limited liability partnership (LLP) with partners who invest in the business) and in having a global network of offices.

Robin Hindle Fisher of Praesta writes:

'2009 was quite a year for me. I ran the London Marathon, turned 50 – no mid-life crisis there, of course – and switched from a full-time career in the City into being an equally full-time coach. I joined Praesta in January 2010. I was clear from the outset of my second career that I wanted to work with other people who had been in senior management positions and be in a business-like, challenging and learning as well as supportive environment. Praesta coaches typically have a 20-year-plus senior-level career behind them before becoming coaches. Many of the partners were board members, CEOs, partners or managing directors of major companies, professional services firms or government departments in their first careers. Once employed, everyone undertakes practitioner-level training and commits to obtaining master coach status after five years. An in-house European Mentoring and Coaching Council (EMCC)-accredited CPD programme and regular professional supervision are mandatory.

The firm's clients reflect the team's seniority. Praesta works with the top echelons of several hundred organisations spanning the City, professional services, FTSE 100 and 250 companies and the civil service. One-to-one coaching is Praesta's principal offering and assignments cover all aspects of senior leaders' agendas and leadership development. Highly tailored psychometric reviews often form part of client assignments. In addition, we also offer structured team coaching and board reviews to client companies and have developed a leading position in working with senior women in business and with companies on their policies and practices in this area.

Praesta operates at the top end of the coaching market – which is where I want my coaching career to be – and, by being a partnership with recruitment strictly limited to highly experienced people, the firm provides a 'business partner' relationship to organisations on top team development. The culture, the team and, most of all, the clients make it a very special place to work.'

Foot-in-both camps transition

When people ask me for advice on transitioning to a 'portfolio career' including coaching, I always advise with all the force I can muster, against going 'cold turkey'. Being a full-time employee working hard, often long hours, but with all the support and fun organisational life provides until one Friday night, then waking up the following Monday morning with it suddenly all gone, and a completely empty life, is to be avoided if at all possible. Far better psychologically, and for the mortgage payments, to transition in some way. Some do it by going down to four days a week with their current employer, using the remaining time to undertake coach training, then build up their private practice, reducing their employed days as their coaching practice grows.

The role model for me in this is Sue Cox, who, when coming up to her last years as Global Head of HR at investment house Schroders, negotiated with her employer to transition down over three years. In year one she worked four days a week; then three days; then finally two. In her increasing amount of non-corporate time, she built up her new life as an independent coach, mentor and consultant, and also established a thriving new network of relationships in her neighbourhood where for most of the previous 20 years, she had virtually only been to catch some sleep. By the time she eventually retired from Schroders, she had established both a portfolio career and a strong local network which stood her in good stead in subsequent years.

Not everyone is able to pull it off this seamlessly, but I encourage those who are the masters of their own Fate to try: the rewards, both in terms of new business life and peace of mind, are considerable.

2. Outside organisations

How can I invoice Thee? Let me count the ways…

If the thought of any organisation, no matter how congenial the place and/ or coaching-focused your role, no longer appeals, then there are many alternatives. People tend to see the options in black and white – either one 'has a job' or is a 'freelance' – but there are in fact almost infinite permutations.

The not-very-freelance

Some leave their firms, but with a contractual relationship to deliver services including coaching back to their former employer. The best deal I know of saw an individual leave his organisation but with a firm contract from them to supply 80 days of consultancy, including some coaching over the next year – not a bad way to launch a business! (Though it may in some jurisdictions have tax implications if you are seen as remaining a *de facto* employee.)

Associations, from tight to loose

In almost 20 years of working with coaches, watching and supporting them as they grow their businesses, I have observed that while most adore the freedom of being their own boss yet still doing the challenging, rewarding work they love, there are two aspects of freelance life many dislike: the marketing, and the loneliness. People who were completely unfazed issuing an invoice for millions when it had the brand name of their global organisation on it, freeze like a rabbit in the headlights when it comes to selling *themselves*. And many miss the buzz and intellectual stimulation of working with capable colleagues. Which is why many coaches gravitate to a 'best of both worlds' situation, where they have the flexibility and freedom of officially working for themselves but the companionship, cover for illness and holidays, and greater marketing muscle of working in association with others.

Every association is different, but overall I see them as ranging from 'tight' to 'loose'.

'Tight' association: The Alliance

One successful coaching business is The Alliance (www.alliancecoaching. co.uk). As the name suggests, the members are all, formally, independent coaches. But they work together very closely indeed, so that to their clients it feels like a solid business that can and does take on major coaching projects. Unusually, Alliance members invested almost a year (part time, while most had commitments elsewhere) when they were setting up, in working together to thrash out not just their unique selling points (USPs), business principles and practice, but also the detail of their values and interpersonal working methods. I thought they were mad and urged them (I knew many of them well) to get out and start finding some business, but they knew what they were doing, quite rightly ignored me and I have since eaten my words: the time they spent 'taking their own medicine' as coaches, i.e. speaking frankly, deeply understanding each other's strengths and forging a strong professional way of working, has paid off. They have grown apace right through the recession, but no matter how busy, they continue to meet for a full day a month to review their work and their process and to update their learning together. For how they view it, see the box below.

The Alliance

At the outset we knew we wanted to create a close-knit cadre of coaches, with an emphasis on high-quality, shared values and impactful work, and to have an organisational vehicle which fitted that. We did not want to build a formal company reminiscent of past constraints and which added only limited value to our potential clients; and we wanted to keep the flexibility to engage individually outside The Alliance in other activities, be they consulting, training, teaching or charity work, along with a wide range of non-work activities.

We are all graduates of the same coach training, which is one of the things that binds us together – yet we have a wide range of collective and individual strengths from our diverse, senior business/professional backgrounds and coaching experience: from the application of in-depth psychology to board-level management; from professional services and consulting to manufacturing; from entrepreneurial to mature blue-chip organisations.

Our early meetings were focused on really understanding each other and our unique qualities and perspectives, agreeing how we would work together, and on creating our sense of what we wanted The Alliance to stand for. We developed a coaching philosophy and an approach that could be tailored to client needs based on a firm basic structure. The Alliance is now just over five years old, and there are currently eight of us who have come to know each other and to value and use our complementary skills and differences very well. It has not all been plain sailing – we have had some challenging situations to deal with – but we have successfully engaged with each other to create rich and often innovative solutions, undoubtedly beyond the reach of us individually.

As well as providing exceptional coaching, we offer our clients our collective observations and insights into their organisation and we provide access to our network, putting them in touch with people we know with a particular expertise. We therefore contribute both to the individual in their organisational context and to the system of the organisation itself.

We recently won a piece of work where the client commented that a decisive factor for them in awarding us the assignment was their observation that we really did exemplify the things we claimed to. So our efforts to create, sustain and develop our Alliance seem to be bearing fruit. But more than this, we have created a space and place for us to collaborate and continue to learn and grow with colleagues and friends we like and trust and respect.

In our previous corporate lives, the expectation was the client was always happy, but often at the price of people sacrificing everything else to the point of utter burnout. In the system we've built over five years we still work hard, the clients are, they tell us, very happy, but we are also fulfilled. We suspect this more balanced approach means clients get a better deal as well.

'Loose' association: freelance coaches with several links

A more frequent model is a group of business people who form a company with coaching as either its main offering or as part of a suite of offerings. They make the sales, and deliver on them through a large group of 'associates' – freelancers who work under the brand of the firm that won the business. Typically there might be from dozens to several hundred associates, with the 'front' business as small as one or two entrepreneurial people, often working from home, or shared office space. The 'front' business which wins the work and organises its delivery then takes 40–60% of the fee* and the freelance coaches who actually deliver the work are paid the balance.

This can be an ideal arrangement for recently trained coaches just starting out: for a few years, the headache of winning the business is someone else's, and they just turn up and coach. It's a win–win: the freelance can build their crucial coaching hours faster than if they had to win all the new business on their own; the coaching company avoids the heavy overheads of having the coaches on their books as employees; and the buying client has the benefit of access to a wide variety of coaches, with a range of different specialisms, but organised into a single point of contact.

Usually a freelance will start with contracted relationships with several different such businesses. Over time, as they build up their own cadre of clients, they resign first one associate relationship, then another, until they realise one day they have their own coaching practice, with both the marketing and business headaches, but also the freedom to retain 100% of the fees earned – before the tax man strikes.

Balancing this greater freedom, there are also drawbacks of the looser association for all parties. Not meeting their coaches regularly, or seeing their work on a regular basis, the providing company is constantly anxious – crossing their fingers behind their backs that John got the message that the venue has changed for Thursday, or Maria's work hasn't 'gone off' since they last worked with her three years ago. The buyer has a wider range of choice – but knows the price of that is no guaranteed consistency of approach or standard. And the coach gets part of what they want – the marketing done and clients handed to them on a plate (but no idea of when or how many) – but their other great desire, for collegiality, remains unmet. You might think the whole set-up is so fragile it's doomed, but in fact it generally works very well indeed, because pretty much everyone in coaching is there from deep vocational choice, loves their work and is highly professional about it – even sometimes going to great lengths, getting up absurdly early, scrambling to reschedule, driving halfway across the country or whatever it takes to cover up or fix the occasional administrative glitch. The client comes first.

---

* You may think that's highway robbery, and so did I when I first was giving it away, but over the years I've realised the overheads of even a small proper business are far higher than people realise, and the cost of marketing is also considerable, so it seems fair. Many people agree, with thousands of business coaches signing on for some such arrangement – for a time.

Referral network

Other coaches don't have formal contractual relationships, but are instead in a group of friends or colleagues who have known each other sometimes for years, and plan to refer work to each other informally when something crops up that they can't handle. In stark contrast to the loose network of associates, which shouldn't work in theory but often does in practice, many people think informal referrals *will* work, but they seldom do. Friendships and mutual support may well continue, and be very congenial, but little business is handed over, and over time the EWOK ('eat what you kill') approach predominates.

The specialists

In the above sections, I talk as if all coaches do general business/leadership coaching, and indeed many do, but mixed up in all these sections – the dedicated coaching companies, the tight and loose alliances and indeed the sole traders below – there is a sub-category: the specialist coaches. These are people who do normal business coaching but also when required deploy specialist expertise. For example, within our own alumni, there is a business coach with a PhD in Pharmacology, 20 years as a strategy director and trained homeopath, who unsurprisingly specialises in helping high-potential executives deal with stress; another who is an expert on coaching business high-achievers with Asperger's syndrome; several specialists in sales/business development, dozens who speak the jargon of, and specialise in, particular sectors such as the law, investment banking, private equity, finance, advertising, the military; one who has expertise working with gay FTSE 100 directors or other public figures who are 'outed'; and of course all those who are first-language speakers and can hence coach in Swedish, German, French, Italian, Portuguese, etc. Others specialise in coaching where diversity is an issue, or in charities, or on returning to work following maternity leave.* And I mention psychologist-coaches in Chapter 6.

Some of these work primarily as specialist coaches, others spend most of their time on mainstream leadership coaching (or in a portfolio, as discussed below) and draw upon their specialism less often. And while the above list might make it begin to seem everyone is a specialist, they are in fact a minority – but an interesting one!

---

* To request being put in touch with any of these specialists, please email info@ meylercampbell.com.

The full-time professional freelance coach/'lone ranger'

So, at last we're at the fantasy life – the full-time coach, jetting around the world, or driving their discreetly expensive Maserati, the confidante of the mighty, in complete control of their diary, with neither boss, nor subordinate nor colleague to cramp their style. And they do exist. A tiny minority even earn the proverbial fortune: several in excess of £250,000 per annum, and I know of one (but only one!) who earns four times that. But they are rare, and to achieve that level of earnings, they work ferociously hard. Part of what enables high earnings is being self-sufficient, doing their own marketing and selling, so not giving away percentages to an intermediary. They are also ruthless delegators, with every scrap of administration done by excellent dedicated administrative support, and have built up a group of devoted corporate clients through providing superb service over many years.

But for many people contemplating a switch to freelance life, if they wanted to work that hard, they could have stayed where they were and where they probably earned significantly more. The treadmill which lone ranger business coaches whizz around daily may be heavily gilded, but it is still a treadmill. For many of those leaving the intense pressure of a successful corporate career, life's too short.

The full-time professional business coach

Asked to comment on the above, experienced business coach Stephen Newton of www.dloassociates.com said:

'Your take on the Lone Ranger ('LR') is interesting – not sure I recognise the Maserati, etc.! You are absolutely right that operating as an LR is not a soft option and one would not go down this line in order to find an easy life as such. However, to my mind, a key reason for doing so which you don't really say, I feel, is the joy of independence and in particular the opportunity to choose with whom you work – note, 'with': being an LR allows one to work with a client as opposed to for them. That allows one to have what may be difficult conversations whilst coaching that would be impossible as an in-house coach, for example. (One of my clients said to me that the greatest value for him in our relationship was that I was the only person that he could trust to tell him the truth, as I saw it, unvarnished, no matter how difficult it might be for either of us.) Being an LR also allows one to fire clients where their values/behaviours/relationships are not congruent with one's own moral compass. In terms of the characteristics of an LR, it seems to me that being self-sufficient is indeed required. However, that should probably not imply undue introversion, as an ability to socialise, market and sell oneself is crucial to success.'

The portfolio career

But there is another dream, and this one many people do indeed live. It is the 'portfolio career': combining different elements, of which business coaching is only one part. Charles Glass, Founding Director of the Professional Career Partnership (PCP), says more about how to put a good portfolio together in Chapter 9, and I discuss how to build a coaching business in Chapter 12; here are just a few initial points.

For many people, the portfolio career is about gaining a significantly better quality of life, typically in the later stages of a demanding career, or earlier on to fit with a young family. And many do live the dream: living in that rose-covered cottage, commuting in a suit to the city some days, on others barefoot on the beach with the kids. They're paid well when they do work, yet still have time for the other things in life. And most importantly, they're their own master. It's important not to have rose-tinted glasses about the economics of this (see Chapter 12) and even the freedom doesn't always work – many strike long summer holidays out of their diary, but then find themselves hunting in the wardrobe for shoes, and struggling into a suit, for a client meeting that just can't be missed, right bang in the middle – but it mostly does, and the rate of satisfaction in this group is very high. Those still in captivity earn more: annual earnings of £150,000–£300,000-plus are common in the City of London, while those who have left those same roles to go portfolio are lucky to reach the bottom of that range. But they don't care: in the wider economy, satisfaction with work rates has been declining sharply since the 1970s, with only 49% of US workers now 'completely or very satisfied'.[4] But in stark contrast, in the 2008 Meyler Campbell Business of Coaching survey, 87% of coaches/portfolio respondents reported complete or very high satisfaction with their work.

As Charles says, the key to portfolio working is getting the mix right. Coaching is highly paid on a per-hour basis, but it is totally unleveraged: to earn, you need to be there, working with an individual or team client, so it isn't possible (apart from the rare exceptions mentioned above – and they are usually making a different life-balance choice) to earn City-type returns from it. But many want to coach because it is, they say, the most profoundly fulfilling work to do. So they mix it up: some coaching, but some other work that earns more, such as consultancy, headhunting, non-executive directorships, etc. In the Meyler Campbell Business of Coaching surveys, we typically find our own freelance graduates coach only 25–45% of their time. It is satisfying, even inspiring work and it can often open doors to other elements of their portfolio, but for most it works best as part of a mix – the portfolio.

So, there's a vast spectrum of ways people use coaching at work, from captive to free-range and everything in between.

Tempted?! If you are, but are wondering whether *you* could really do it, then the next chapter might be right up your alley: it asks, are you suited to be a coach?

3

Do you have what it takes?

People often come and talk to me about business coaching as a career. I take them through the various training options and different possible career paths. As the conversation draws to a close, they sometimes ask, perhaps hesitantly, 'So, do you think I've got what it takes to be a coach?'

If they have the humility to ask the question, then the answer is almost certainly yes.

So this is a very short chapter. It covers, first, the substantive *abilities* you need to be a coach, then says a little about *personality* and *commercial nous*. (I am assuming you have the openness to learning, self-awareness and preparedness to be challenged that would be needed when embarking on any new learning venture, becoming a coach very much included!)

1. Ability

Coaching isn't difficult. Yes, there are some things to learn, and as you'll see in Chapter 5, a lot to 'unlearn'. But most normal business people should be perfectly capable of that.

So when we select candidates for our own Business Coach Programme, with regard to ability, we are looking for evidence of just three things:

- business credibility;
- prior demonstrated interest in business coaching;
- and being 'more or less sane'(!)*

---

* A fourth criterion, 'fit with the community', isn't about ability, it's instead about maintaining our own particular brand, much of which rests on the calibre of our diverse and remarkable alumni community. But that's unique to us; a quirk, not generic.

Business credibility

To be a successful business coach, you need to be credible with business-people and at the level at which you are going to coach.

Credibility takes many forms. For most, it just means you've been in organisations long enough to earn your stripes: when you walk in the door, your presence is that of someone familiar with the complexities of organisational life. Others get their credibility from outside business: they're a world-class sports star, for example. Or it might be from their personal qualities, or sheer raw coaching ability: I know a coach who is a Head Teacher for 11/12ths of his year and takes only a few business coaching clients at a time. His coaching is such that he has a devoted following. But outsiders like this still have to convince an HR director, or maybe present to a board, so they still need to know the rules, the jargon, even something as simple as the dress codes.

A decent coach training (see Chapter 4) will of course help you develop, clarify and articulate your arguments and 'pitch' specifically with regard to coaching, but you still need the basics to build upon.

You'll notice I'm not saying the business credibility is needed for the substance of the coaching – as you will see in Chapter 5, one of the hallmarks of good coaching is the ability to pull answers out of the client, rather than advising them from any expertise base. It's to get you in the door and to win clients' respect so you are able to coach.

All of the above presumes the person is external to the organisation – a freelance coach perhaps. But the vast majority of coaching is done by people already working within organisations. The credibility point still stands. If you are a leader, you can (maybe) require people to do things from the power base of your title, job role, etc. But if you want to switch to coaching them, then you too need to win a different kind of respect. We talk about that more in later chapters – for the moment the credibility I'm talking about here is at the entry level of business credibility such that you don't need to have explained to you, business in general, or the specific sector you are working in, or even the nuances; you know the ropes.

Prior interest in coaching

The science is clear, that the best predictor of future performance is past performance. So we look for evidence that you have been interested and involved in coaching-type activity – often people say to us, 'I think I've been doing this for years, now I want to learn how to do it right!'

So you may never have called it coaching, but if you have always had an interest in people and what makes them tick, or if people open up and talk to you about things, and/or if you have even taken a few courses out of interest, then you are probably suited.

'More or less sane'

And third, we require that candidates be 'more or less sane': will organisations and coachees be safe in your hands? So if, for example, you are in the emotional turbulence of a major bereavement, or a heart-wrenching divorce, now is probably not the right time for you to be coaching.

It's more than just a situational issue: to be a business coach, you need the personality trait of reasonable emotional stability. Of course we all have good days and bad days, but for people in organisations to feel safe that coaches can be trusted with whatever they throw at us, we need to have our feet on the ground. The opposite of this trait is 'neuroticism'; that is, being emotionally very up and down (it used to be called 'highly strung'). So if you are prone to fly off the handle more than most, if you're forever tense, frustrated or angry, or your highs are sky-high but then you plunge to the depths, then coaching may not be for you.

The danger here is that perfectly normal people who would make fine coaches, read that previous paragraph and wonder, blimey, am I neurotic? Again, if you're asking the question, you're probably not. People who are so emotionally unstable that it would make them unsuited to coaching, know it. They've probably also been told many times over the years that they always take things too personally, or overreact. Unless you've been aware of a sizeable amount of that in yourself since you were old enough to remember, then you're not.

Why am I picking on neuroticism, you might ask, when there are so many other aspects of personality that could make people unsuited to becoming a business coach? Because, as the wise and wonderful Adrian Furnham points out, neurotics 'seem drawn to jobs that are about emotions, such as counselling, the dramatic arts and the visual arts'.[1] Coaching hasn't attracted too many yet, but we're on the alert.

2. Personality

Of course, the last of our three criteria is more a question of personality than ability.* But does any other personality variable matter? Are good coaches naturally extraverted, or introverted, or anything else? In other words, is there such a thing as a typical business coach?

Having trained people to coach for almost two decades, I think not. In our own community we have business leaders, coaches and advisers of every possible hue, range and stripe, from bouncy extraverts to deep introverts, and pretty much every variant on humanity one can think of, including a 50:50 gender balance, and representatives from most countries in Europe and many beyond, plus all major creeds and none. The only factor that does seem to be statistically interesting is there are far more people with an MBTI 'N' preference than 'S' (for explanation of MBTI see Chapter 6.) But 'S's can make excellent coaches – and they have a built-in advantage of rarity when looking to define their USP as a coach. For example, one S coach I know has combined her coaching with a detailed specialist knowledge of a particular area of employment law. Her (many) clients do indeed want to be coached, not advised, but they also take comfort that she is always right up to date on the relevant background – it differentiates her. But having said that, it does seem to be the case that many more Ns have an interest in coaching, as both consumers and producers.

3. Commercial nous

Another very important part of the question 'have I got what it takes' relates to your ability to earn a living from coaching.

This is a completely different question from ability and personality. It has already been touched on in Chapter 2, but to recap, the coaches who are the most successful commercially, who flick off recessions as if they were an irritating midge, who rise to high levels in their organisations, and/or make fortunes as external coaches, are those who know what to do to succeed, and do it in a disciplined and consistent manner, week in week out. If you can do that, more or less, in your current business life, then you

---

* Yes, I know, there are all sorts of debates on personality, including even whether it exists at all (or is situationally constructed). I'm ducking that question altogether here, just seeing our third criterion at the behavioural level, i.e. the ability to keep your head when all around are losing theirs. For more on personality see Chapter 7.

should be able to apply it to coaching. It's tougher post-credit crunch, but it's still perfectly possible. (Chapter 12 should help.)

Right, that reassured you? If you have the three ability components, i.e. business credibility, have been interested in all this for quite a while; and are more or less sane – apart, of course, from when the computer crashes *again*, that's perfectly understandable – then you're fine, let's move on. In the next chapter, we discuss how you can explore coaching further.

4

Developing your coaching: first steps

How do you develop your ability to coach?

This chapter takes you through four key steps:

1 Experience great coaching yourself.

2 Dip your toe in the water!

3 Get trained.

4 Continue learning.

Step 1: Experience great coaching yourself

The crucial first step is to experience good coaching yourself. Ideally, you would go one better than that and feel the full-on astonishing experience of working with a *great* coach.

So how do you find one?

1. Word of mouth

If something horrid happened and you had to find the very best lawyer in the business, how would you do it? Exactly – you'd ask around for recommendations. Do the same to find a coach.

2. HR

In larger organisations, someone in HR, L&D or Talent Management will be responsible for the quality and provision of business coaching within the organisation. Top HR directors' 'little black book' of good coaches is now one of their most important assets, even becoming part of why they're hired. Not only do the internal experts know who is around and what they're particularly good at, they also often have a knack for suggesting 'matches' with a coach or two they think would work well with you. Typically they will give you 2–3 CVs, from which you choose one or two for a 'chemistry' meeting (see below).

3. Referral sources

As with any other professional, word of mouth and personal recommendations, especially by people who know the local market well, are by far the best. Failing that, you can try referral sources, particularly the various accrediting bodies, and coaching brokers.

Accrediting organisations

There are many bodies involved in coaching accreditation (on which more below), but the most relevant source of accredited business coaches is the Worldwide Association of Business Coaches (WABC). Its accredited coaches are listed on www.wabccoaches.com. It may be worth scanning the sites of some of the others, but be aware they mix business and 'life' coaching – WABC is one of the few to date to focus solely on business, and the only one with global reach.

Training organisations

Good coach training organisations may make a public register available; it's worth checking their website. Others don't make their graduates' details publicly available, but would be happy to suggest names of potential coaches on request.

Coaching and Mentoring Network

This organisation has been running since 1999 and has remained determinedly independent. It seeks to maintain a neutral space where people looking for coaches and mentors can find them, and usefully, it has distinct sections for personal and business coaches. See www.coaching network.org.uk.

Coaching brokers

The expanding coaching market has unsurprisingly spawned many ancillary services, including a number of attempts to broker coaching to corporates. One which has weathered several years of operation is TXG; their website is www.txgltd.com.

4. 'Chemistry' sessions

Once you have identified a possible coach, the form is to meet them in person – 'for a coffee' (i.e. informally.) Normally this is free (but not always, so check). Be aware the chemistry works both ways: you are trying out whether you can trust and work with this person, but so is the coach. If they suggest someone else it might be that the 'chemistry' doesn't work for them (they're allowed!) but more commonly it's because they think someone else would be better qualified to work with you and the particular issues you mentioned.

5. Having found one, how do I know they're good?

Trust your instincts. If you find yourself opening up and telling them things you wouldn't normally; if that feels fine; and if by the end of the chemistry meeting you find to your surprise you've already had some good practical insights or action points, or things are clearer, it's a pretty good sign. If the coach hasn't been pre-screened for you by HR, and you need to do your own checking, again do what you would do for any consultant: see a CV, check credentials, take up references. For some questions that sort the genuinely accomplished business coach from the wannabe, see the box below.

Ten tough questions to ask a business coach

1. Where were you trained?

Don't consider a coach without an externally accredited well-established formal training. There are excellent coaches who haven't got this, because they started 15 or 20 years ago when it didn't exist – but their vast experience means they're in such demand they never advertise, so you're unlikely to stumble across one (except maybe through personal recommendation). A formal training lasting at least one year is the norm, plus evidence of active CPD thereafter. For the merits of different training courses and different accrediting bodies, see below. For a full list, see Tables 4.1 and 4.2 at the end of the chapter.

2. Who is your supervisor?

Decent coaches are 'in supervision' – in the professional sense, not the factory floor sense. (The term, and concept, originally came from the worlds of therapy and psychology, but it doesn't mean coaches are in therapy. On the contrary, supervision here describes a very focused set of checks and balances which can be applied to any professional context involving people.) In other words, they pay an expert to work with them regularly to maintain an independent check on the quality of their work for the client, paying organisation and coach; and to keep learning. In the UK, the specialist body for coaching supervisors is APECS (www.apecs.org) and a provider of coaching supervision training is the Bath Consultancy Group (www.bathconsultancygroup.com). For more on supervision, see later in this chapter.

3. What Code of Ethics do you subscribe to?

Many coaching organisations, and even individual coaches, will say they have developed their own Code of Ethics. This is impressive, and is typical of the dedication and great care which is a hallmark of the business coaching field. But a professional indemnity insurance specialist advised me years ago that 'grow your own' is a bad idea. The world changes fast, new issues come to the fore, hence maintaining a current Code of Ethics is a full-time professional task in itself, and individuals or small businesses are unlikely to have the resources to remain current right across all the necessary domains. Far better, he advises, to affiliate to an established professional body which can make the substantial investment necessary to keep right up to date.

If so, which one? The various accrediting bodies are actively raising their game – both AC and EMCC announced new entry requirements in 2010. But it remains true that some are far easier to get into than others, and many still fail the Groucho Marx ('I wouldn't want to join any club that'd be prepared to have me') test. The one with the most stringent requirements is the WABC, particularly with regard to the business aspects of coaching, hence many senior business coaches choose to be members and adhere to its Code. But the coach may have good reasons for choosing another: a key organisation for them may require EMCC membership; or they work in markets such as the USA where the ICF is dominant. For more on accreditation and the pros and cons of different bodies, see below, here you're just using it to torment, sorry I mean test, a prospective coach.

4. What CPD have you done within the last year and what do you plan for this year?

Fascinating if they just *happened* not to get around to any last year ('Gosh, it was a really busy year…') but have lots of plans for the future! As a guide of what to expect, several accrediting bodies require around 40 hours a year of CPD. A tougher measure is percentage of income; Meyler Campbell research in 2009 found leading coaches typically spend 5% of their annual income on keeping up to date. Coaches are a dedicated lot: many commit to one major investment in ongoing learning a year (e.g. training in a new psychometric or tool) and/or are in book clubs, peer sharing or learning communities, and deadly earnest about their commitment to learning through active supervision.

5. Tell me about one of your coaching 'success stories'.

Is what they describe the kind of thing you are looking for?

6. When has your coaching failed?

Even people with a few years' experience might be floored by this one: properly contracted and decent coaching is pretty indestructible and usually goes well, so it takes years of experience to accumulate enough mishaps to have a decent answer. But eventually it happens; listen for what they did about it, and what they learned. Alternatively they may describe a tricky situation that needed a few attempts to get it right, or where they went down one track and eventually pursued another before getting results.

7. Who are your clients?

Confidentiality matters, so watch how they refrain from disclosing the identities of the organisations and individuals they have worked with – it could be you in future; are you comfortable your commercial and personal information will be protected?

8. How do you evaluate your coaching?

Important if you have to account for corporate spend. Calculating return on invest-ment (ROI) of coaching is a sub-world in itself; see Chapter 11.

9. Tell me in what situation you would not coach.

The clearer and more comprehensive the answer, the happier you feel. Beginner coaches get so excited by its power, they want to coach anyone who comes within a hundred yards. Over the years experienced coaches tend to shrink the categories of work they take on, and great coaches will be able to give you recent examples of work which they thought would be better done by others, and which they therefore referred on.

10. What kind of client do you work best with?

Does that sound like you?!

6. If it doesn't work, move on

Business coaching works fast: some coaching topics are cracked in a single session, or just 2–3. Even with huge or long-term topics, if you don't feel there are good results on the way within the first few meetings, raise this with the coach. If they don't have a convincing explanation, politely move on.

We're a start-up business/charity and funds are tight – how do we find a good but inexpensive coach?

Good coach training courses are like hairdressing schools, they need 'prac-tice clients' for their students to experiment on. Find the best business coach training in your area/country (see page 55) and they are likely to be a source of acceptable coaching – it might be unpolished, but if the train-ing is sound, it will be closely monitored and it's usually free or low cost. This might sound alarming, but it's like buying art at academies' graduating shows: somewhere in there are the stars of the next generation. They won't be a great coach yet, that takes years, but there will be some who are already good – you just need to be very alert in the chemistry and vetting process!

Step 2: Dip your toe in the water

If you're serious, a proper training course is essential. But if you can't right now – too busy, too broke, too pregnant – then there are useful things you can be doing in the meantime. And as Herminia Ibarra advises in her terrific book on successful career transitions,[1] it's wise to test a new field with small experiments before taking the deep plunge. Depending on your preferences and time you could try:

- *Reading.* Love reading? Try Jenny Rogers' excellent *Coaching Skills*,[2] which gives a great introduction to the whole field, and/or Sir John Whitmore's *Coaching for Performance*,[3] the classic on one of the core tools, the GROW Model, for starters. For more, see the references later in this book, and for even more, ask around to see if there is a coaching book club in your area – or start one!

- *Training school sample events.* If on the other hand you prefer to try things out for real rather than just read about it, training organisations typically run short events which are open to the public. Avoid the naked selling events, but all the good schools offer short learning opportunities such as coaching 'fishbowls' (where you can watch top business coaches coaching live clients, for real) lectures, briefings and networking, either free or at moderate cost. These have many advantages: you can pick up some useful tips; you look at the people and imagine being one of them (good? Not good?!); you can check out the 'feel' of the specific training provider in case you later want to take the plunge, and most importantly at this stage, you can see if the field feels right for you.

- *Short courses.* The world is full of two-day coach training courses. They do *not* make you a business coach (and avoid any which say they do), but they can give you a good boost up. Typically such courses will explain GROW and get you practising it, run a listening exercise, etc. The skills won't last – behaviour change takes repetition and time – but the jargon will stick, and it should start tuning your antennae in to coaching. Long ago I paid a lot of money for a week-long course in a grubby hotel near the airport, with a broken window and a creepy little man leering from a bar stool talking about NLP. It doesn't appear on my CV – but it got me started.

Step 3: Get trained

You've experienced great coaching; there's pressure in your firm to develop a coaching style of leadership; and/or you've heard of people who've made a successful switch to coaching as a flexible 'portfolio career'. How do you step up to that level?

If you're serious, you need to undergo formal training. Twenty, even ten years ago you could break into coaching without it. But today with large numbers of people coming onto the market with solid business credentials *and* training, why would anyone hire anyone without it? (See the box on Ten Tough Questions!)

Formal training matters for deeper than just competitive reasons. Even with great natural talent, structured training puts you through your paces, exposes weaknesses you were unaware of, and brings out unexpected potential. Training also brings you up to date, plugging you into current best practice in the field, and gives you robust processes and a well-filled toolkit. It can also give you a community: some training organisations do, some don't, but at its best the alumni group you gain of graduates from X or Y training school can be a rich source of referrals, introductions and business help.

The elements of a good training course

We consider the detailed tools and techniques taught on coach training courses in the next chapter; here we outline the key elements.

Training courses will vary widely in what they cover, and how they do it, but any good course will have all of the following elements: structured learning, theory, practice, supervision, feedback, accreditation and a learning community. (And one of the advantages of a formal training is they will require you to try even the elements you wouldn't naturally be drawn to!)

Structured learning

There is an emerging international consensus on the core competencies of a business coach: see www.wabccoaches.com for the WABC's comprehensive list which applies globally, and as an example of a regional framework, www.emccaccreditation.org. A training course that is accredited by an organisation such as WABC or EMCC will have been grilled by the accreditation provider to ensure that each competency is covered somewhere in the training, so you don't need to worry about it.

Theory

What deep theoretical roots will your work have? All good courses will include some consideration of the theory underpinning coaching. Some focus mostly on the practical aspects and have a minimal theoretical content, others major on it. Don't expect this to be handed to you on a plate however: there will also be quite a bit of asking you to reflect, think through and articulate the theory *you* bring to business coaching, and even (especially on a Master's course) to push your learning further in your specialism.

This is because all coaches need a 'rock on which to stand': something that gives their work deep foundations, and sets them apart. This is especially important in senior-level business coaching, where you will be expected to have something unique that you bring, possibly from an earlier or parallel part of your life. Psychology happens to be mine, for two of my colleagues it's business strategy, and for many of our graduates it's their deep experience in business, or being a lawyer; different people build their coaching on different rocks.

I mentioned psychology. It is *not* essential to have studied psychology to be a coach; psychology degrees to this day contain almost nothing directly on coaching, and psychologists have to do specialised training to coach like everyone else. But if you are interested to study this further, perhaps to make it the rock on which you stand, see the box below.

Making psychology a foundation of your coaching?

When people come and talk to me about developing their coaching, we often stray into a side-conversation on psychology. As already noted, psychology is not a requirement for coaching. But coaches have an instinctive interest in people, and often a long-standing interest in psychology, the people science. So when they confess this, my coaching antennae twitch: do they really want to study coaching, or is their dream actually to study psychology? So this becomes a mini-coaching conversation and as ever the outcomes vary widely.

In addition to connecting with your inner wishes, there are some further factors to weigh up. If you are in your 20s or 30s and want to coach, full training in psychology may be worth considering because by the time you are at your career peak, there's an outside chance it could be a mandatory requirement to be a coach. And if you're older, recent neuroscience research[4] shows learning a demanding new subject in later life delays Alzheimer's, improves memory and sharpens brain function. I am hopelessly biased here – I retrained as a psychologist starting in my 40s and have found it one of the most profoundly satisfying things I have ever done, but you might find the same exhilaration and renewal from studying another field that underpins coaching, such as decision science or business strategy, in comparable depth.

But beware: psychology is tightly regulated in most countries. In case you get completely hooked and want to end up practising as a psychologist – and the new field of 'coaching psychology' is emerging so you might – then be extremely careful that the course you embark upon is fully recognised by the local psychology regulator. For example, in the UK many universities offer psychology degrees, but the British Psychological Society (BPS; www.bps.org.uk) does *not* recognise all of them. It would be deeply frustrating, after three years' hard undergraduate work, to discover that you can't be accepted on to a Coaching Psychology Master's because the undergraduate degree wasn't BPS accredited. The BPS is pitiless about this: if your undergraduate degree is not BPS accredited, they will insist you start again and repeat the entire three years to gain a degree that is. So check very carefully with your local regulatory body before embarking on any course of studies. (Then enjoy!)

If you would love to study psychology but now is not the time to do a full degree, then in every city there are usually excellent short courses at universities and adult education centres. Or get yourself a copy of D.G. Myers' outstanding textbook, *Psychology*,[5] currently in its ninth edition: impeccable scholarship, yet clearly explained and fresh and engaging to read – and great cartoons!*

Practice

Practice is at the heart of all good coaching training. The essential skills of good coaching can almost be written on the back of the proverbial envelope, but actually doing it is much harder – partly as there is so much to *un*learn. The absolute essential for becoming significantly better is putting in the coaching hours. I notice coaches in training seem to improve, not steadily, but in sudden upward leaps. The first comes after about 9–12 practice coaching sessions, then another at about 20 sessions, and another after about three times that. Jenny Rogers[6] says it takes 2,000 hours to become really competent; recent research says 10,000 hours to mastery of most things.[7]

Take care, however, who you practise with. There are lots of trade-offs to balance: working with people in your office who agree to be 'guinea pigs' saves time, which for a solo parent juggling work and heavy home responsibilities might be the single most important factor – but working with people who already know you, and expect you to behave in a certain way, isn't the best space to feel free to try completely new things. Conversely working with people you have never met, in fields which are totally foreign, is very valuable as you might feel much more free to experiment. And if you are right outside your professional expertise it *forces* you to be non-directive (see Chapter 5) – but there is a much heavier cost in terms of time, finding, vetting and briefing them, and possibly travelling distances to meet.

The two absolute essentials in a 'practice client' are that they be business-credible – there's no point training on pussycats if you work with lions;

---

* I have deliberately linked many of the Psychology references throughout this book to Myers, partly as it's brilliant, partly so if you have it to hand, you can easily follow the references in parallel from a single source.

and that they be currently in good mental health. It's challenging enough juggling the new tools all at once, without the client suddenly bursting into tears or screams.

This might sound alarming, and so it should. The boundaries with counselling or therapy, or 'what do I do if a client strays into territory I'm not trained to deal with', are among the worries most people bring to coach training. But good courses deal with this very firmly and early, building up your own awareness of your personal boundaries and your techniques to ensure you stay well within them. A further 'belt and braces' safeguard here is the next crucial element of the training course, namely:

Supervision

Even to become an OK coach, let alone a great one, you need someone to keep a close eye on you as you're learning; somewhere to take questions and problems and explore forming ideas.

This is true when you're developing your skill at anything, but in coaching, because we're working with people's minds, there *must* be an extra layer of protection built in. It is called 'supervision' and the concept came from the worlds of therapy and counselling. There are many elements to it. First, your supervisor is someone who watches out for the interests of *all three parties* to any business coaching: the coach, the client and the paying organisation. Are you the coach even subtly seeing your issues in the coachee, rather than theirs? Is the client a bad egg, manipulating you as part of her devious schemes? Is the organisation getting what they are paying for, or are coach and coachee drifting off into a happy little oblivion somewhere else?

A good supervisor should also help the trainee coach learn, pointing out new areas to explore, giving sage advice, an occasional rap over the knuckles and (hopefully more often!) pointing out where the coach has particular gifts which they were hitherto quite unaware were unique to them.

Feedback

An indispensable part of a training programme is feedback, ideally live in the moment, on your real coaching. It needs to be delivered sensitively, but straight between the eyes.

Community

Even the most committed introverts benefit from a chance to exchange ideas with others while developing their coaching. In fact, introverts can find communities of coaches quite congenial: for once, they're in a group of people who are trained to shut up, and listen properly.

Accreditation

I am not going to toe the party line here. The politically correct thing to say is accreditation bodies are a Good Thing. But a Princess once famously said three is too many in a marriage – and nine accrediting bodies, as there are in the UK at present,* and many more worldwide, is too many in a market. One solid professional body with tough standards, and sharp teeth to enforce them, would give buyers more confidence, but there is as yet no such institution. Admittedly it takes time for a profession to get this nailed down: doctors have largely achieved it, but they have been formally constituted for over 200 years. Psychologists haven't managed yet and they have just celebrated their centenary. So in an occupational field only 25–30 years old, it is unfortunate but unsurprising that we happen to be living in the period when multiple accrediting bodies are still to some extent banging different drums.

I am constantly asked whether given this, accreditation actually matters, and if so, which one is best. The answer to the first question is, it depends. Within organisations, typically one of two situations applies: either no accrediting body has taken hold, so you are free to take your own decision, or, often because a single influential person has become a 'true believer' in one particular accreditor, you can't coach there (officially) without being accredited by that organisation – or an internal process the organisation has set up in response to the lack of a single powerful external body. The former, open, situation is far more common, but the latter is increasing. So freelance coaches can and do face a situation where prospective clients are ruled out because they require coaches to be AC, or WABC, or EMCC accredited, but their own accreditation is with ICF, and vice versa. Or, as happened in 2009 in one European capital, experienced coaches were asked to attend an internal assessment centre in one part of town in the morning, then cross town to a not dissimilar process, but in a completely different organisation, in the afternoon, none of it paid for and none of it guaranteeing to lead to work.

---

* AC; APECS; CIPD; EMCC; ENTO; ICF; SGCP of the BPS; SCP; WABC – for full details see Table 4.2 (which has yet more as it covers the English-speaking world.)

However in practice, individuals often bypass a need for formal accreditation if they have an irresistible lure in their CV (famous businessperson; famous sports win; vast wealth) and/or they have been careful to keep their network alive and fresh and have excellent contacts and a proven track record with the buyers who count.

It is also largely irrelevant for external coaches engaged directly by leaders from the 'C-suite' (CEOs, COOs, etc.), who are seldom even aware of accrediting bodies and who take their own decisions, well above the reach of all but the most influential HR or L&D enforcers.

Even if the coaching engagement is being handled by HR or L&D departments, two very different attitudes to accreditation are apparent. The world-class HR or L&D practitioners found in leading organisations in the world's financial capitals tend to buy very discerningly, assessing each potential coach on their individual merits, rather than relying on just one factor, such as accreditation, alone. Putting forward a coach for the worldwide CEO or another senior leader in the organisation may not be the most important thing they will do in a year, but it may well be the most visible and high-risk, so savvy buyers will grill and assess coaches for individual fit and are unswayed by badges.

But if you are dealing with more junior HR personnel who have had less experience of the complexities of the coaching market, and/or who are further away from the centres of excellence, and/or in firms where someone has decided that coaching procurement must be systematised, then you are likely to face 'box-ticking', where accreditation suddenly switches from irrelevant to essential. To get through the first – usually computer-based – stage of such screening, you need to attest that you have formal training, and accreditation, and supervision, even if the computer couldn't tell a good one if it bit its nose. (Formal assessment processes vary of course; the superb Unilever process led by then-Global Head of Coaching Sam Humphrey is still many years later regarded by the industry as the 'gold standard', but at the other end of the quality spectrum there has been an outbreak of pro forma box-ticking in recent years.)

So whether accreditation matters or not, depends.

The question of which is the right one is easier to answer. It depends on what type of coaching you are doing, and where. For top-level business coaching, you may wish to consider the WABC, which is focused exclusively on business coaching, and in particular the senior, executive end of the market. It is also genuinely global, with coverage of every relevant continent including fast-expanding growth in the world's exploding market, China. You may or may not plan to work globally yourself, but if your organisation or clients are global organisations, WABC is worth investigating.

The ICF has a minority of business coach members, but remains largely focused on raising standards on what used to be called life coaching; the preferred term these days is personal coaching. In the US, where this is a large section of the market, the ICF is the leading accreditation body by far. In the UK the ICF is relatively small, and across Europe it is important in some countries and less so in others. The EMCC is as its name says, important in Europe. (The EMCC's conflating of coaching and mentoring was of some concern to me, as it could potentially perpetuate confusion between the two, but it matters less now, as people have become much clearer on the distinction.)

If you are a psychologist, you will be aware of the usually complex accreditation requirements prevailing in your country. In the UK, the BPS has a Special Group in Coaching Psychology (SGCP) but has decreed that for the moment it does not plan a route to chartering as a coaching psychologist. Hence a splinter group, the Society for Coaching Psychology (SCP), has recently formed and offers a route to accreditation.

The organisation to watch for the future in my view is the AC, which announced carefully considered new three-level accreditation standards in 2010. It is growing fast around the world, runs inexpensive CPD activities in widespread locations and has a thriving programme of quality publications.

By far the simplest way to gain accreditation by any of these bodies is to undertake a course which has been approved by the relevant accrediting body (because the accrediting body has, behind the scenes, exhaustively investigated the training provider and satisfied itself that its graduates are up to standard). There is then usually just a simple process where the training provider confirms to the accrediting body that you are a bona fide graduate, you pay the accrediting institution a fee, and you're in.

Some accrediting organisations, including the WABC, also have a route to accreditation for people who have *not* undertaken such a training course. This is deliberately not easy, as they are staking their reputation on accrediting an individual without the safeguard of having a reputable and pre-approved training provider backing them, but for those prepared to conduct a sustained paper war, it can be done.

Information on these and other accrediting bodies throughout the English-speaking world is summarised in the Table of Accreditation Providers: see Table 4.2 at the end of the chapter.

Choosing the right course for you/your organisation

The Table of Training Providers, Table 4.1, lists those generally regarded as the main courses currently available across the English-speaking world. This was winnowed down from many more: Meyler Campbell research in 2009 identified an astonishing 311 coach training courses on offer in the UK alone.[8] Even eliminating the long tail of courses mentioned by only one respondent, there is still a sizeable number to choose between.

Given this cornucopia, how on earth to choose? As with finding an individual coach, by far the most important method is word of mouth. Where did the people you respect, train? Which course has the best reputation in the sector you want to work in? Who did other organisations like yours turn to?

Obviously as with any prospective course you study their brochure and website: are the faculty experienced, does it seem well organised, is the content listed the type of material you want to cover? In addition, there are at least six other filters that may help you get to a shortlist: life v. business, level, cost/ROI, rigour, practicalities and community.

1. Life v. business coach training

Since you're reading a book on *business* coaching, you're probably interested in courses for business. (For the personal/business coaching distinction, see Chapter 1.) Or not: you might want to draw on your business background to help people as an exceptionally good personal coach. Either way, you need to be clear on which sector the course is preparing you for. Unfortunately, this often isn't clear. Most trainers fail to distinguish between the two, or even claim it's the same thing. I disagree: some of the basics are indeed the same, but business coaching is considerably more complex: for a start there are almost always many parties involved in the initial contracting (as opposed to a single individual in life coaching.) Table 4.1 identifies the courses – only about 5–10% of the whole – which focus on business coach training. You might want to take this one stage further and look not just for a training that specialises in business or organisational coaching, but also to identify the leading brand in your chosen business sector which takes you back to asking around.

2. Level: Master's or Practitioner?

The training and accrediting bodies have done good work in recent years in forging a consensus on two broad levels of coaching practice and training: Practitioner and Master's. The labels are self-explanatory: Practitioner-level courses should have a sound basis in theory, but the main emphasis will be on actually coaching. They are usually one year part-time. Master's degrees, as you would expect, have a much greater emphasis on and depth in the academic theory, and they are also usually longer (typically two years) and more expensive.

Have no illusions that a Master's/PhD will offer any guarantees: someone said to me years ago she was working for a PhD in coaching 'because I don't have any business experience, but I want to be a business coach because it pays more and this will get me in the door'. It won't – as noted above, savvy organisational buyers look at much more than a single piece of paper, however weighty.

Instead, in deciding which level is right for you, I suggest you use the coaching trick of following your *intrinsic interest*. Whichever route you choose, it will be hard work and you'll need good motivation. Some people have fretted for years that they don't have a degree and now's their chance. Or they just love studying in a university environment, with essays and assignments, theoretical depth and a Master's degree at the end. For others that's the last thing they need – they want a course that's practical and high-energy, with a real focus on putting the learning to use. Follow your dream – that will give you the energy to flourish in the training, even if, as for most people, you have to juggle it with full-time work and other commitments, such as family.

3. Cost – and return on investment

Table 4.1 also indicates the cost of each coach training: fully accredited coach training is typically around £10,000 + VAT (at 2010 levels) for a Practitioner-level course and £15,000–£25,000 for a Master's-level programme. If the training is funded by your organisation, then you will likely be weighing up the benefits described in Chapter 2 of having strong internal coaching capability, including among the leadership teams.

If you are paying as an individual, to know whether you will get value for that investment you need to know your reasons for wanting to develop your coaching: do you need to pay the mortgage and feed your family as a result of this, or is it just for your personal interest? If you want the training to lift you to a new level in your organisation, or to convert you into a successful freelance business coach, then look for evidence that substantial numbers of previous graduates are making a good living.

What you can typically earn as a coach, and the many ways people do it, are discussed in Chapter 12. In brief, there is a very wide range: I know one business coach who earns £1 million a year solely from their coaching – but at the other extreme, one primarily life coach training organisation told me with great honesty that having surveyed its graduates, 95% of them weren't able to earn their living from coaching alone. In between, from the results of several market surveys including our own on the business of coaching, plus my observation of generations of graduates over 15 years, most can and do earn a reasonable (but not huge) living. In terms of recovering their initial investment, most graduates of our own programme are working at a level in the European business coaching market where they can charge £10,000 upwards (2010 prices) for a single six-month coaching assignment – but it typically takes them 18–24 months to get up to that level of full professional charging. And the ones who worked solidly on their coaching but also crucially their marketing and business development, sustained and even grew their businesses despite the 'Great Recession'. For more on all this, see Chapter 12.

If however you are considering coaching for personal interest and fulfilment, then the 'ROI' will be different, and scrutinising your shortlist perhaps the angle on the material covered, and the type of people you will be working with, will matter more. Again, what have previous graduates of your shortlisted courses done with their training: is it encouraging, even inspiring?

4. Rigour

At a basic level, indicators of a rigorous training are straightforward: is the approach clearly grounded in well-established, empirically-evidenced approaches? Is the faculty of high calibre? Is the selection process tough? Rigorous selection processes are one of the big differences between general coach training, where usually you pay your fee and are in, and specialist business coaching courses. For example, on our own programme only about 40% of those who contact the company each year are offered a place. (For the selection criteria, see Chapter 3, 'Do you have what it takes?'.)

Beyond that, rigour may manifest differently for different people. As a young diplomat I had the job of taking the then Singapore Minister of Finance, Dr Tony Tan Keng Yam, around the country for a week. At the end of his visit, he said he wanted to give me a present, to say thank you. It was a piece of advice: 'Anne,' he said, gravely, 'always be the *third* owner of a hotel'. As an underpaid young diplomat, I'd rather have had fifty quid*, but actually the subtle wisdom of his gift, the metaphor, has stayed with me. I prefer training with a well-established organisation that has had time to settle down and get things consistently right but on the other hand *you* might prefer the funky new kid on the block, who trains in innovative, crazy ways. One firm I knew used camels.

5. Practicalities

The research is abundantly clear that the way of learning any new skill is to learn a bit; put it into practice; mull over it; learn a bit more; try it out and mull again. The conscious and unconscious processing and absorption that goes on between learning modules is just as important as the times when you are actually concentrating on learning aspects of the new skill. For this reason most coach trainings are modular, with days or half-days spread out over time. That's the optimal way to learn, and for the learning to stick, and for most people this also fits well with the rest of their working and personal lives, as they can manage a module a month, for example. But even though this is the optimal way to learn, it may not suit some people's diaries – learning in one intensive blast may be better for them.

Similarly, with the format of the training – do you flourish in a small-group environment where things are very bespoke and personally crafted for your or your organisation's unique needs – or would you much prefer to sit anonymously at the back of a large lecture theatre, watching and observing with wry detachment the follies of others?

6. Community

Most people want to get on with the people they're training with, but when you're grappling with something new and challenging – maybe for the first time in decades! – it can make a powerful difference to be with congenial fellow-sufferers to share the highs and lows, and for tools, tips, resources and contacts.

This goes from a 'nice to have' to almost essential if you are making the leap out of full-time work. The people you train with can become your

---

* Just kidding – we were of course not permitted to accept gifts of any monetary value, though most of us had collections of kitsch that defied description.

instant new community, partly replacing some of those no-longer-around work colleagues. And they have much more than social value: if this is a career change, will these people be able to help open doors for you, and enrich the quality of your work? And is the ethos of the community a generous one of mutual self-help, or do people just scurry to lectures and scurry out again, keeping their contacts close to their chest? This is where going to trial events is invaluable – do you feel at home with these people, what is the 'spirit' of the gathering, and is it right for you?

Step 4: Continue learning ...

Having trained, you are still only, in that wonderful Churchillian phrase, at 'the end of the beginning'. The next two years post-training in particular are absolutely crucial, to keep practising and learning, until it becomes fluid and unconscious and you can flick in and out of coaching mode in an instant.

This is particularly important for the majority of people who do business coach training not to become a professional coach but to develop their management and leadership skills: for them, coaching might just be the few-minute opportunity that suddenly opens up standing by the water cooler. Paradoxically, to be able to coach well in those 2–3 minutes takes hours of more formal coaching sessions. The training course will teach you what to do and get you started; you then need to keep going, to build that rapid-response capability.

The pieces for ongoing learning are mostly the same as in the training: practice, supervision, formal learning and support/community.

Practice post-training

Fortunately for most people coaching becomes instinctive, and is so fulfilling that it is no hardship to keep doing it. Sometimes the deepest rewards come outside the workplace: one older male participant had the rest of us almost in tears halfway through one course, when he said quietly: 'Over the weekend I had the first real conversation I've ever had with my 14-year-old son.'

Nevertheless you need to ensure you have formal coaching arrangements in place, to build up your hours. Within an organisation there is usually no difficulty: once word spreads that you can coach there's a queue outside your door. The Coaches in Government Network is a clever arrangement in the UK civil service. It is a group of trained coaches who want to keep coaching, but they recognise that senior people are often more prepared to work with an external coach. So they swap: a network member in, say, The Department for Environment, Food and Rural Affairs (DEFRA) will have a client or two in the Education Ministry, and vice versa. The coaching is not charged, but is in all other ways fully professional and properly contracted. All the coaches have 'day jobs', so can't take on a large client list, but it's still a neat solution, providing access to quality coaching, from people familiar with the unique culture and jargon of the UK government, yet external to the client's particular department.

Freelance coaches who don't have an immediate pool of potential clients on their doorstep come up with a variety of solutions to keep building their hours. Many have 'transition clients' where they charge lower fees than a more established coach. It's a win/win: the client gets coaching from a qualified source but more cheaply, and the coach is building their experience. Others volunteer, in local schools (head teachers have the same intense performance pressure as CEOs, with far less money to achieve it) or churches or arts and community organisations.

Formal new learning, or CPD

Accreditation and training bodies recognise that ongoing learning is an indispensable part of professional practice, and most require an average of 40 hours a year logged CPD. They will give credit hours for a mix of activities, including attending courses, supervision and reading.

Refresher courses and new techniques

I notice after their initial coach training, the next course coaches typically undertake is training in the Myers–Briggs Type Indicator (MBTI®). (For more on MBTI, including the debate over MBTI *v.* trait personality measures, see Chapter 7.) The 'gold standard' coaching toolkit was in the past MBTI, FIRO-B® and a good method for 360-degree feedback. Or to put it differently, one intrapersonal psychometric (i.e. one that gives an overall picture of individual personality); one interpersonal (i.e. that measures people's needs with regards to others); and something to get reliable data from the context. The advent of Positive Psychology means the goalposts have moved and a good coach is now expected to have a Strengths instrument in their toolkit as well, such as the VIA, Gallup's StrengthsFinder or Realise2. (For more on all this, see Chapter 7.) Apart from MBTI, none of these is expensive to train in, but there is a significant other cost in adding them to one's toolkit, as every new approach needs time to practise, absorb and integrate. For that reason most coaches add about one a year, in the meantime pairing up with others to cover the gap.

Supervision

You will have had a taste of supervision on the training, but there were plenty of other people around then to keep an eye on you, and for you to turn to – now, supervision *really* matters. It's a comforting feeling to know there's someone there for regular contact and updates – and to call in emergencies.

As noted above, there are several ways to find a business coaching supervisor. The simplest is to pay one. This sub-domain of business coaching is rapidly professionalising. In our 2008 Business of Coaching Survey, 40% of supervision was on an unpaid peer-sharing basis, and average UK fees for paid work were £100–£200 per session. Only a year later, in the 2009 Survey, unpaid supervision had dropped to 28%, and fees for paid work had risen considerably: 18% were still paying £50–100 a session, 19% £100–300 and a new category of elite supervisors earning £300–750 a session had broken cover.

Reading

It is said that Sir Francis Bacon was the last scholar in Europe to know everything; an insomniac, he walked in the Palace grounds by night, reading, and by the end of his life had read everything in the then-known world. In the early days in coaching when so little was published that was almost possible, but since the mid-1990s an avalanche of information has poured down on us. Books, blogs, Twitter, articles – the trick is to pick up on the indispensable new tools and approaches without drowning. There are several ways to do this: I scan the very useful journal *Coaching at Work* (www.coaching-at-work) to keep an eye on what people are actually doing in organisations, and industry gossip, and the *Consulting Psychology Journal* (www.apa.org) to keep up with the latest global best practice and research. Other journals include *Coaching: An International Journal of Theory and Practice* (www.tandf.co.uk), *The Coaching Psychologist* (www.sgcp.org.uk), and the *International Coaching Psychology Review* (www.sgcp.org.uk). When I worked briefly in the United Nations before my coaching life, each member of our team took responsibility to follow one key industry journal and update the others with anything important. If you are in a team this approach might still be valuable – or maybe Twitter has superseded it!

Support/community

Groups who have come together in training courses often want to keep in touch post-programme. You might think this matters most for people embarking on freelance coaching careers, and indeed they do often need and want it. But it is equally important for people within organisations, to help keep their coaching active, and as a counterforce to all the other organisational demands. I have seen groups form a LinkedIn network; and/or meet once a month for ongoing learning; invite in outside speakers; and keep meeting for co-coaching and supervision.

Support can be business as well as socially focused: over the years we calculate that over 30 businesses large and small have been formed by people who met initially on our programme. This can range from formally becoming fellow directors in corporate coaching companies to co-operative arrangements to help each other out on bigger coaching projects.

Another fun and fast-growing new way of keeping in touch with both people and industry trends is the coaching book group. One group I know consists of just three friends, all experienced coaches. Asked how they organise it, one member said: 'Three of us, over a sandwich lunch, a couple of hours, having read a book/article, leads into conversations about our coaching experiences/sharing what's worked/hasn't worked, etc. It's great – we love it!'

But what is underneath all this hive of activity? What exactly do coaches *do* behind closed doors?!

They start with the essentials: listening more, asking penetrating questions, having people stop and think for themselves. These are the basics of coaching: if you want to learn about these practical tools, go to Chapter 5. Or if you're the kind of person who prefers to know first *why* something works, see Chapter 11. Or you may have dropped the book already, and rushed out to find yourself a great coach and get started!

Table 4.1 Table of training providers

Training Provider	Website	Cost /Cost Range[1, 2]	Highest Level Course Name	Programme Timescale[3]	Accreditation[4]
Academy of Executive Coaching	www.aoec.com	££ – ££££	Master Practitioner in Executive Coaching	15 months	EMCC, ICF, AC
Ashridge College of Management Studies	www.ashridge.org.uk	£££ – £££££	Masters (MSc) in Executive Coaching	24 months	EMCC
Coaches Training Institute (CTI)	www.thecoaches.com	£ – £££ ($)	Co-active® Coach Training	12 months	ICF
College of Executive Coaching	www.executivecoachcollege.com	£ – £££ ($)	Advanced Certified Personal and Executive Coach	6 months	ICF
Henley Business School (University of Reading)	www.henley.reading.ac.uk	££ – £££££	Masters (MSc) in Coaching & Behavioural Change	30 months	
I-Coach	www.i-coachacademy.com	£ – £££	Masters in Professional Coaching	12 months+	EMCC
INSEAD	www.insead.edu	££££££ (€)	Consulting & Coaching for Change	14 months	
Management Futures	www.managementfutures.co.uk	£££	Diploma in Coaching	12–24 months	EMCC
Meyler Campbell	www.meylercampbell.com	££££	The Business Coach Programme©	12 months	WABC, AC, SRA
School of Coaching	www.theschoolofcoaching.com	££££	Coach's Programme	6 months	EMCC

Table 4.1 *Continued*

Training Provider	Website	Cost /Cost Range[1, 2]	Highest Level Course Name	Programme Timescale[3]	Accreditation[4]
Tavistock Institute	www.tavinstitute.org	£££	Coaching for Leadership & Professional Development	4 months	
University of Oxford (Saïd Business School)/HEC School of Management – Paris	www.sbs.ox.ac.uk www.exed.hec.edu/en	£££££ (€)	Masters (MSc) in Consulting & Coaching for Change	11 months	

[1] The pricing key is as follows:

£:	Up to £ 2,500
££:	Up to £ 5,000
£££	Up to £ 7,500
££££	Up to £ 10,000
£££££	In excess of £ 10,000
££££££	In excess of £ 20,000

The figures exclude VAT. The relevant currency indicator (€ or $) is shown to indicate that we have converted from the original currency.

[2] We have given details of the highest level of coach training provided by each organisation but, where more than one level of course is offered, we have indicated the relevant price range according to the key listed above. (Pricing does not include conversion to full Masters (MSc/MA) qualifications unless the training is specifically at that level.)

[3] The timescales shown relate to the highest level of training provided. Courses at lower levels may well take less time to complete. Most programmes are delivered part-time, with specific face-to-face (or other medium) training.

[4] We have listed primarily accrediting bodies that correspond with the Table of Accrediting Organisations. Some providers' courses may be accredited by individual Universities or other organisations. SRA (column 6) is the Solicitors' Regulation Authority (UK), formerly the Law Society of England & Wales.

Disclaimer: The above Table has been designed to provide preliminary information on coach training providers using information drawn from publicly available website content as at July 2010. It is not intended that the Table should provide detail on all issues relevant to training providers, nor is it intended to be an exhaustive list of all organisations offering some form of coach training. The information is liable to change and we do not guarantee its accuracy.

Table 4.2 Table of coaching accreditation organisations

Accrediting Body	Status & Date of Establishment	Geographical Reach	Accreditation offered		Coaching Sector Emphasis
			Training Organisations	Individuals	
Association for Coaching (AC) www.associationforcoaching.com	Not-for-profit Established 2002	Global focus	Course Recognition available	From 1st October 2010: Executive Coach and General Coach Schemes: 3 levels in each: Accredited Coach, Accredited Professional Coach and Accredited Master Coach	Non-specific: personal and business/executive coaching
Association for Professional Executive Coaching & Supervision (APECS) www.apecs.org	Not-for-profit Established 2005	UK based + international membership	No	Yes: Accredited Executive Coach and Accredited Executive Coach Supervisor	Specific focus: business/ executive coaching and coaching supervision
British Psychological Society: Special Group in Coaching Psychology (SGCP) www.bps.org.uk/coachingpsy www.sgcp.org.uk	Special group of representative body Established 2004	UK based + global reach with international members	No, but under review	Currently have Chartered Psychologists who specialise in coaching psychology Other routes under development and review	Forum for coaching psychologists and non-psychologist coaches interested in using psychology in their coaching

Table 4.2 *Continued*

Accrediting Body	Status & Date of Establishment	Geographical Reach	Accreditation offered		Coaching Sector Emphasis
			Training Organisations	*Individuals*	
Coaches & Mentors of South Africa (COMENSA) http://www.comensa.org.za	Not-for-profit Established 2006	South Africa based with local and international members	No, but implementing Member Criteria & Standards of Competence Framework	No, but roll-out of new Member Criteria & Standards of Competence Framework will define levels of competence & expertise	Non-specific: personal and business/executive coaching
European Mentoring and Coaching Council (EMCC) www.emccouncil.org www.emccaccreditation.org	Not-for-profit Established (in current form) 2002	Pan-European Membership across 18+ European countries	Yes at 4 levels – Foundation, Practitioner, Senior Practitioner and Master Practitioner	Yes at 4 levels – Foundation, Practitioner, Senior Practitioner and Master Practitioner	Non-specific: professional coaching and mentoring
Institute of Leadership and Management (ILM) www.i-l-m.com	Registered charity Established 2001	UK based + global focus	Yes: 2 levels – Approved Centre Status (approval to deliver ILM qualifications) Recognised Provider Status (relevant to external or in-house development programmes)	No	Broad spectrum vocational training to manager across all sectors & industries

Table 4.2 *Continued*

Accrediting Body	Status & Date of Establishment	Geographical Reach	Training Accreditation Organisations	Accreditation offered Individuals	Coaching Sector Emphasis
International Association of Coaching (IAC) www.certifiedcoach.org	Not-for-profit Established 2003	US based + global focus Membership across 15+ countries	No – although provide licenses for coach training organisations to incorporate the IAC Coaching Masteries™ into their training programs	Yes: Certified Coach	Non-specific: personal and business/executive coaching
International Coach Federation (ICF) www.coachfederation.org	Not-for-profit Established 1995	US based + global focus Membership across 90 countries	Yes: 2 designations – ACTP (Accredited Coach Training Provider) and ACSTH (Approved Coach Specific Training Hours)	Yes: three designations – Associate Certified Coach, Professional Certified Coach and Master Certified Coach	Non-specific: personal and business/executive coaching
International Institute of Coaching (IIC) (originally ECI – European Coaching Institute) www.internationalinstituteofcoaching.org	Not-for-profit Established 1999	Founded in UK + global focus Membership across 75 countries	Course recognition available at 5 levels: Accredited Full Coach Training Programme, Accredited Foundation Coach Training Programme (Levels 1 & 2), Accredited Short Course, Accredited Workshop	Yes: 4 levels – Accredited Practitioner Coach, Accredited Senior Coach, Accredited Master Coach and Accredited Fellow Coach	Non-specific: personal and business/executive coaching

Table 4.2 Continued

Accrediting Body	Status & Date of Establishment	Geographical Reach	Accreditation offered		Coaching Sector Emphasis
			Training Organisations	Individuals	
Society for Coaching Psychology (SCP) www.societyforcoachingpsychology.net	Not-for-profit Established 2008	UK based + international focus	Course recognition available	Yes	Specific focus: coaching psychology
Worldwide Association of Business Coaches (WABC) www.wabccoaches.com	Private Canadian Corp since 2002 (Originally established as NABC in 1997 in US)	Canadian HQ + global focus Membership across 30+ countries	Yes: WABC Accredited at 3 levels – Practitioner, Master and Chartered	Yes: 4 levels – Registered Corporate Coach™ WABC Certified Business Coach™ WABC Certified Master Business Coach™ Chartered Business Coach™	Specific focus: senior business/executive coaching

© Copyright Meyler Campbell 2010. Reproduced with permission.

5

Building your basic coaching skills: the 'Big Five'

So when the door closes, and coach and coachee are finally left alone together, what actually happens? In this chapter, we cover the five absolute basics. In the next we talk about some bells and whistles you can add on – but if you did just this chapter's five simple (but not easy!) things really well, you would be astonished by the results. The 'Big Five'* alone can be transformational.

In fact, I would be so radical as to say, the other things are sometimes added in to make the coach feel better. The Big Five are like a Picasso drawing: others would cram more onto the page, but only the master has the confidence to draw a single, perfect line. The coaching equivalent is:

1 contracting;
2 the GROW model;
3 listening;
4 questioning, and
5 non-directive.

I say more about each below. In the real world they blend, and you might need to flip back and forth a little to get results, but I describe them here in their 'pure' state so you get the clearest picture.

1. Contracting

On the rare occasions that something goes wrong in coaching and people come to me for help, 99% of the time it was a failure of *contracting*. Good

---

* Not the psychometricians 'Big Five', or the 'Big Five' safari animals – the coaching Big Five!

contracting has three main elements: *commercial*, *psychological*, and *within the work itself*.

The *commercial* aspects are the same as everything else in business: what is the service to be delivered here, by whom to whom, what are the end results/deliverables, and the details such as location, cancellation charges, etc. This takes some thought and work to hammer out, and research on best practice in your particular sector/context, but it is a straightforward business task. Nevertheless, many coaches in training still have to be reminded about this piece – they get so absorbed in the thrill of actual coaching, they need to be gently reconnected with the standard business 'hygiene factors' they had temporarily forgotten.

By contrast, the *psychological contract* is almost never spelled out in business, but it is there all the time, underlying – or undermining! – the overt work being done. In coaching some of it though must be explicitly spelled out: for example, contracting around confidentiality. Is everything that is said between these walls utterly confidential, not to be revealed by you the coach, even unto your dying day? Or is there a requirement that some information, perhaps at key milestone points, will go back to the organisation that is, after all, paying? (If the latter, a simple trick that saves much grief is to ensure that all reporting goes through the coachee: so the organisation gets what it needs, but trust is maintained as the coachee sees everything.)

The psychological contract begins to be formed in the many – seemingly trivial – initial administrative exchanges between all the parties, and then particularly in the 'chemistry' session. The very existence of such a session – where the prospective individual client has the chance to meet the coach and decide if they feel comfortable working with them – goes a long way towards building a workable psychological contract. If forced into coaching, people remain wary. If they have real choice, they are more likely to engage.

The essence of the psychological contract is trust: the client has to trust the coach to the extent that they feel able to open up, disclose sensitive information, and try and explore new things. How do you build trust? For coaching, which is a relatively straightforward part of business life, I think you just need to be a more or less decent person, seem competent at the task and have an inner confidence in what you're doing. The first of these – being basically decent – was already touched on in Chapter 3. As for the others, I observe it takes about 3–6 months of a coach training for people to build basic competence in coaching, but much longer for them to believe it: building that crucial inner confidence takes many practice sessions over, typically, 6–12 months. But it pays off: sensible business people have an acute 'nose' and can tell instantly if you're authentic or not.

The third element of contracting is *during the work itself.* The coach constantly keeps an eye on whether the topic worked on, is actually what the corporate client is paying for. And even within the session, minute by minute, whether what's being discussed right now is actually relevant to the goal set at the beginning of the session (on which more below.)

So far so good. But now we get to *simple* contracting *v. complex* contracting – i.e. the difference between 'life' and business coaching.

Simple contracting

Where there is just one coach contracting with one client – in personal coaching for example, or in business coaching where the client is a sole trader, or the proprietor of a small business where there isn't anyone else involved – contracting is usually very straightforward. Coach and client can work out together what is involved, the price for the work, and the deliverables. And in addition to the commercial contracting, the 'psychological contract' is usually also clear: I as the client will trust you and be pretty open about even my most sensitive business issues, maybe even personal ones where relevant; you as the coach will respect that confidence absolutely, and create a really practical and effective environment for us to do good work together and deliver the outcomes I want.

Complex contracting: both the individual *and* the organisation

Contracting at the individual level is of course also necessary in complex organisational coaching. Typically the coach's first contact is with the corporate 'buyer' or initiator of the coaching. When the coach is briefed by them, there are some questions about the prospective individual client so simple that it might seem naïve, even a bit embarrassing, to ask – usually these are of course the most important! Does the person actually want to be coached? Did anyone ask them? What is the purpose of the coaching? As coaching becomes ever more 'sexy', it is becoming increasingly common for it to be suggested rather than another intervention that would in fact be better for that particular task. If there is for example a simple skill deficit – Jo's new role requires them to do X or Y and they don't know how – then targeted training to plug the gap might be a better starting point.

Once the coach is briefed, and is onto the next stage of meeting the prospective coachee directly in the 'chemistry' session, they might get quite different answers to the individual-level questions. It sometimes turns out the prospective individual client *didn't* feel they had a real choice about being coached – maybe they feigned acceptance but internally felt resentful. Or they might have really wanted coaching, but not had any choice as to the coach.* Both of these can be a waste of money: coaching depends so much on the client being actively involved, that foisting anything on them, whether it's being coached, or a coach of someone else's choosing, is pointless. So as much as possible, the coach who finds themselves in this position has to name it, open the subject right up again and give the client real choice, saying something like: 'Well, we seem to be in a less than ideal situation. Let's figure out what your real options might be here, and how you could manage each of them…'

But assuming there wasn't any such hitch, the client was keen to be coached, and 'clicked' with one of the prospective coaches they were offered, the next task is to contract on the actual work to be done within the coaching sessions – what are the goals for the coaching work overall, and for individual sessions therein. With a client in personal coaching, job done, and you launch into the work.

In the *organisational* context though you're only part way there: the coach needs to be contracting in parallel with the many others involved. The paying client, the organisation, will have objectives for the coaching. Those objectives may be clear or unclear, and they may or may not be aligned with those of the individual person (or team) being coached. And there are usually several different stakeholders: the client, their line manager/Chairman/CEO; the HR and/or L&D specialist or occasionally both; and perhaps a separate budget holder, to name just a few. This is one of the major differences between life and business coaching: in business coaching, with multiple stakeholders, there is far greater complexity. (And more again if, as is often the case, the players are in different cultures/time zones.)

There is also the sometimes tricky contractual matter that the real client is not the person sitting in front of you, it's the organisation paying the bill.

----

* One small professional-services organisation I knew offered coaching to all people promoted to partner level – but the only coach allowed was the wife of the Senior Partner. She had done a short training course and wanted clients. I am not making this up.

Some people, usually former therapists who in my view haven't properly switched to operating under the rules of business, disagree, and maintain that the 'client' to whom they have primary and sole responsibility is the person sitting in front of them. I feel quite passionately that this is wrong: ethically, and indeed legally, if the coach is contracted with the organisation, then the organisation is the client. (While in theory it might be possible for a business coach to be hired by an *individual* in an organisation, in practice you would ask why this is happening: usually it's because the individual wants to leave, or there has been a breakdown in trust with their employer. If the employer is an existing client firm, facilitating the departure of a valued employee would presumably be a breach of the contract with the firm. In which case the coach has to choose between taking on the individual and renouncing the corporate client, or keeping the corporate relationship and declining the individual.) Yes of course we do our level best for the person sitting in front of us, but our paymaster is the organisation. We coach the individual to the very best of our ability – but it would be wrong to coach them, even if they set that as the goal, on anything inimical to the interests of the organisation.

The usual situation – and it crops up all the time – is where they are tired, or exhausted, or stressed, or feel unappreciated, and consider leaving. Assuming they are a valued employee the firm wants to retain, it would of course be highly improper for a coach to assist them to move to a competitor, while being paid by their present employer – but while this sounds a nightmare in theory, in practice the problem seldom arises: good clients have a sense of propriety too and generally don't stray beyond the limits, and experienced coaches know that giving them some space to vent is often all that is needed. The really tricky issues are usually more nuanced and complicated. Dealing with the challenges this throws up, when the objectives and even the wellbeing of organisation and individual client diverge, is one of the most common subjects coaches take to supervision (see Chapter 4). It really helps to have expert, dispassionate guidance to tease out where the ethical responsibilities lie and to plot the correct path, especially in 'grey areas'.

In addition, working in organisations there is the need to *understand the context* and contract well in the shifting political sands of organisational life. The hazards of this are well known to people in business, so I won't say much more, but have summarised some useful questions in the box on the next page to jog your memory.

Contracting around the sandtraps

There is always more to surprise us, but asking yourself the following questions should help:

- Who are the key stakeholders?
- How can I find out what they want from the coaching?
- How will I manage the contracting process with the various stakeholders?
- How will I balance confidentiality and an organisation's desire to have feedback on progress?
- Are there any key aspects of 'how things are done around here' that I need to know?
- What is the stimulus for the coaching request? And who initiated it?
- What is the need of the organisational client?
- How does it relate to their current or future business needs and drivers?
- What are likely to be the issues for coaching, from their point of view?
- Is coaching the best approach to meeting the various needs and expectations, or would, for example, counselling or training be more suitable interventions?
- Are the organisation's and individual's goals in alignment?

How to find answers to these questions may not be apparent, or easy. In practice there are often things which the coach is not told. One of the hallmarks of a very experienced business coach is the ways they have developed of finding out more. Practice (and sadly, a sorry lesson or two I'm afraid) will help your antennae get much more acute.

2. GROW model

The GROW model is by far the most widely used coaching tool in the world.

It looks deceptively simple – but don't be fooled. At one level it *is* simple: that's part of its appeal. Even the busiest or most forgetful of us can manage to remember G-R-O-W. But on the other hand it has immense depth and power.

It's also like an accordion: it can expand in or out as much as you want – GROW works to structure a long, formal coaching session of an hour or two, but you can use it just as well (well, pieces of it – or the whole thing if you're dazzlingly good!) for a two-minute conversation by the coffee machine.

Let me outline it briefly first, then we'll go through each section in more detail.

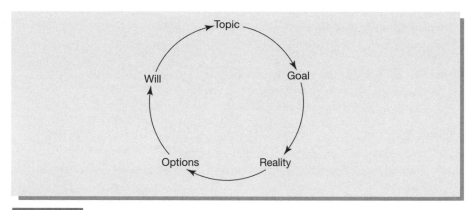

Figure 5.1 The GROW model

GROW: brief outline

■ *Topic*. It actually starts with 'Topic' – the client comes in and says what they want to talk about today. (Yes I know, so it's really the 'TGROW' model – but like so many movie stars, it had to change its name to be famous.)

■ *Goal*. From that broad topic, the coach gets the client really clear on what they want from *this* session: e.g., 'what is the specific outcome you want today, and how will we know we have succeeded?'

■ *Reality*. In the 'R' stage the coach asks the client to get the key facts out on the table. Military strategists would call this stage 'reconnaissance' (as in, 'time spent in reconnaissance is never wasted').

■ *Options*. This is familiar territory for business people: what are the options, and what are the costs, benefits, upsides, downsides, risks, etc. of each.

■ *Will*. And finally, what will you do, i.e. what is your action plan? But also crucially, the 'W' uses *both* meanings of 'Will' – i.e. not just 'Will' as in action but also what is your 'Will' around this, i.e. your motivation.

How do you take a client through it? Simply by asking them the questions appropriate to each stage (then stopping and *listening* properly to their answer – see below!). Some good questions to ask in each stage are in the box on the next page – coaches in training often find it useful to compile their own unique set, noting good questions wherever they spot them, trying different ones out, and settling on the ones that work best for them.

Some GROW questions:*

Topic

- What brought you to coaching? What would you like to explore?
- What would you like to work on today?
- What else?

Goal

- What do you want from this particular coaching session?
- What specifically do you want to have when you walk out that door, that you don't have now?
- How does that contribute to your overall work objective(s) and current challenges?
- What will achievement of the goal be like? What will you/others see, feel, hear, touch?
- How will you/we know we've succeeded?

Reality

- What are the key facts we need to be aware of?
- Briefly, what is the background and current context of this goal?
- What else is relevant?
- Who else is involved?
- Where?
- When?
- How?

Options

- What might you do?
- What have you already considered?
- What else could you do?
- The 'miracle question' – if you had a magic wand/had unlimited time or budget, what would you do?
- What are the upsides/downsides/risks of each?
- Which option(s) will you test further, or act upon?

Will

- What will you do? When? How?
- What might get in the way?
- What support do you need to stick at it, and where can you get it from?
- What is your commitment to going ahead?

---

* For more, see Sir John Whitmore, *Coaching for Performance*, at the end of which there are several pages on questions for each stage. Whitmore, J. (1996) *Coaching for Performance*, 2nd edn., London: Nicholas Brealey Publishing.

More on GROW

Now you have a preliminary sense of how it works, let's dig a little deeper.

Topic

As Alison Hardingham so helpfully reminds us[1], the client doesn't walk in the door as a blank slate: they turn up amidst a very busy life, their head buzzing with all that's going on. Some of it is noise – they got frustrated in bad traffic, the cat was sick this morning, a key employee is leaving – but somewhere in there is this session's topic. How to tell the difference? Ask the client! This is a core underlying assumption of business coaching: the client is presumed to be well, and perfectly capable of disentangling things for themselves, if we just create the right conditions.

So even the simple starting question, 'what would you like to talk about today?' can open a can of worms. Myles Downey then makes it even tougher: he suggests we ask it *again*.[2] I saw him once doing a live coaching demonstration. The first topic was very sensible and would clearly have made a difference to the client sitting there. Myles noted it respectfully, then asked again. After a moment's pause, a second topic emerged. Again, respect – but then Myles asked, 'Anything else?' – and out blurted a third topic that was clearly 'the one'. The coaching session was set alight. Asked afterwards by the audience if he had suspected the 'real' topic was underneath, Myles said courteously not at all, it is simply his practice to ask, several times, in order to check. A discipline.

Goal

By now, with perhaps several big meaty topics on the table, a consultant would be in mental overdrive, following all the threads, hothousing solutions, worrying how to get through the load in such a short time. But Myles just calmly asks a simple question: 'Which of these do you want to work on today?' This is the essence of coaching: it seems innocuous, but it throws the responsibility for the *content* of the coaching onto the client. Only they know the vast complexity of all the factors, history, data, hopes, fears, contradictions, of the matter in hand. Putting the question to them causes them to drop their thinking from surface brain functioning down into deeper processing: often they fall silent briefly while their brain crunches it all. Then they look up, into your eyes, and firmly state the topic.

In a normal conversation, both sides would regard that as that. But GROW differs massively from normal conversations, at two points: the beginning, and the end, the 'G' and the 'W'.

In a normal business conversation, or indeed over a glass of wine with friends, 'topics' come up all the time, but you wouldn't then require them to distil that down into a single, pinpoint goal for the conversation. In coaching, you must. If you did nothing else from this book other than just go around your organisation requiring a far higher standard of clear goal-setting, that alone would be transformational. There is powerful scientific evidence for this (see Chapter 11) and it is cross-culturally valid: the more specific the goal set at the beginning, the higher the performance outcome at the end. Of all the vast amount of research from organisational psychology, this is one of the few pieces that has jumped over the wall into mainstream business, in the acronym 'SMART'. SMART goals are variously defined, but the acronym is usually something like Specific, Measurable, Achievable, Realistic (ah! we'll come back to that!) and Timed.

But no one applies this as determinedly as coaches must in the 'G' of GROW. Getting it right is often uncomfortable. Clients who aren't used to it generally need to experience it in several sessions before they get the hang of it. It often feels awkward for coaches in training too – so much so that initially they almost always duck out too early, and fail to get a proper 'G'. Experienced coaches are supportive, patient – but tough. My own preferred method is to make it as tangible as possible. Gesturing at the door, I ask, 'What do you want to have when you walk out that door, that you don't have now?' Clients thereby get what I mean by a goal – it might be clarity, or a plan, or three bullet points, but it's inside their head. I'm not offering a magic wand, to change the world outside; but what *is* on offer is sharpening up the only tool they really have to make that change, i.e. themselves.

The goal is utterly key. It does all the heavy lifting of the session – so if you don't have a good clear goal, you don't have a coaching session. I once watched a colleague do a coaching demonstration, in a large hall in a hard-edged industrial town, in front of a cynical audience of 200 people. He had only 30 minutes for the demonstration. The minutes ticked by. Ten minutes, fifteen, and he's still working patiently to get the goal. Twenty minutes, and his colleagues in the audience are beginning to sweat. Finally at minute 25, he got it – and in the remaining five minutes, the rest of the session fell into place like dominoes: Reality, Options, Will, click click click, and a great result. With a great goal, the rest of the session falls into place.

Why is it so powerful? It's like light. When the light waves are all over the place, as normal, it's light. When with great effort, all the waves are brought into focus, it's a laser and can cut through steel. That's what we are doing with 'G': it's as if we're picking up the entire content of the client's brain, and turning it to focus laser-like with the same searing power on a single topic.

Because this demanding precision of goalsetting is unfamiliar, there is a big difference between clients who are 'trained' and 'untrained'. A client who has never experienced coaching before will have no idea what they're meant to do, and the coach needs to guide them through. By contrast, coaching someone who has been coached many times before, and/or where this is their third or fourth session with you, is much easier. They know the rules: they tell you briefly what the key things are they want to work on ('Topic') and know they then need to focus this or part of it into a crisp 'Goal'. Often they come with a pre-prepared G. If so you have 'transferred the technology' and they have a tool for life.

But sometimes even the most 'trained' client comes in absolutely steaming: something big or bad, or good, has happened, and they have to get it off their chest. You need to let them vent. Sometimes the chance to vent, with the coach not interrupting, is itself the value of that session, and the whole session can be eaten up by it. Practice helps here: experienced coaches have the confidence to judge when it's time to move the client onto the task for today, and very experienced coaches can do it deftly and surprisingly fast, even where the subject of the venting would seem overwhelming.

Note there is a difference between the *overall goal(s)* your client brings to coaching, and the *individual goal for each session* (different writers use different terms for each). So for example, Client A comes for six months' coaching, with the brief to prepare them for, say, their first board-level position. That's the overall (sometimes 'programme') goal. Within that, individual goals are set for each session. Over time the series of achievements session by session (including the work that is done by the client between sessions) adds up to delivering the overall goal. In the GROW model, we are referring to the individual goal for *this session*. (And in the first one or maybe even two sessions of a six-month programme, the G goal for that individual session might be to define, refine and crisp up to SMART standards, the overall programme goals for the six months. If you see what I mean.)

How do you know if you have a sharp enough goal? If you haven't, the session feels out of control – to both people. The discussion goes round and round. It is often low-energy, uninspiring, flat. The reward of hanging out for a really defined goal, is a turbo-charged remainder of the session: it's shorter, because everything is tightly focused, energising, even fun – maybe exhausting, but still exhilarating.

Getting the goal: some tips

- Have courage: bring the client back to goalsetting until it's sharp.
- Require specifics: 'be clearer about what I need to do' is not a G (unless measured – see below); 'three actionable bullet points written in my notebook' is.
- Honour individual difference (see Chapter 7) – some people need tangible takeaways – a plan, bullet points; for others it's feeling different (e.g. less anxious).
- If the latter, drive for measurable results using 1–10, i.e. for subjective goals (e.g. higher clarity; self-confidence; lower anxiety), benchmark using the scale of 1–10; i.e. 'on a scale of 1–10, where are you now and where do you want to be by the end of the session?' Then set it aside and get to work, only revisiting it at the end.
- Don't assume you're both clear on the G, but test it out, e.g. 'so, given what you've said, could you state for me what your goal is for this session?'
- Write the goal down once established, so you can track if it morphs during the session (and check, and if necessary recontract for a new G).

Reality

Now you have the Goal, the task in Reality is to get the facts out on the table. Again, this piece on its own can make a dramatic difference: in this busy world, we very rarely stop and give the important parts of our lives, a good hard think.

If we try it on our own, we might not spot that our thinking has got stuck in a rut – or we do sense that, but can't find a way out. But working with a coach, who methodically encourages us to consider *all* the key domains – finance, people, technology, operations, etc. – there are often 'Ah-hah!' moments; 'I hadn't thought of this before, but actually...' The coach is on the lookout for habitual patterns of thinking, that might unknowingly blinker the client. 'People people', for example, are often on full alert to the ramifications for others, but might not have considered properly the operational or financial constraints. Technocrats, on the other hand, might have a brilliant plan which fails to take sufficient account of human risks or needs.

There are three traps to avoid here. First, this is not, as some people think, about being 'realistic'. The coach may privately think an aspect of the goal is unattainable, but who are they to know – they may be blithely unaware that the client's cousin is a Russian oligarch. Unless there is a clear breach of the law, moral or ethical codes, or the coaching contract, this is not the place for the coach to impose their own limiting beliefs on the client; evaluation of options comes in the next stage (and even then, it's done largely by the client – if you want to be paid for your opinions, become a mentor!).

(If you do have serious concerns about an Option – or indeed a Goal – being feasible, there are two possible things you can do. Ideally, jot it down in your notes in a corner where you put 'things to come back to later'. When you check that towards the end of the session, you'll often find the concern has already been dealt with. Or, if you are really worried, say it, but own it as yours: 'Myrtle, this may just be me, but what concerns me about X is Y.' They can then either explain more background which satisfies your concern, or agree you have a point. The trick is to state your view neutrally, so it remains a proper challenge to their thinking, rather than telling them what to think.)

Second, some beginners think this fact-gathering is for the coach. But in purist GROW coaching, the coach needs to know very little of the background and present situation – all this digging is for the sake of the *client*. As the main facts are pulled out, the client often gains insight. That insight, the higher quality perspective, is the objective, not feeding an analysis process of the coach. (The latter is consulting.)

And third, note that in Reality, good questions begin 'what', 'who', 'how', etc. – but *not* 'why'. If you ask 'why', people will leap happily into self-justification, digging themselves deeper into the hole they're currently in. (This is one of the differences between coaching and therapy; the subject of some schools of therapy is often or even exclusively 'why'.) 'What' type questions are more likely to keep the client objective, and able to look dispassionately at the facts. (OK, I accept there are occasions when 'why' can be valid, if asked neutrally simply as part of the fact-gathering. But it is a healthy discipline for novices to avoid it – and thereby to notice how habituated we are to ask it!)

Options

Having clarified their goal and considered the facts, only now does the client consider their options. The coach has two tasks here: first, to broaden the options, and second, to narrow them down.

Broadening options can add great value to the client's thinking. Often people will say (metaphorically, or even literally with their head in their hands), 'there's nothing I can do.' But as Viktor Frankl has so soberingly pointed out[3], in even the grimmest situations there is always *something* one can do; in the concentration camps, he noted some people when able to control nothing else, could still choose their inner reaction to events. Or they will say, 'there's only one option' which the coach must challenge – what other alternatives are there? Or clients often say 'I've really only got two choices' – you get the picture.

The 'O' is where coaches who love technique can have a field day. There are dozens of great questions to help clients break out of their mental constraints. The 'miracle question' often works. I was coaching a client once and both of us were stuck, going round and round on a seemingly intractable problem. Then I asked, for no particular reason, 'If you had a completely free hand, what would you do?' and the client almost spat straight back, 'I'd *fire* the bitch!' She clapped her hand to her mouth, giggled shamefacedly, and said she had no idea until that moment she felt so strongly about this particular individual. The topic had suddenly became a lot clearer! There are dozens of variants on the 'miracle question': 'if you had unlimited time/unlimited budget what would you do; if you could wave a magic wand; if you woke up in the morning and the problem was solved...' – each has unblocked many a log-jammed client.

Here's another favourite of mine. The client says, and they mean it: 'I don't know.' You flip back quickly with, 'If you did know, what it would be?' – but you have to keep a perfectly straight face. Astonishingly, 50% of the time they will come straight back with the answer – because the question has got in under their radar, and triggered a hitherto buried thought. The other 50% of the time, when they spot the question is absurd, they gaze at you in astonishment, or laugh, and it doesn't work. But a 50% strike rate is not to be sneezed at – try it! But keep a straight face.

Once the client has been freed up to consider a full range of options, the task is then to narrow the field down, by evaluating the pros and cons of each. Again, the criteria against which the various options are judged is for the client to determine – these may also need to be coached out of them. For some clients/topics/contexts, safety first is absolutely paramount. For others, the best option is the most innovative. Each to their own.

Will

As noted above, this has two parts: what *will* you do, and what is your *will* or motivation on this.

First, the action plan part of 'W'. This again is where coaching is different from a normal conversation. The coach wants to know, having talked the matter through properly, what action the client is now going to take, and by when, etc. This may not need to be as tough as you were on 'G' because if everything has gone well the client is by now energised, clear and determined. But you do need to push harder than you would in normal conversation, for the client to articulate the action to which they are now committed.

Then, we need to check the level of that commitment – the will, or motivation part of 'W'. Sir John Whitmore's scale of motivation[4] really does work here. You ask the client on a scale of 1–10 how likely they are to do it. If the number is 8/10 or above, they probably will; if it's 7 or below, they probably won't. I have asked this question hundreds, perhaps into the thousands, of times, and Sir John is absolutely right. If it's 7 or below, I tell them his wise words, they look sheepish, and it emerges that back in G, or R, we missed something, and we need to cycle through again. And high-achiever coaches and clients, even if it's 8 or above, usually then ask, 'so what do we need to do to make it a 10?!'.

3. Listening and hearing

In the 1960s Carl Rogers pointed out that just being deeply listened to is enough for many people to resolve their problems – *without* any other intervention.

This is so utterly crucial…

… let me pause for you to take it in. Just being deeply listened to is enough to bring about change.

And fifty years on it's even more true, and more rare. Everyone and everything – email, BlackBerries, Twitter, blogs, .txt, SMS, RSS feed – is on transmit mode, and each of us inhabits our own personal cacophony.

By contrast, when I was first deeply listened to as an adult, by an expert trained to listen acutely, the experience felt such a privilege, and was so productive, I was moved almost to tears. I suspect neuroscientists will soon find cells in the brain which fire under conditions of real listening, explaining why it is so liberating and creative. For whatever reason it works, it works: problems that were stuck work loose, unexpected new ideas pop up, you think more deeply and see further.

So it is an absolutely central coaching tool.

The coach's ability to listen and beyond that, to *hear* – that is, to listen such that they really understand the client, can imagine being in their world – creates trust and authenticity. Listening is key to non-directive coaching, which we consider below: real listening switches the focus so the session is guided by what the client says and what the coach hears, rather than by any prior agenda of the coach.

How do you listen better?

Step 1: stop talking!

Step 2: just listen. There is the term 'active listening', but the phrase annoys me: it's a contradiction in terms. True listening isn't a 'doing' state, it's a 'being' state where everything else is shut down, and you are just utterly absorbed in what the other person is saying. One hears about things like paraphrasing, or straight parroting back what the person has just said to show you have heard.* If you're *really* listening, the clients don't need that signalled, they already know.

As with everything else in coaching, it gets better with practice. If it feels really difficult at the beginning, then it might help to 'fake it till you make it' – in other words, just do the behaviours (fall silent; attend closely to the client) and over time the inner chatter will die down, and the ability to develop a genuinely listening state, build. If you have ever learned meditation, it's the same technique: if a distracting thought comes into your mind, then don't fight it, just note it and allow it to pass away, coming back to, in this case, the listening.

There's a distinction you may find helpful. Listening as we do it in normal life and business is *'listening to respond'*. They say something; we say something back. Like tennis – back, forth, back forth, always on edge, always looking to hit the great return. Sometimes this is relevant in coaching, but you can doubtless do it already. The skill to deepen instead is the ability to *listen to understand*.

To contrast the two in coaching:

- ■ *Listening to respond*. The coach's focus is on their own next step rather than on the client. Typically novice coaches might hear the client's

---

* Nothing wrong with these techniques per se: used discriminatingly, they can be very effective, for example to check we have heard correctly. But done mindlessly and repetitively, 'because that's what I should do in active listening', they drive clients crazy.

words but are to some extent distracted by their own needs and concerns (e.g. what am I going to say or ask next; how does what he's telling me fit with what I know about the organisation; what on earth does that acronym mean; does she expect me to have the answers; I don't approve of what he's telling me). At worst – as someone said in a famous investment bank – 'around here we don't listen – we reload!'

■ *Listening to understand.* Here the coach and client are in conversation, with the client doing most of the talking, and the coach simply absorbed in what the client is saying. The coach is not distracted by worrying about the process, so they have more channels open to receive information, and are more likely to pick up, without trying, what is said, and also what is not said, and 'body language'. The coach will probably also pick up any emotional aspects associated with the content of the discussion. And they are more able to notice patterns, perhaps in the client's language (e.g. a frequent use of negatives) or across sessions. Coach and client are probably in 'the zone', or 'Flow' (see Chapter 6).

Being able to flex from listening to respond, to listening to understand, is necessary for proper Big Five coaching. Listening to understand is most likely when the coach:

■ has a belief in the client's ability to help themselves;

■ follows the client's agenda rather than their own;

■ does not judge the client;

■ is comfortable with structuring the session (with a light touch);

■ asks open questions;

■ moves beyond needing to have an answer or to be right.

If you would like to explore this further, some good references for further reading are listed at the end of the chapter. Standing head and shoulders above the others, in fact on its very own mountain, is Nancy Kline's wonderful and eminently practical book, *Time to Think*.[5] Her coaching method engenders a quality and length of listening which is so generative, it can be all that is needed. The subtitle of her book is 'Listening to ignite the human mind', and it does.

4. Questioning

Questioning – at last! You probably think you've got to the most important section of the chapter – but *au contraire.*

A small story, if I may. I had a coaching client once who was a public servant, relatively young, but exceptionally gifted. He had been 'fast tracked' to very great responsibility, and was working in a policy field he cared deeply about, but his work was stressful almost beyond endurance: the subject matter was inherently distressing, and his particular office was also notoriously toxic, with a bullying leader and seething political crosscurrents. Coaching was a rare place he could open up. He refused to let me come to his office, preferring to walk across the park to ours and thereby get some fresh air and distance from work. He always arrived with several clear topics, worked incredibly hard in the sessions, and would stride back across the park, recharged to go back into battle. I learned how crucial it was for him, when on one occasion he turned down a summons to a meeting with his Cabinet Minister, in order to come to coaching.

Then one day when we were scheduled to meet, I got a bad migraine – but knowing how much he gave up to attend our sessions, I hauled myself to the office. Once there, I explained: 'Fred' (not his name, of course), 'I'm so very sorry, I have a bad migraine. I would have cancelled anyone else, but I know how important these sessions are to you, and that you can do it on your own. Go.' Then sat for the rest of the session, with my head in my hands, in a blur. Through the fog, I could hear him, initially disconcerted, then saying 'OK, you usually ask me what my Goal is. I have been thinking about that and ...' and off he went. After about 20 minutes I heard a voice through the fog saying, 'Annc, I'm stuck, what do I do?' I muttered I had no idea and he had to get on with it. So he did. At the end of an hour and a half, the voice through the fog said: 'Thanks, that was *great*! I've got a lot out of that!' And indeed he had – the next session, when I was back to normal, he showed me his notes, and reported on the results. I wouldn't have done it with any other client – it was late on in our coaching programme, he knew and had internalised the process well, and needed the thinking space desperately. Perhaps I shouldn't own up to it! But it does illustrate that an awful lot can be done with contracting, GROW, and listening (or in this case, huddled in a heap) – you need those frightfully clever questions a lot less than you think.

They do add something. But, at their best, if the contracting is thorough, the GROW clear and tough, and the listening profound, they needn't be more than a light touch on the rudder.

Open and closed questions

Often the most powerful questions are very simple, short and open. They begin with *what, where, when,* and *how*; they elicit information and take the conversation forward. Closed questions by contrast may be a statement disguised as a question, and can often be answered yes or no; this doesn't usually take the client's insight forward, though there are exceptions to every rule.

Different questions for different tasks

No matter how light the touch on the rudder, questions do control the direction of a conversation, and different types of questions have different results. To know which type to deploy, ask yourself what would help the client most in this particular moment. Is it to:

- focus attention;
- follow interest;
- raise awareness; or
- generate responsibility?

May we consider each in turn.

Focus attention

There are two tasks here, the obvious one and the deeper one. Clearly the coach will use some questions to bring the client back to the task in hand if they have strayed, to keep them on the point. (Or to 'recontract' verbally in the moment so they're focused on a new point... 'we seem to be in a different domain here. Your original Goal was X, but am I hearing that Y has now emerged? Which is more important?') But there is also a deeper purpose.

Focus can get the client's mind into its most highly productive state, that of relaxed concentration. Tim Gallwey calls it 'focused attention'.[6] Norman Doidge's gripping book *The Brain That Changes Itself,* reports neuroscience research showing that focused attention is 'essential to long-term plastic change' in the brain.[7] Sustained intensely focused attention is one of the radical new methods used by leading clinicians around the world with results including some 'blind people restored to sight; learning disorders cured; IQs raised; ageing brains rejuvenated; lifelong anxiety and repression relieved; and stroke patients written off as beyond help recovering their faculties'.[8] (For more, see Chapter 11 – and I can't recommend the Doidge book highly enough: it blows wide open the boundaries of what is possible.)

To me this could be the first hard evidence, backed up by brain scans, of why coaching using the same techniques* also achieves astonishing change and transformation in business clients. A hitherto diffident lawyer newly promoted to partner in his firm has his innate talent unlocked and soars; a team which has been fighting for years pulls together to grapple with recession issues just in the nick of time – we see it all the time in coaching, it's one of reasons why it is so profoundly satisfying. Neuroscience may be beginning to explain the underlying reasons why it works, and focused attention is certainly one of them.

Examples of questions that help to focus are:

- All the 'G' questions, including:
    - What would be a useful outcome for this meeting?
    - What would you like to have at the end of this meeting that you don't have right now?
    - What would success look like?
    - What would the benefit be of achieving today's goal?
    - Where are you now on a scale of 1–10? …
    - … and what number do you want to get to by the end of this session?
- Where are we? (It's allowed! If you have got confused, it's likely the client has too, so just name it.)
- Could you draw the threads of that together for me?
- Can you summarise the key insights from today, and your action points?

Following interest

The coach needs to be wary of following their own interest rather than that of the client. This can occur at quite subtle levels – as people go through coaching training, they are often embarrassed to realise they do it more than they first thought. One called it 'stealth coaching' – i.e. asking questions that nudge the client to where the coach thinks they 'should' be, but without them spotting they're being led. It doesn't work. For coaching conversations to 'fly' they have to follow the client's interest. Good questions are clean, moving the process along, but in the direction chosen by the client. Using their language and keeping questions simple achieves this.

---

* Although not as intensively as Doidge describes – I wonder what would happen if we did?

Examples of questions that follow interest are:

■ [If several possible topics have been raised] Which is most interesting to you?

■ What did you notice?

■ You said ..., – tell me more? (Or more simply: Say more?)

■ Where do we go from here?

You might think questions like 'which is most 'relevant'' might be better, but I would counsel you to explore what happens when you stick with the word 'interest'. In the question, '...which of these interests you', it is a very precise and clever little word. 'Relevant' can knock the client sideways into judgement, or what they 'should' do. 'Interest' is more innocent. It sends the client down into their own storehouse of experience, data and preferences. They come back up with something of intrinsic value and importance to them – and we shall see in Chapter 10 that intrinsic interest is one of the core requirements for real motivation. So following interest sets them up to succeed.

Raising awareness

One aim of the coach is to help the client discover something new, from a simple insight to life-changing thoughts. The most powerful, as we saw above, are those which lie within, but are currently buried. The task is to bring them back into awareness.

The most powerful questions to do this are those that build on the client's own words, simply reflecting (or repeating) back words or statements e.g. 'you said you found the meeting *difficult?*' Or 'what do you mean by *difficult?*' Or even – and less is definitely more – '*difficult?*'* This encourages the client to go deeper into their own thinking. Examples of questions that raise awareness are:

■ When you said ..., what does that mean to you?

■ What did you mean by ...?

■ When you said/did ..., how did others react?

■ What have you observed (seen/heard) that tells you that ...?

---

* I know, I was critical earlier of 'parroting back' – the difference is the intent. Mindless parroting is fit only for parrots, but repeating a word sensitively to get the client to think about it more deeply, is sometimes right for humans.

- What did you feel about ...?
- How is this connected to ...?
- If you did know the answer, what would it be?

Generating responsibility

Although the issue is the client's, a common pitfall is for the coach to take on responsibility for solving it. This is hard to avoid initially, until you develop ways of deflecting clients' requests. It can be so tempting to help, when a client is asking for your advice, and/or genuinely does not seem able to come up with an answer or solution of their own. But the client is going to have to walk out the door and carry out their plans on their own, without you, and even if it seems tough, the thoughts and plans that stick are the ones that come from them.

Questions that generate responsibility include:

- What could you do?
- What would you encourage your boss/colleague/team member to do?
- What will you do?
- When?
- What needs to happen so that ...?
- What support do you need?
- What would prevent you from doing this, and what's your fall-back plan to deal with it?
- If you did know the answer what would it be?
- How committed are you to this, on a scale of 1–10?

(And if clients are pressing:)

- I'm happy to share what I think, but first ...
- Let's discuss your ideas first: what will you do?

5. Non-directive coaching

By now you might be protesting – even exploding! Am I allowed to say *nothing*?! What's the point of my 30 years of experience, wouldn't it be useful for them to hear some of that? I could save them so much time/protect them from mistakes/it would just be so much faster if I ...

Indeed. And of course, in practice, senior coaches do mix up asking and telling. Particularly at leadership coaching level, clients prefer, even require, their coaches to 'bring something to the party'. It varies the pace, makes things interesting. But giving advice in coaching is like sugar: a sprinkling livens things up, but too much over too long is unhealthy. The task is not to abandon directive coaching, but to add in the full power of non-directive: to learn it so thoroughly that you can do it just as fast and well as you can directive – in a split second, without thinking. Then you have the *full* range at your fingertips.

So at last we have arrived at the biggest of them all. Contracting, GROW, listening, questioning are all techniques, but non-directive is a principle.

The distinction is between *directive* and *non-directive* coaching. As we said in Chapter 1, at its crudest, this is the difference between tell and ask. In directive coaching, the coach in some way tells the client what to do: *puts in* advice, guidance, content. In non-directive coaching, by contrast the coach *pulls out* the thoughts, capabilities, potential, plans, inspirations from the client.

Why is non-directive so important? Because it works better! If only for the simple reason that people, particularly intelligent high-achieving people, don't like being told what to do. They may ask your advice – but have you ever noticed, they then ignore it?! People are far more energised by plans they've developed themselves.

It's also a critical time-management technique for busy managers. If an employee comes to your door and asks for a quick bit of advice, and you give it, then next time they're right back at your door. But if instead you consistently flip it back to them (as in, perhaps, 'what have you thought of already?'), then eventually they develop their own capability and stay at their desks. Their morale and productivity are higher, because people appreciate having a bigger stake in what they do – and you have more time. What's not to like?!

I can teach the GROW model in workshops to people who've never heard of it before, in 15 minutes. Coaching, on paper, is extremely simple. Yet it takes between six months to a year for capable businesspeople to learn to do it tolerably well. Yes, there are more techniques than the basics in this chapter to be grappled with (including those in later chapters), but what takes a year is not the learning, it's the *un*learning. And 90% of the unlearning is needed to master non-directive coaching.

Almost everyone who comes to train on our own Programme, whatever their job – lawyer, leader, consultant, manager, HR specialist, psychologist, professor – has earned their living to date by telling. It's a habit of 20 or 30 years, which would take some time to break in any event, but it goes beyond that. When I ask a world-class management consultant of 35 years' success to stop transmitting, I am asking him to cease using the weapon that has been the whole basis of his success to date, and he is likely to feel naked, exposed and uncomfortable without it. For many of us, it goes even further, as telling, guiding, advising others has become a part of our very 'ego identity' – it's just part of who we are. So it takes great effort to stop doing it, in order to try out the new approach.

But despite all this, our faculty know all we have to do – and it can take quite a bit of effort! – is to get students to try it, and stick at it, until they experience the client having one of those magical 'ah-hah' moments. It's like a shark tasting blood: they have the thrill of seeing light spill across a client's face, and they're hooked. Pontificating has its own charms, I know, but it's not a patch on seeing your clients becoming fully alive again, reconnected and energised by their renewed purpose, fresh clarity, even joy.

How do you do it? You've already learned – it's the principle underlying the basics above – contracting, GROW, listening, questioning. Those things are what you do, non-directive is the spirit in which you do it: believing the healthy capable businessperson sitting in front of you has the resources they need, and all you are there to do is unleash them. Curious to try it?!

Further reading

Contracting

Some interesting case studies of contracting in complex organisations include:

Frisch, M. H. (2001) 'The Emerging Role of the Internal Coach', *Consulting Psychology Journal*, Vol 53, No 4, Fall, pp. 240–250. Excellent advice on confidentiality: 'impossible ... the issue therefore is to clearly identify what is confidential and what will be shared' (p. 246).

Wasylyshyn, K. M. (2005) 'The Reluctant President', *Consulting Psychology Journal*, Vol 57, No 1, Winter, pp. 57–70. Shows the coach carefully assessing the corporate culture; a thorough process is described in detail.

Winum, P. C. (2005) 'Effectiveness of a High-Potential African American Executive: The Anatomy of a Coaching Engagement', *Consulting Psychology*

Journal, Vol 57, No 1, Winter, pp. 71–89. Officially a (great) case study on coaching and diversity, but also an excellent outline (pp. 76–77) of the contracting process.

Witherspoon R. and White, R. P. (1996) 'Executive Coaching: A Continuum of Roles', *Consulting Psychology Journal*, Vol 48, No 2, Spring, pp. 124–3. Describes 4-step process: commitment/assessment/action/continuous improvement.

Listening and questioning

Kline, N. (1999) *Time to Think: Listening to Ignite the Human Mind*, London: Cassell.
Chapter 3: 'Attention' on listening. Chapter 4: Incisive Questions.

Scott, S. (2002) *Fierce Conversations*, London: Piatkus.
Pp. 109–18: common mistakes in one-to-one coaching.

Whitmore, Sir J. (2002) Coaching for Performance, 3rd edn, London: Nicholas Brealey.
Pp 46–52: types of questions.

Whitworth, L., Kimsey-House, H., Sandahl, P. (1998) Co-active Coaching, Palo Alto, CA: Davies Black.
Pp. 34–38: Levels I, II and III dialogue.

6

Building coaching skills: the different approaches

If Big Five coaching is the tree, then what baubles would you like to hang on it? If any? Some people think all trees, including this one, are beautiful in their own right and leave it well alone; they coach using the core elements of contracting, GROW, listening, etc. and do good work. Others add so many baubles and ornaments the tree groans under their weight. Others again just set a single star atop the tree – an approach or guru who illuminates their coaching.

This chapter sets out some of the possibilities, so you can decorate your own tree, or not, as you wish. There are countless different options, so I have grouped them into approaches from:

1 sport;
2 psychology;
3 'NLP', and
4 business – then finish with ...
5 a bit of fun – what are the 'Top Ten Tools' in business coaching?!

1. Sport

The tree metaphor applies perfectly to the main originators of business coaching in the UK, Sir John Whitmore, Tim Gallwey, and colleagues. On the surface, they look like, and indeed are, high-performance sportspeople: Sir John Whitmore was a successful racing car driver, winning the European Saloon Car Championship in 1965;[1] Graham Alexander was junior tennis champion at Wimbledon;[2] Myles Downey a world top 100-level tennis player; David Hemery won Olympic Gold in Mexico City in 1968. In the succeeding generation, Adrian Moorhouse won Gold at the Seoul Olympics in 1988 and Alison Gill is a not once but three-times Olympian.

But underneath that surface glitter, there is a lot of tree. For some of them it is Big Five – indeed they invented part of it. Others, particularly in the second generation, have blended in aspects of peak performance sports science.

Simon Jenkins of Leeds Metropolitan University has done the nascent profession of business coaching a great service by capturing the detailed history of its first 40 years while it is still clear and fresh.[3] The story is fascinating, and isn't about solitary individual achievement. Rather it's a tapestry woven over time by these experts working together in alliances, constantly developing their approaches, with regular fresh infusions from deep theoretical or empirical sources: Sir John Whitmore went to the Esalen Institute in 1970 when it was visited by Carl Rogers and Abraham Maslow[4]; Tim Gallwey, as we see below, trained as a Harvard psychologist; Adrian Moorhouse co-founded his business Lane 4 with sports scientist Professor Graham Jones; and Alison Gill, the founder of Getfeedback and Crelos, is an organisational consultant and psychologist. Someone once said to me, in marketing you 'sell the sizzle not the sausage'. Their high-performance sports achievements gave many of the early leaders in European business coaching great sizzle, but their work has longevity because of its substance.

The 'Inner Game' approach

The 'Inner Game' approach may not have been the absolute beginning of the field (scattered references to business coaching go back far earlier in the century) but it gave it a major boost. The first Inner Game coaching training was run in the UK in 1979 at the initiative of Sir John Whitmore, who had trained with Tim Gallwey in California.[5] Gallwey in turn trained originally as an educational psychologist at Harvard, actually taking classes with the founder of modern behaviourism B.F. Skinner. But while Skinner and his pioneering colleagues to some extent regarded the mind as a 'black box' which one needn't concern oneself with, explaining behaviour and development in other ways, Gallwey's approach is the complete opposite: he encourages us to look within for radically improved performance.

One concept from Gallwey which many business coaches have found useful is his distinction between *'Self 1'*, the inner critic who can hold our performance back, and *'Self 2'*, the natural ability to perform which if allowed to operate freely (i.e. unimpeded by Self 1) can lead to peak performance. The task of the coach is first to help the client to understand the concepts and see them operating in themselves, and then to develop techniques to allow Self 2 to be in play more often and at key moments. For more, see his classic *Inner Game of Tennis*.[6]

Sports science

The Gallwey approach, though formative, has not been tested empirically, but mainstream sports science does infuse the work of many other executive coaches. Business psychologist Alison Hardingham co-authored her book *The Coach's Coach*[7] with three leading sportsmen, including Mike Brearley, former England cricket captain and now a psychoanalyst. Professor Graham Jones, Professor of Elite Performance at Bangor University in Wales and co-founder of Lane 4 has published on the psychology of high achievers (HAs), whether in sport or in business. In a very useful article[8] he outlines in clear, simple and easily remembered terms how a coach has to adapt to work successfully with them. He lists common characteristics of HAs, including being 'self-focused; goal-driven; demanding; a sponge for information', and how coaches must respond: lack of 'ego' in the coach; delivering rapid results; and providing detailed and instant feedback: 'They are not afraid of feedback. They are more open than non-HAs to you watching them, warts and all.'[9]

Sandra Foster, a psychologist and principal at executive search firm Korn Ferry has translated mental training skills used by Olympic and elite athletes, into techniques for use with organisational executives. Approaches she describes include developing performance routines (of the kind rugby player Jonny Wilkinson briefly made famous, while it worked for him), developing the ability to focus despite distractions, the correct use of mental imagery, 'activation control', i.e. learning how to regulate one's level of arousal at will, and finding the 'IZOF' ('individual zone of optimal functioning').[10]

Bruce Peltier includes in his book, *The Psychology of Executive Coaching*, a thought-provoking chapter on 'Lessons from athletic coaches', which includes sections on thorny issues like drive, and learning from defeat, as well as practical techniques such as working with video recording.[11]

And bringing it right up to date, coach Sarah Fenwick uses mental toughness and resilience techniques with both her business leader and high-performance sports clients: a short case study on her website (www. sarah-fenwick.com) on clients crossing the Patagonian ice cap describes the approach. Sports science is also a rich resource for tackling the 'P' of the PERFECT model (see page 97). If for example a client is experiencing nerves before having to make a major conference speech, Sarah advocates matching the techniques used to the symptoms: for example, using cognitive approaches if the problem is (mental) worry, but somatic ones, such as breathing techniques, if it is physical, e.g. manifesting as bad 'butterflies'. She writes: 'a line I love from a sports psychology paper on anxiety management is, "Butterflies are not a problem, it's just a case of getting them to fly in formation".'[12]

Most of the books and articles mentioned in this section include lists of references, so those who might want to have a sports focus to their 'tree' can find plenty to explore further. It is to be hoped many will: sports science, especially high-performance sport, still has enormous untapped potential for business and leadership coaching.

2. Psychology

Psychology too offers a great wealth of approaches to business coaches. The few examples discussed here, to whet your appetite, are:

- the professional ethos;
- how people change;
- career transition;
- positive psychology.

Professional ethos

Of all the gifts psychology can give us as business coaches, perhaps the most valuable is the least obvious. It's not one of the many approaches discussed below, though they are useful: it's the professional ethos inculcated over years of training, supervised practice, and peer expectation. Without it being explicitly spelled out, neophyte psychologists pick up strong tacit messages. For example, never overclaim. Be crystal clear about your boundaries, and if something is not within your proper field of training and practice, refer it on. And most valuable of all: don't necessarily believe what you're told. Instead of accepting the 'presenting issue' at face value, psychologists are taught to build into their quotes for work, sufficient time at the outset to conduct their own analysis of what is going on, in order to come up with their own thoughtful proposed solution.

Putting it another way, in terms of the Big Five, they are taught to be exceptionally strong at contracting, in its broadest sense. (And they're also very strong on psychometrics/assessment, but that has a chapter all to itself: Chapter 7.)

When it comes to the approaches themselves, there is a super-abundance of choice. In addition to the humanistic approach touched on above, 'psychodynamic' psychologists offer us, for example, insight into resistances and defences which may block change; behaviourists challenge us to take close account of what might be reinforcing existing behaviour, and how to structure and reward detailed steps for improvement; cognitive psychologists specialise in thinking, attention and memory; health psychologists have salutary things to say about the need for exercise and proper hydration if our clients (and we!) are to remain at our peak. And so on.

There's so much, it could be overwhelming, but fortunately there is help at hand: later in this chapter, in the section on Positive Psychology (PP), we discuss Carol Kauffman's 'PERFECT' tool, which herds it all into useable shape.

But first, I want to mention two other approaches from less well-known corners of psychology. Whether they know it or not, from their training or their intuition, coaches often already draw on cognitive approaches (e.g. GROW), behaviourism (structured action planning) and psychodynamic (from their supervisors, who often have this background.) So I have chosen examples from two other fields: James Prochaska's method of facilitating change, from *health/clinical* psychology, and *developmental* psychologist Herminia Ibarra's approach to career transition.

How people change

An important addition to the Big Five that most business coaches will want for their tree is a way of dealing with change, whether for themselves, their clients, their teams, their organisations, or indeed their world.

Science doesn't yet have a definitive prescription for how we can make people change. (Good!) But one approach, Prochaska's Stages of Change model, was originally developed to help people succeed at a very difficult task: giving up smoking, where people are battling not just the usual challenges of any behaviour change but also physical nicotine addiction.[13] Since then the model has spread far afield including to business coaching, where it can make a significant difference in coaching clients through tough change. It is described in more detail in Chapter 10, on Motivation and Change, but I mention it briefly here to prompt consideration of a change tool to add to your kit.

The Prochaska approach has five stages at its core (plus relapse, which can happen, and success, which he calls 'permanent exit' – i.e. from the cycle). The five at the heart of the model are:

▪ Pre-contemplation.
▪ Contemplation.
▪ Preparation.
▪ Action.
▪ Maintenance.

For more detail, including coaching questions for each stage, see Chapter 10.

How people develop: career transition

Another untapped source of approaches is developmental psychology. Some of it is focused on the early stages of life, but Professor Herminia Ibarra of INSEAD is a developmental psychologist who works not just with adults but with those at the peak of their careers, and especially as they go through important *transitions*.

Ibarra investigated career success, researching the careers of people who have truly made it, who adore what they do, who have achieved everything they want from work – material or worldly success, spiritual satisfaction, deep peace – the kind of people who say, 'work is more fun than fun'. She found *none* of them had got there by the traditional planned route. Instead the process was iterative – exploring here, learning there, stepping forward and back, taking time to think and equally making time to act. From the research she has developed a series of guidelines, or 'unconventional career strategies'.

Her book *Working Identity* describes the process in full.[14] The box summarises it and there's more on career coaching in Chapter 9 for those who might want to make this a significant branch of their tree.

Ibarra's unconventional career strategies

- **Unconventional Strategy 1.** Act your way into a new way of thinking and being. You cannot discover yourself by introspection.

- **Unconventional Strategy 2.** Stop trying to find your one true self. Focus your attention on which of your many *possible selves* you want to test and learn more about.

- **Unconventional Strategy 3.** Allow yourself a *transition period* in which it is okay to oscillate between holding on and letting go. Better to live the contradictions than to come to a premature resolution.

- **Unconventional Strategy 4.** Resist the temptation to start by making a big decision that will change everything in one fell swoop. Use instead a strategy of *small* wins, in which incremental gains lead you to more profound changes.

- **Unconventional Strategy 5.** Try things out as extracurricular activities or parallel paths so that you can experiment seriously without making a commitment.

- **Unconventional Strategy 6.** Don't just focus on the work. Find people who are already what you want to be; but don't expect to find them in your same old social circles.

- **Unconventional Strategy 7.** Don't wait for a cataclysmic moment when the truth is revealed. Use everyday occurrences to find meaning in the changes you are going through. Practise telling and retelling your story. Over time, it will clarify.

- **Unconventional Strategy 8.** Step back. But not for too long.

- **Unconventional Strategy 9.** Change happens in bursts and starts. There are times when you are open to big change and times when you are not. Seize opportunities.

Adapted from: Ibarra, H. (2004) *Working Identity*, Boston, MA: Harvard Business School Press, pp. 167–170.

Positive Psychology*

In the last ten years the new field of Positive Psychology (PP) – which is not 'positive thinking' but rather the science of successful function and peak performance – has burst upon the coaching scene. It was developed by the distinguished scientists Martin Seligman, a former President of the American Psychological Association (APA), and Mihaly Csikszentmihalyi. They noted psychology in its first 100 years had focused on pathology, or what's *wrong* with people, and much had thereby been achieved to help relieve suffering. But they wanted to balance that with comparably rigorous research on the remaining 95% of society who aren't mentally ill, to

---

* Initially this American term was unpalatable to some in Europe: too 'rah rah'. With the passing of time we've perhaps now become used to it, but if it still sticks in your craw, think of it instead as 'functional psychology', an appropriate balance to psychology's hitherto focus on dysfunction.

help them develop and strengthen what's *right*: character, strengths, the sound and the positive in individuals, organisations and societies. PP does not advocate a simple switch from negative to positive, but simply to get back to a *balanced* analysis of people and situations.

Seligman and Csikszentmihalyi have raised vast amounts of research funding, because the topics being researched – peak performance, character strength, resilience – are attractive to corporate donors who see them as providing competitive edge. The result is large-scale research studies on myriad aspects of optimal human functioning, and for the first time coaches are at the forefront of the researchers' minds, as Seligman has identified coaching as one of the core delivery mechanisms for bringing about personal, organisational and societal change. Hence downstream from the research we are beginning to see an outpouring of scientifically-validated tools and interventions developed specifically for our and our clients' needs.

In this section there are just three examples of PP tools of potentially considerable use to business coaches, the second and third of which were developed explicitly for coaching by my Meyler Campbell colleague and Harvard Professor Carol Kauffman. They are:

■ Flow.
■ 4 steps to confidence.
■ The PERFECT model.

Flow

Mihaly Csikszentmihalyi, now Distinguished Professor of Psychology at Claremont Graduate University in the US, and formerly of the University of Chicago, has spent almost 30 years researching how people attain optimum performance – the best that the individual can achieve, often way beyond what they can do in their normal state. Others refer to it as *optimal experience* or being *in the zone*.

Many people have experienced Flow in their work or personal lives. One client said to me a little sheepishly, that for him it's building spreadsheets. He can develop them for hours, working even late into the night, with total accuracy, drawing in the complexities, fluidly and fluently building piece by piece. For others, flow comes more often outside work, in sport or hobbies: negotiating a difficult rock climb, or being part of a demanding choral performance. Many people report experiencing flow while skiing – can you think of such times in your own life?

Csikszentmihalyi's research also uncovered what it takes to get *into* this highly productive state. His teams used technology to contact thousands of participants around the world at random times. When their pager/mobile went off, people reported back on what precisely they were doing in that moment, and how they felt. Csikszentmihalyi extracted from the millions of data points generated, the occasions when people reported performing at their peak, and analysed them to reveal *nine conditions of Flow*. Armed with this knowledge, we and our clients can get into the flow state more often and more 'at will'.

The nine conditions of flow, and a little more about each, are described in the box below.

The first four are the most important for coaches. These are in fact what I call the *preconditions* of flow: the things that need to be in place before it happens – the things we can make more likely through coaching.

The next four are *outcomes*, or what happens in the brain in flow. You'll see many processes, even those we think are core, are put by the brain into 'quiet mode' so that our concentration on the task or activity in hand becomes almost total.

So far so good: there are four conditions of flow we can help clients set up more regularly, the Flow state then happens, with four conditions showing you're there. But the final condition is the sting in the tail: flow happens only when we are doing something we find inherently interesting! Does this mean all those people who don't really like their work, are doomed never to be in flow, only ever in the 'zone' outside work, in their hobbies – is it pigeon-fancying for ever? Or can coaching also help with this ninth condition?

Nine conditions of Flow

The nine conditions of Flow are:

1 *Balance between challenge and skill*
   Challenge high, skill low = stress; skill high, challenge low = boredom. High challenge but with the skill to meet it is the first precondition for flow.

2 *Clear goals every step of the way*
   Big unattainable-seeming goals need to be coached down into more manageable ones.

3 *There are clear rules or boundaries*
   This may seem paradoxical, but think of tennis: without observing the white lines, it's just a hit across the net; only with the lines observed does it become tennis, and exciting.

4 *Immediate feedback*
Not in three months' time, or once a year, but immediately. Surgeons attain flow more often than most other workers, and they get instant feedback on their work, e.g. the constant bleep of heart-rate machines (or not …).

5 *Concentration is so intense that there is no attention left over to think about anything irrelevant*
Extraneous thinking shuts down.

6 *Or to worry*
Emotions aren't present in flow either: pleasure or satisfaction may be felt in having achieved or completed something important afterwards, and/or anxiety felt beforehand, but no mental energy is diverted to emotion when within the flow state itself.

7 *And even self-consciousness disappears*
No mental energy is wasted even on something as core as being aware of one-self – *all* is focused on the present activity.

8 *The sense of time becomes distorted*
This is one of the defining characteristics of being in flow.

9 *The activity is, in Csikszentmihalyi's word, 'autotelic', i.e. it is intrinsically moti-vating, such that people do it for its own sake*
Ay, there's the rub.

Adapted from: Csikszentmihalyi, M. (1990) *Flow: The Psychology of Optimal Experience*, New York: Harper & Row

Carol Kauffman's '4 steps to confidence'

Professor Carol Kauffman, the founder and Director of the Institute of Coaching at Harvard, is one of the world's leading scientist-practitioners in the field. She has developed both of the next two tools discussed here, the '4 steps to confidence' approach and the PERFECT model.

Whatever you call it – confidence, self-belief, self-efficacy, 'Imposter Syndrome', 'fear of being found out' – it is *astonishing* how many of our senior business coaching clients, and we, are held back by it. Sometimes, with the 'insecure overachievers' the top management consultancies noto-riously seek to recruit, it has positive benefits, driving people to work and achieve at almost super-human levels. But for others, lack of confidence holds them back from achieving their full potential.

For these people, and more particularly to equip the business coaches working with them, Carol has combed the latest research and distilled it down into four simple but soundly-evidenced steps to build this crucial resource up to the levels our clients need to function at their best. The approach is summarised and described further below.

Carol Kauffman's 4 steps to confidence*

1   Reverse the focus.
2   Enhance positive emotion.
3   Play to Strengths.
4   Develop hope and access Flow states.

In more detail:

1. Reverse the focus

The brain is hardwired to negativity, but focus on what's wrong engenders anxiety, which limits optimal thinking. The research is clear that positive emotion leads to more productive outcomes: but because of the hard wiring, we have to make a constant effort to switch our focus to it. (And back: the negative needs to be dealt with as well but in balance.)

So step 1 is for the client to reverse the focus as often as possible, and the coach to model and support this.

2. Enhance positive emotion

Positive emotion isn't a transitory experience, it is a resource that buffers people from stress and increases health, wellbeing and level of function. In particular, positive emotion has been shown to enhance performance in many areas, building cognitive, emotional and physical resilience. This links with step 1: if clients (and indeed coaches) reverse the focus on a regular basis they are by definition spending more time in a positive state. For more on this, and for further exercises to use in coaching, see Martin Seligman's seminal books.[15]

3. Play to strengths

True confidence builds, securely grounded in reality, if we play to our strengths. Again the coach can assist by helping the client identify their own unique combination of strengths (see Chapter 7), then encouraging/reminding/setting 'homework' tasks so clients use them more often.

4. Develop hope and access Flow states

One of the strongest predictors of success and overcoming adversity is having hope. Cognitive research into hope has broken it down into two

---

clear aspects: 'Will' power, and 'Way' power. The first is self-efficacy, or the sense that 'I can' and the second encourages people to identify multiple pathways to a goal.

One core way to build self-efficacy is to use the first elements of Flow (see page 94), particularly ensuring the right balance between challenge and skill. 'Way' power is about routes to achievement. First, it is useful to understand that paths to success are not necessarily linear. For example, when climbing the Leaning Tower of Pisa, at some points it feels like you are walking down (and you are!) but you are in fact still making progress towards its summit. Second, the research indicates successful people have on average around six possible pathways to reach their goal. So not just one (because if that is blocked, they're stuck) – but not 12 either, or they'd be running round in circles. Pathways thinking means coaches should help clients (in 'O' of GROW for example) generate enough serious ways of getting to their objective that they have several real alternatives, but not too many.

PERFECT

Already the potential toolkit for business coaches is brimming over – and there's more to come in this book, and infinitely more in all of what you already know, have tried, experienced, been taught and just picked up along the way. With this abundance, and particularly when working with challenging complex clients, or at speed, or under pressure, it can sometimes be difficult to keep a clear focus on precisely which approach to use.

PERFECT is a mnemonic which guides us on *what to do, and in what order*. It isn't a tool in itself: it's a toolkit, or somewhere you can store and organise tidily away all the things you use. (In England, we'd call it a shed.) It brings together many different insights and approaches – see Figure 6.1.

The suggestion is that one works from the bottom up. This is not sacrosanct, but it does make logical sense, even if just as a useful order for the coach to run through in their mind at a key decision point.

Physical

The foundation for everything else: what from their medical or genetic history, or in their current physical or mental health, nutrition, level of exercise, etc. is affecting the client's performance? It may even be something as simple as drinking enough water; insufficient hydration causes a very sharp performance decline. But business coaches seldom venture into such domains: we

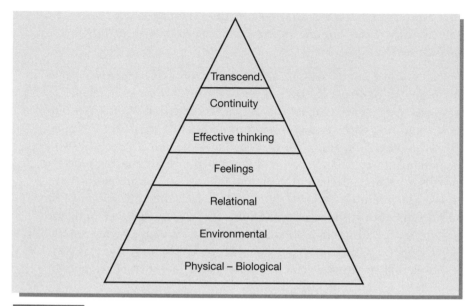

Figure 6.1   **The PERFECT model**

don't dare as we feel unqualified. But Carol has done us a service with the reminder that the solution can just be good coaching questions, for example:

- Given what you know about yourself, what do you need to address on a physical level to optimise your performance and energy level?
- What would you need to have in place to regain your sense of physical vitality?
- What activities energise you?

Environment

The context matters – we say much more about this in Chapter 8. What systemic or cultural factors and forces do coach and clients need to be aware of? Overt ones include governance and legislative requirements and those of key stakeholders and constituencies, less obvious might be where the power lies, and cultural differences.

Relational

What matters in interpersonal relationships for this particular coaching contract? The coaching relationship itself is a tool some coaches use to help the client: if for example, when a client is using a coaching session to do a 'dry run' of a board presentation: 'I'm suddenly feeling confused – it may just be me, but are you making too many points at once here?' Or the client's interpersonal needs, as revealed by the FIRO-B tool (see next chapter) might be key. Or there may be a conflict management issue – there often is! In which case plain coaching just to tease out the real issues to clarity, mediation skills and/or the Thomas Kilman instrument (see www. opp.eu.com) can all be useful.

Feelings

Emotions matter; the whole 'rational markets' theory of economics has crashed, and taken whole countries down with it, for failing to take account of human non-rationality. 'Behavioural economics' is growing up in its stead, but in my view still fails to comprehend fully the deep powerful forces of emotion in individuals, teams and organisations. There is an enormous amount here: one simple beginning, Carol suggests, is for a coach to raise their awareness of emotional triggers and contagion: which emotions can *you* observe in a client, yet remain fairly detached, and which ones 'hook' you? For example, you might realise you can work with a client who is often anxious, without picking it up, but find a depressed mood or state more contagious. Supervisors can often be very useful in helping identify these patterns and work with them. They might question, for example, if the feelings are soundly based, or the right size for the situation.

Effective thinking

Coaches are often already very alert to this, and GROW helps structure it; what other techniques do you have to help clients broaden and sharpen their thinking? One might be MBTI (see next chapter) which is officially a personality instrument, but can also be seen as a tool for understanding (and hence being able to work with) cognitive style, i.e. habitual thinking patterns.

Continuity

The past, the present and the future – how does each of them impinge on the current coaching topic? While much of coaching is about building towards the future, something in the past may be affecting the present situation more than we realise. With regard to the present, we can help clients raise their awareness of the here and now through mindfulness training and techniques (see, for example, www.michaelchaskalason.com).

Transcendence

Meaning, purpose, reason for existence, mission: again, as for 'Physical' at the bottom of the pyramid, coaches may shy away from this. Or they may feel it is too 'airy-fairy' for coaching. But there is a gathering evidence base in science* that performance is enhanced when goals are intrinsically rather than extrinsically motivated, i.e. when they are linked to what the person deeply values. The VIA Strengths Inventory (see next chapter) offers a practical route into this, as five of its 'Strengths' (appreciation of beauty and excellence; gratitude; hope; and humour, as well as spirituality) are aspects of transcendence. If a client happens to have one of these as a core strength, coaching could consider how best to play to it.

Both '4 steps to confidence' and PERFECT are so new there isn't yet much published material to direct you to for further information.** For more detail on PERFECT, see Carol's 2010 Editorial in *Coaching: an International Journal of Theory, Research and Practice*[16] and for more on '4 steps to confidence', you may wish to keep an eye on her website, www.carolkauffman.com.

Here end the brief dips into some potential approaches from psychology to add to your Big Five coaching. If they whet your appetite for more from this vast field, try Diane Stober's *Evidence-Based Coaching Handbook*[17] or Bruce Peltier's *The Psychology of Executive Coaching*.[18]

3. Coaching approaches: Neuro-Linguistic Programming (NLP)

While Positive Psychology is the hot new field, NLP is the problem child of business coaching: people love it or loathe it. Some, including many life coaches and some business coaches, are zealous advocates; others, including some buyers, are wary or even hostile.

Caution is to some extent justified as the NLP world can on occasion have a 'cultish' whiff to it and some of its advocates have been known to overclaim. And it is true that while it was originally based on sound

---

* For example, in Self-Determination Theory (SDT); Kauffman, C. (2010) 'Editorial,' *Coaching: An International Review of Theory, Research and Practice* (in press).

** Both were, may I say with quiet pride, first launched at Meyler Campbell Masterclasses in 2008 and 2009 respectively.

cognitive-behavioural psychology of the 1970s and 1980s, it has long since sailed off in its own little boat far away from the scientific world, and hence also out of reach of mainstream psychology's checks and balances of empirical research, ethical guidelines and peer review.

However, it is included in this book for two reasons: first, it's out there in the market and one might need to take a view on it. Second, and more importantly, carefully used, it has many useful tools and insights to offer coaches.

Language

One key NLP demand is that we pay much more precise attention to language. In normal conversation, if we hear an acronym or a term we don't understand, the social convention is to say nothing, pretend to know it, and keep listening hoping it will become clear. This is not appropriate in coaching: one has to have the courage to say 'I'm sorry I didn't understand that term, could you explain it please'. This may be helpful for the client because in truth they don't understand it either; or if through your challenge they realise they are in the habit of using jargon others may not follow. NLP also cautions us to stay particularly alert to parts of speech, such as generalisations ('this always happens'; 'everyone says') which can mask considerable lack of precision.

Visual, auditory, kinaesthetic

Another useful concept from NLP draws a distinction between people with 'visual', 'auditory' or 'kinaesthetic' preferences. The NLP world claims that approximately 70% of us have a visual preference, with the balance mostly auditory, and a small percentage kinaesthetic. Each has a preferred vocabulary – 'I see what you mean'; 'so, without wanting to put words in your mouth, …'; 'my gut feel on this is …'

Again, the value is being made aware and on the alert. Many people with the majority 'visual' preference, who can imagine clearly in pictures and use visual words, find it hardest to communicate naturally with those with a minority kinaesthetic preference, i.e. those who, according to NLP, process primarily using their feelings, or physical sensations. Making a conscious effort to adjust their language to that of feelings and physical sensations can improve matters very quickly.

If you wish to explore NLP further, a good place to start might be Sue Knight's book, *NLP at Work*,[19] and courses on the approach abound. (This, indeed, is another of the positives of NLP – it has taken cognitive/

behavioural approaches to a far wider audience than would have been reached by academic psychology alone.)

4. Approaches from business

New friends are exciting, but old friends are true. So when seeking to identify your own particular suite of approaches to coaching, don't forget the ones you had already: perhaps a deep understanding of strategy, or doing business in China, or the particular complex culture, jargon, promotion and equity structures of the legal sector.

This is hard for us to see: we take it for granted as it has always been there. But it is crucially important as it is often this shared experience which wins us the initial trust to coach. Whatever our particular background is – private equity, manufacturing, FMCG – it gives us a general business understanding that an outsider doesn't have. We know the broad rules, the jargon, the structures and the no-go areas. If, for example, a client mutters, 'this is getting towards being a matter of advice to the Stock Exchange', we realise the gravity of what they are saying. We know the rules, the pecking order, some of the unseen codes, pressures and pleasures. This tacit knowledge gets us in the door, enables us to pass the initial 'sniff test' with prospective clients.

And as well as that wealth of tacit knowledge, people whose careers have been in business, in public sector organisations or as entrepreneurs, also have a plethora of *explicit* tools as well, perhaps for business planning, post-merger integration, employment law, succession planning, financial analysis, or whatever it may be. That sense of 'this person understands' is a powerful beginning to good business coaching, and the approaches and tools you brought to your enquiry into coaching, may in the end be just as important a part of your 'tree' as anything new you learn. Furthermore, there is your own individuality: 'Big Five' is different in your hands from anyone else, and your unique background and personality may be exactly what a particular client needs.

Ah, personality: that is a chapter to itself, and we go on to consider this in Chapter 7.

But first, a little fun to finish off with and to draw the threads together: my personal list of the 'Top Ten Tools in business coaching'. It's not definitive, everyone's list will be different, but rather it is to provoke your thinking: what is your list to be?

5. My Top Ten Tools for business coaching

1. Silence

Silence can be companionable – waiting while the coachee thinks something through, both of us relaxed. Or it can be assertive, they know I am going to sit it out for *their* answer. But it is top of my list for a third reason: consistently allowing a tiny gap after the coachee speaks yields gold on those occasions when they breathe in and say, 'actually …'

2. Big Five

See Chapter 5.

3. MBTI

The most widely used method for calibrating how best to adjust to each new coaching client, but not the only one; some coaches use a Strengths approach. For both, see the next chapter.

4. Spark

The unique personality and business background of the coach. We are not coaching machines, and some spark of our individuality might be exactly what the client needs to help the work along.

5. Ryan & Deci

Builds motivation: see Chapter 10.

6. 4 steps to confidence

See above.

7. Prochaska

See page 91.

8. Ibarra

And again, page 91!

9. Flow

Another trusted standby: whenever there is a block to progress, one good place to start is the first four steps of Flow – and often one need go no further than the first, 'balance between challenge and skill'. With the world changing so fast, many business people are just not equipped with the skills they need to tackle their many challenges. No one but a coach is going to voice that; doing so can be very liberating.

10. PERFECT

This could well become the standard means of integration for all our other approaches.

Further reading

Tim Gallwey and the Inner Game approach

www.theinnergame.com – the Tim Gallwey/Inner Game website.

Downey, M. (1999) *Effective Coaching*, London: Orion Business Books. Applies the Inner Game approach.

Gallwey, W. T. (2000) *The Inner Game of Work*, New York: Random House.

Flow

Csikszentmihalyi, M. (1990) *Flow: The Psychology of Optimal Experience*, New York: Harper & Row.

Csikszentmihalyi, M. (1997) *Finding Flow*, New York Basic Books.

Seligman, M. (2003) *Authentic Happiness*, London: Nicholas Brealey.

NLP

Knight, S. (2002) *NLP at Work*, London: Nicholas Brealey.

7

Deepening coaching skills: working with individual difference

Up to now, we have been presuming that coaching is 'one size fits all' – that the same approach works for everyone. But it doesn't.

As is apparent to anyone who looks up from their newspaper while travelling on the London Underground, human beings vary rather considerably. Sophisticated coaching must flex to adapt.

'Individual difference' is what the scientists call it, as they are dispassionately interested in objective assessment of individual variation. But in coaching, we're not using psychometrics, or any other tool, for the sake of it: we're usually doing it for a very particular and subjective purpose, namely to raise *self-awareness*.

Self-awareness is important in coaching for three reasons:

- from the coach's perspective, the more we know our **own** personality/ issues, the more we can set them aside and hence become less of an 'interference' to our coachee;
- from the individual or organisational **client's** perspective, having greater awareness of themselves and their impact on others is often in itself a goal for coaching;
- and sometimes most valuable of all in business terms, having experimented on themselves, clients can put their deepened knowledge of how people tick towards significantly better management and leadership of **others**.

We consider here a number of different ways of deepening self-awareness, from simple pen-and-paper methods, through to more complex psychometric approaches; then finally take a look at how in practice some coaches put them all together.

1. Pen-and-paper approaches

We presume the client is healthy and well; so if raising self-awareness is an issue, they should be able to figure it out for themselves, and indeed they can.

Johari

One well-known method is the 'Johari Window'. The Johari Window (see Figure 7.1) is not an ancient mystical technique, but a simple two-by-two matrix developed apparently by two Californians called Joe and Harry.[1] It is a quick and effective way to gather information about ourselves.

The matrix illustrates that in any situation, logically there must be things that:

- I know and you know: the *Arena*.
- I know and you don't know: the *Façade*.
- You know and I don't: the *Blind Spot*.
- and the *Unknown*, which we both don't know!

Being asked to fill in the Arena box about a particular situation; for example, 'how I am perceived as a team leader', might of itself generate some insight – it is really just another way of asking a coaching question. And should one want to find out the perspective of others, one does so by pushing back the vertical line in the matrix, i.e. requesting feedback; to have others made more aware of oneself, one pushes down the horizontal line, i.e. by making more disclosure.

For some, including I confess myself, this is too simplistic a model, but I include it as every now and then a coach or client says they find it exceptionally useful.

Wheels

Similarly some decry the various 'wheel of life' diagrams, but others find them indispensable. Jenny Rogers describes in depth how several variants of the approach can be used.[2] Coaches who use this technique often develop their own standard blank template and ask the client to fill it in.

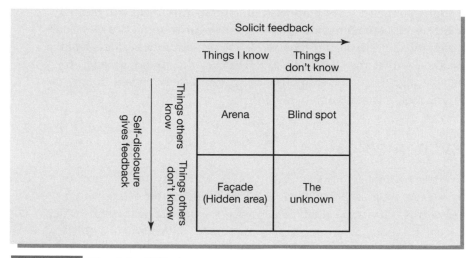

Figure 7.1   The Johari Window

Adapted from: Luft, J. (1970) *Group Processes: An Introduction to Group Dynamics*, Palo Alto, CA: National Press Books.

This has its merits but, as Jenny notes, a different and potentially better way is to give the client a blank page and ask them to draw and label their own wheel – and to draw each segment's size according to its current importance in their life. Then they repeat the exercise, drawing the segments how they wish them to be. You'll see what happens: clients are confronted with sometimes very imbalanced wheels, but entirely of their own drawing. (A good moment, perhaps, for allowing them to sit in contemplative silence, as mentioned in Chapter 6.)

But it's 'horses for courses'. We discuss personality difference below: clients who prefer the established order of things, and relish structure, might like the security of a pre-printed chart; others would prefer the freedom to design their own.

Life v. business?

The above techniques both owe more to 'life' coaching. There is vigorous debate as to how much one needs to know about broader life background, family, past, etc. in business coaching. Some business coaches believe firmly that it is essential to know this at the outset irrespective of the coaching contract, while others are equally firmly of the view that for much short-term coaching on straightforward issues, none whatsoever is required. Where there is a specific need for this information, as in career coaching, you will see in Chapter 9 that Charles Glass addresses it by working through a set of proprietary questions. This 'structured interview' approach perhaps represents a halfway house between the two views: any necessary and relevant information is sought, but in a business-familiar manner. And as the client goes through the background material, there may be 'ah hahs' of self-awareness; as in 'R' of GROW, merely pulling the information together can generate insight.

2. Psychometrics

As its name implies, a psychometric measures the psyche, in whole or in part. There are probably millions of them out there, from fun tests in magazines which have no validity whatsoever, to scientific instruments which have quite strong power to predict how people will behave in a variety of ways. (Strictly, not all psychometrics are tests, particularly personality: a test suggests right or wrong answers, hence the word instrument is preferred by psychologists. I use test here as that tends to be the generic term used among coaches.)

Defining quality in psychometrics

While this diversity is interesting, and it might be tempting to use wacky or untried tests, in the US, organisations have been sued for using poor tests or those that unfairly discriminate in assessment situations, and coaches using them for development should also stick to the reputable. Some key determinants of quality are that the test is:

- *Objective*: the results are not influenced by a scorer's personal preferences or biases.
- *Reliable:* repeat testing yields a similar result – i.e. it captures something in the person which is relatively stable over time, rather than a transient mood or situation; it is measuring 'trait not state', in the jargon.
- *Valid*: it 'does what it says on the tin' – i.e. it actually measures what it claims to measure. For example, a test of literacy should in fact predict how well people can read.
- *Discriminating*: the test should *be discriminating*, showing clear differences between individuals on the behaviour being tested, for example sorting out people who can process in 3-D sufficiently to be a safe air-traffic controller, compared with those who can't. It should not be *discriminatory*, i.e. unfairly discriminating against minority or any groups on the basis of irrelevant characteristics.

(Adapted from opp.eu.com)

What tests measure

The assessment consultancy Getfeedback puts it neatly: see their Bullseye diagram in Figure 7.2 and the explanation of each circle below. There are tests for every level, but the closer to the centre of the bullseye, the harder the thing is to change.

▦ *Motivation*: 'will do'. An individual's motivation is formed at an early age and usually doesn't change much. It might be based on things like the strength of their desire for power, or need for structure.

▦ *Capability*: 'can do'. The classic was shorthand/typing speed tests, where very precise measures could be obtained. At executive level, 'can do' tests will typically measure clients' capability to make strategic decisions or value judgements under challenging conditions.

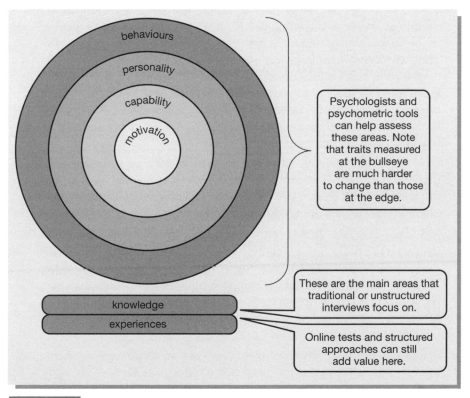

| Figure 7.2 | The Bullseye diagram |

Source: Adapted with permission from: Getfeedback, *Guide to Effective Selection*, see www. getfeedback.net.

- *Personality*: 'likes doing'. Personality or character traits are those that we generally recognise about people: a characteristic pattern of thinking, behaviour and feeling.
- *Behaviour*: 'does!'. The easiest to change.

(Adapted from www.getfeedback.net)

Access to tests

To protect the public (and perhaps also for a smidge of commerciality) there are several levels of access to tests, from freely available to anyone, to those only available to medically trained doctors and psychiatrists.

The five levels of access in the UK are:

1 *Open access*. A few good psychometrics for specific purposes are available to everyone, simply by paying a small fee per test. Three that are useful for business coaching, are Schein's Career Anchors, available at www.careeranchorsonline.com or in hard copy from Amazon; the Thomas-Kilman Conflict Mode Instrument (TKI), available at www.opp.eu.com; and Realise2, an online strengths assessment and development tool (on which more below), available at www.cappeu.com. As pressure on budgets increases, these rarities – soundly research-based tools, which add value to coaching but where no costly training is required – will be even more prized.

2 *Open access, after training*. Anyone can also use tests including the popular MBTI and FIRO-B, provided they undertake a training with the distributors (OPP in Europe; CPP in the US). Trainings typically take 2–5 days per test and are not inexpensive.

3 *BPS level A required*. 'BPS Level A' is a qualification to administer *ability* tests, which are not generally relevant to business coaching, with the exception of a few such as the Watson Glaser Critical Thinking Analysis. For business coaches, the main purpose of undertaking Level A training is as a prerequisite to the more commonly used Level B. (The BPS Level A and B system is currently under review: see www.bps.org.uk for updates.)

4 *BPS Level B required*. 'BPS Level B' qualifies one to administer *personality* assessments, although some may still require product-specific certification before the publishers will allow someone to buy them. There are many reputable tests of overall personality, including the NEO (www.hogrefe.co.uk), the Hogan suite (www.psychological-consultancy.com), 16PF, etc. (www.opp.eu.com/16pf).

5   *Only available to medical practitioners.* The full MBTI five-scale version, the TDI (explained page 114), is only available to qualified clinicians, as are tests such as the MMPI (Minnesota Multiphasic Personality Inventory) a comprehensive mental health-oriented personality assessment which measures everything from soup to nuts, including all the major pathologies, and the Beck Depression Inventory, a short and very useful test which could be invaluable in mid-career business coaching.

Indirect access to tests

If you are not Level B qualified but want to use a test that requires it, the simplest way is to pair up with a colleague who is. They deliver the test and give the client the feedback, ideally with you present as well so you hear it in full; you and the client then take it forward into the coaching. Many Level B qualified people are likely to be found in the alumni of any good coach training, so you may have colleagues who can readily do this for you.

Alternatively organisations such as Getfeedback (www.getfeedback.net) offer a test bureau, delivering online testing to your clients, with appropriately trained organisational psychologists giving the feedback, and again you take it on from there in the coaching.

The tests business coaches use

The inner rings of the bullseye diagram are more relevant to selection: as the things most unlikely to change, these are the ones targeted in selection decisions. Once the person is hired, business coaching comes into play, perhaps to help them settle and/or get to peak performance. Tests used by coaches tend to concentrate on the third ring of the diagram, *personality*. (All this fine teamwork leading hopefully to ideal outcomes on the outer circle, behaviours!)

The 'gold standard' of what good-quality business coaches are expected to have at their disposal used to be MBTI, FIRO-B and a method of 360° feedback. That is, as we shall see below, a measure of overall personality (MBTI); one for how the client relates to others (FIRO-B) plus data-gathering from the client's context (the crucial importance of which is discussed in the next chapter). Things have moved on, and with the Positive Psychology resources coming onstream, the 'gold standard' now includes the above three plus a Strengths inventory.

360° feedback is discussed in the next chapter; here we consider each of the other three in turn.

1. Overall personality: the MBTI controversy

By far the most popular tool in coaching for raising awareness of overall personality is the MBTI. I presume most readers are familiar with it, but if not it is, in essence, a general personality assessment based on the work of the Swiss psychologist Carl Jung, and developed by Americans Katherine Briggs and Isabel Myers. It is built upon four core dimensions of how people prefer to manage energy, information and decision-making (i.e. E/I, or extraversion/introversion; S/N, sensing or intuition, according to how we take in information; T/F, thinking or feeling, according to how we use information, i.e. take decisions; and J/P, judging or perceiving, i.e. whether we take pleasure in completion and closure; or curiosity and the journey). This results in 16 possible personality types, such as 'ENFP' or 'ISTJ'. The 16 types are not intended to be a label or a box to put people in – the useful metaphor is rather to think of them as rooms in a house: we need to be able to occupy them all. Some of us prefer to live out on the front porch, some prefer the quiet of the library, but we all need to use the kitchen.

The MBTI is the most widely used personality instrument in the world, taken by more than 2 million people a year. Its fans may therefore be surprised to learn it is a pariah among psychometricians! It is largely absent from reputable psychology textbooks and degree courses, is not accepted as a measure in psychology research, and is *certainly* not mentionable in mainstream academic peer-reviewed scientific journals.

Why?!

The case against

There are three strikes against the MBTI:

- *Type v. trait*. Psychologists as you will have discerned in earlier chapters don't agree about anything: Freudians, behaviourists, humanistic psychologists, etc. have been fighting like ferrets in a sack about the fundamentals of psychology for 100 years. Except, that is, in the area of personality, where there is a rare level of agreement. Personality psychologists are in almost complete accord, and have been for 30 years, that there are five basic building blocks of personality which combine (like the four components of DNA) to form the infinite variety of human beings. (Hence the 'Big Five' theory of personality – but this is the psychometric Big Five, not the coaching one.) This is the 'trait' world, and it has captured all the citadels of psychology – universities, peer-reviewed journals, prizes, scholarships. MBTI is, officially, not a trait measure but a 'type' instrument; the psychometricians say no such thing exists.

■ *Five v. four scales*. Mainstream trait theorists are agreed there are five core building blocks; the MBTI has only four scales. This matters more than being one short on the numbers: the missing fifth scale is, the trait theorists say, crucial, as it is the scale which runs from emotional stability to neuroticism (the normal half of the scale) and then on from neuroticism to psychoticism (the abnormal half). MBTI lacks this fifth scale they say, and therefore cannot be a comprehensive personality instrument such as the researchers' gold standard, the NEO.

■ *Normal distribution v. bimodal*. Trait psychometricians insist personality characteristics, such as introversion, are normally distributed, i.e. people's scores range across a bell curve, with most bunched in the middle phasing out to a few strays at either end. Type says the distribution is bimodal, i.e. people are at either end – either one thing or the other – so an extravert or an introvert with no shades of grey between.

The rebuttal

■ *Type v. trait*. Guilty as charged. There is no such thing as type; the MBTI, some would say, is a good trait instrument.*

Why then does the MBTI industry cling to the type label, which keeps it beyond the scientific pale? Partly for historic reasons, but partly because the simplification which the type approach enables is one reason for the MBTI's great usefulness. If, following the trait approach, you are an O12, C26, E32, etc. then the numbers are essentially meaningless to a lay person and require constant expert interpretation. But if, as in MBTI, you have a forced choice of either E or I, either S or N, etc., ending up with a 'best fit' type, such as say ENFP, you have something readily understandable and useable (see 'Applications for coaching' below). Trait keeps power with the white coats; type hands it over to the clients.

■ *Five v. four scales*. False. The MBTI world is perfectly aware of the fifth scale, and a version exists with it included, the Type Differentiation Indicator (TDI). But the purpose of the MBTI was to make information about personality widely available, to bring about greater understand-

* Type adherents don't of course agree. Commenting on this section OPP made the following good point: 'Type reflects how most people understand others. "He's an introvert". "She's a caring sort". In this respect type is very real. It may be that they are made up of underlying traits, however the human experience is to categorise to create meaning and understanding and to reduce complexity down to a useful set of data for navigating everyday life.' (E-mail to author, 30 July 2010.)

ing and harmony in the world. It was therefore designed from the outset to be delivered by (trained) lay people. The designers did not however think it right for lay people to be running around saying, 'I'm afraid, Mr Smith, you are psychotic'. So the form most of us are familiar with does indeed lack the fifth scale, and the full-scale TDI is available only to licensed clinical psychologists and psychiatrists. So the MBTI is a five-scale instrument, with one scale removed from the most commonly used version, for perfectly good reasons. (The lack of this fifth-scale data to non-medics is of course a drawback of the MBTI: there are times when I am working with a client and can sense something is horribly wrong, or at the least clouding the picture, and wish I had that fifth scale to confirm/disconfirm my hypothesis.

■ *Normal curve v. bimodal.* The jury's out: looking at the scatterplots of the data in detail, one could in fact argue the case either way. If you look at it with your head to one side, you could discern a bunching in the middle, but if you tilt your head the other way, there is a case for seeing a bunching at either end. Anyway this is a technicality of interest only to the boffins. The great value of the bimodal approach is that it lays the platform for a superb suite of *applications* for us as business coaches (see below).

Value of MBTI in coaching

Having explained the controversy, why has MBTI, despite the disdain of science, become the most widely used instrument in coaching worldwide? There are in my view three reasons:

1 *Non-judgemental.* If the Beck Depression Inventory scores you as clinically depressed, or even if the NEO says you are high on emotional instability (i.e. neuroticism), then this has practical implications: such material appearing in your personnel files may affect your chances of getting a job, promotion, etc. (The tests could well be entirely right of course, and you shouldn't get the job!) Trait approaches imply judgement; indeed, that in some cases is their purpose.

By contrast I suspect a major reason why the MBTI has been so successful for 70 years (or 90, depending on whether you date its origins from the original research in the 1920s, or the first version of the current test in the 1940s) is that it goes to great lengths to be judgement-free. Each of the 16 'types' is treated with scrupulous even-handedness, with an equal measure of pluses and minuses. But there are no cut-off points, and no reference to one type or another being suitable for a particular occupation: whether you are an ISFP or an ENTJ in a manufacturing company, you are just a different type of employee, with different things to offer. (Hence its usefulness in development, but not selection.) Rogerians have long held that the human soul shrinks in the presence of judgement; Frederickson has solid research evidence that we flourish in the presence of positive emotion (see Chapter 11); and countless people over the years have said to me MBTI worked for them because it felt true, but not judgemental.

2 *Applications for coaching*

(a) *How to coach, by personality type*

The advantage of simplifying responses into either/or preferences, is that you can build detailed and comprehensive support materials from that base. The most crucial for business coaching – I would suggest, one of the most important references in this entire book – is *Introduction to Type and Coaching* (available from www. opp.eu.com), one of a series of almost two dozen substantial booklets which help put the MBTI to practical use.

The coaching booklet is based on the solid data set built up over the decades, from millions of people taking the MBTI each year. Based on that, the booklet sets out detailed guidance on the strengths of each preference; what typically goes wrong for them; and, very usefully, what the research evidence says is the best way of tackling the deficits. The material is highly accessible, presented in short bullet-point format. And best of all, for each preference, there is a section on how best to coach them! This might sound appallingly prescriptive, but it somehow manages to strike the right balance of offering extremely useful tips, yet without cramping coach or coachee's individual style. Indispensable.

(b) *Stress and getting out of it*

That very useful coaching guideline is becoming well known, but much of the other supporting material remains untapped by coaches. For example, another booklet in the series, *In the Grip* (also available from www.opp.eu.com), is about stress. Others talk about 'coping' with stress, but the MBTI isn't content with mere toleration: it offers tried-and-tested means (again based on decades of experience and data) of how to get each type *out* of it. The business benefit, to say nothing of the reduction in human suffering, of having methods which consistently and reliably shorten times in anger, depression, or any of the other ways different types react to chronic or acute pressure, are very significant.

(c) *Change*

Similarly, there is detailed guidance available to assist coaches working with people going through change, in *Type and Change* (also from www.opp.eu.com). One learns in that, for example, that of all the types, it is ISFJs who have by far the most difficulty coping with change, particularly if it is suddenly imposed from the outside. The counsel is to back off – exactly the reverse of what, in misguided helpfulness and concern, colleagues, consultants or coaches might otherwise do. Again, it's not prescriptive, but provides valuable food for thought in dealing with an unfamiliar personality make-up, or a puzzling reaction to a situation.

(d) *Conflict*

Here I refer you not to a helpful booklet, but back to the original Jung. In *Psychological Types*[3] – which I warmly recommend not just for its insight but as classic literature – he says in cases of conflict, look to the middle two scales, S/N and T/F, which are about how we process information. Often if two people are irritating each other, one of these is the culprit. Ss drown Ns in too much data; conversely, Ns never give Ss enough information – so both chafe, and think the other incompetent. Similarly, if needing to take a joint decision, Ts may get irritated at Fs' subjectivity, while the Fs get cross at the Ts' detachment. No one here is setting out to be difficult, all are people of goodwill, they are simply processing data differently.

In any event, if a coaching client reports being consistently wounded by another person, investigate a possible S/N or T/F mismatch. If this is indeed the problem, sighs of relief all round as with quick explanations, and agreement to try and remember the other's requirements, the tension can vanish almost overnight. (Until the next time – so a memory-jogger might be helpful too!)

3 *Development*

Jung was most unusual among psychologists: instead of studying babies, or the mentally ill, he had a particular interest in adults, and especially the highest performers. A central feature of his account of personality is therefore a description of how we develop in mid-life, and I notice clients find it uncommonly liberating. Jung said the tasks of the first half of life – forming relationships, earning a living – are carried out using the genetic preferences – I and S and F and J, for example, if you are an ISFJ. But the task of the second half of life is to bring out the other hitherto undeveloped preferences, the E, N, T and P, in this case, to become, as he puts it, a whole human.

Lovely – and exactly how many of my clients experience it. People who have been extravert all their life become more reflective – the extraversion hasn't gone away, they're just developing another piece. In my own mid-40s (right on schedule, Jung would say) my natural N stayed very much with me, but suddenly I developed a passionate interest in two very S hobbies, gardening and family history, and both have given me great pleasure ever since. Jung wouldn't see it as a 'mid-life crisis', just as normal human development.

This is important in coaching senior executives: people at later career stages are often unrecognisable in standard MBTI terms. Their results tend to be quite undifferentiated (E4, N8, T3, J22, for example), and asked to choose between preferences they say, 'but I can do both'. To which the reply is yes, they clearly do, but which was there from the beginning, and which has developed over time? Usually they can answer instantly. Hence the 'development needs' section of *Type and Coaching* is largely irrelevant – they have already knocked the rough edges off. But the booklet still remains very useful in helping them understand and work better with other members of their team.

Intelligence as confound

A final caveat: another aspect of raising self-awareness in senior executive coaching is that high intelligence can cut across almost everything we are mentioning in this chapter. So those familiar with MBTI will have a view of what a 'typical' type – say an ISTJ – is like, but for many of the individuals we coach, their intelligence is such that it almost wipes the other pieces off the board.

Professor Adrian Furnham of University College London, says in fact in job performance only three things matter: 'High G but not too high; High C but not too high; and low N'.[4] That is to say, high intelligence ('G'), but not to the point where it becomes disabling; high Conscientiousness but not to the point of obsession; and low Neuroticism, or being emotionally stable. Others don't agree, and see individual difference in more complex terms, but there are times when I think to myself he's right. Intelligence does indeed give a positive cast to other features; emotional instability/neuroticism gives a negative one; and many of our driven high-achiever clients wobble on the edge between conscientiousness and over-perfectionism. But only someone with Adrian's great authority (and charm) can get away with handling the nitroglycerine of testing leaders for their intelligence; the rest of us must plough on with more conventional means of raising awareness in coaching.

MBTI and your coaching

If you are familiar with the MBTI, to bring this section to a close you might like to think about some of the following questions:

- What assets do you bring to your coaching as a result of your preferences?
- And which aspects of your profile present the greatest challenges in coaching?
- How might you mitigate these?
- How might your preferences affect your approach to the *business* of coaching (e.g. marketing, selling, contracting, chemistry meetings, documenting coaching sessions, closing assignments, providing organisational feedback)?

2. FIRO-B

The MBTI is the first psychometric many people turn to in coaching, The second is usually 'FIRO-B' (which stands for Fundamental Interpersonal Relations Orientation-Behaviour; for more information, and how to train, see www.opp.eu.com). Whereas MBTI is an intra-personal instrument, i.e. it looks at the personality within us, FIRO-B by contrast is an inter-personal one, looking at the needs we have in relationships with other people.

The brainchild of Will Schutz, FIRO-B was developed at the time of the first long-range nuclear submarines. They were designed to submerge below the surface of the seas and stay there, invisible for up to eight months at a time. The designers realised the greatest 'risk to mission' was not a failure of the hardware, but the risk of what might happen among the men cooped up in a steel tube for eight months. As a result, Schutz was commissioned to undertake a research project of enormous scale, researching everything known on interpersonal relations and conflict, not just in psychology and science, but across the world's great classic literature and religions as well.

Having boiled it all down, Schutz said the essence of interpersonal relations is a function of three things: inclusion, control and affection (I, C and A), and the extent to which we differ in our individual needs for each. His great stroke of genius, the thing which makes FIRO so exceptionally useful, was to then go on to split the scores from his test into two. He called them the 'Expressed' and 'Wanted' scores, i.e. what we signal to the outside world, and what we want within, for each of I, C and A.

The result is a simple 3 × 2 matrix, which he claimed, and research over the subsequent half-century has tended to support, gives the essence of an individual's interpersonal make-up.

FIRO-B is of course useful in raising self-awareness in individual coaching, but its main application is in working with more than one person, or teams. The psychometric (FIRO-B is well within the 'trait' pale) shows how pairs or groups of people fit together – or not! – like the pieces of a jigsaw puzzle. If I have a high 'Expressed Inclusion', for example – naturally wanting to include most people in most things I do – and you have a high 'Wanted Inclusion' – naturally wanting most people to include you in most things – then our needs match beautifully and we'll get along fine. But if we don't have a good match, then two people of goodwill can rub each other up the wrong way, quite without meaning to. If, in the Gestalt saying, 'simple awareness is often curative' then FIRO-B is a peacemaker.

3. Strengths Inventories

Most of us are well aware of our weaknesses, and these are often highlighted in appraisals or other assessments. But particularly in historically modest Britain, we are often less clear about our *strengths* – yet knowing these is often required in coaching. The problem is, while we have clear and detailed language to describe what's wrong with people, we had until a decade ago, much less developed ability to describe and understand strengths. If you went to a psychiatrist, they could consult the *DSM IV*, the *Diagnostic and Statistical Manual*, a vast heavy tome which could detail with great precision which sub-variant of complex pathology you had – but there was nothing to chart human strengths with equal comprehensiveness and authority. Positive Psychology has invested enormous amounts of research effort to redress this balance. As a result there are now three major tools for coaches to use in raising awareness of strengths:[5]

■ *The VIA (Values in Action) Inventory of Strengths.* This is the result of extensive research by Martin Seligman, Chris Peterson and their teams of researchers at a number of top US universities, including the University of Pennsylvania and the University of Michigan. More than 1 million people have already completed the inventory, which looks at 24 *overall* human strengths and virtues, identified by Peterson and Seligman (2004) in their landmark study.

Thanks to a generous donation by a philanthropist who wanted this material (called affectionately by some, the 'un-DSM') to be in the public domain, there is no charge for completing the inventory. To try it, go to www.viacharacter.org, follow the link to the VIA and take the test. You'll receive a one-page report listing your own personal top five strengths. (Some may surprise you!) It is also useful to click further to produce your report on your top *24* strengths: the website keeps changing slightly, so you may have to hunt around for the click for this. The site also has a free library of further information.

■ *The Gallup StrengthsFinder™ Instrument.* Over the last two decades the Gallup Organisation has poured millions of dollars into research on strengths in the workplace, and has published its own strengths profiling instrument, the Gallup StrengthsFinder, now available in several versions. To access it at individual level buy one of the Gallup publications, either the original book, *Now Discover Your Strengths*, or *StrengthsFinder 2.0*, or *Strengths-Based Leadership.* Inside the dust jacket is a code number, which is used to take the test online. Again a report will be generated and you can refer to the book for more information on each of the 34 strengths measured. To access it at organisational level, which yields much more comprehensive reports, see www.gallup.com. The Gallup instrument focuses on strengths relevant to *work.*

■ *Realise2: the second generation.* Professor Alex Linley and his colleagues at the Centre for Applied Positive Psychology (CAPP) have researched strengths in the *European* context. There are several interesting aspects to the CAPP instrument, Realise2 (see www.capp.eu.com). They identified further strengths not found in the VIA or StrengthsFinder.* Also, and very interestingly for coaches on the lookout for ways to deliver transformational results in clients, the Realise2 report also breaks strengths down into 'realised' and 'unrealised' strengths – that is, the ones you know about and play to, but also those strengths that currently lie untapped. Equally useful for leaders and coaches of hardworking businesspeople, another report category is 'learned behaviours', i.e. the things which we believe to be strengths, as we do them well and use them all the time, but which in fact drain our energy. A very important awareness to raise!

Individual difference: the future?

While best practice is currently to understand individual differences in coaching by using an intrapersonal + an interpersonal psychometric + a strengths instrument + 360° feedback, what new tests are the innovative coaches using already, which may represent trends for the future? Perhaps:

---

* Such as 'bounceback' – perhaps something we have had to develop through Europe's long and often difficult history? Realise2 also reports on weaknesses, so is the only strengths tool to provide people with a holistic, overall assessment of strengths, weaknesses and learned behaviours.

■ *The 'dark side'.* The full Hogan suite of personality instruments (see www.psychological-consulting.com) is comprehensive, including measures of personality and motivation, and famously including the Hogan Development Survey (HDS), which measures the 'dark side' of leadership. The HDS is unique as a reliable measure of management 'derailers' in the normal business population, and it is explicitly intended to support coaches called in to tackle individuals with dysfunctional interpersonal skills, or to fix damaged teams.

■ *Entrepreneurial ability.* In a turbulent recession-hit world many people are reconsidering their careers, with some considering setting up their own business. Dr Shailendra Vyakarnam, Director of the Centre for Entrepreneurial Learning at the Judge Business School at Cambridge and his multidisciplinary team have developed a tool, Tristart (see www.tristart.co.uk), which enables would-be entrepreneurs to test out at minimal cost online, both their entrepreneurial ability and the viability of their current business plan – testing, in other words, whether both the individual (or the team) and the plan 'have what it takes'. Again the tool was designed explicitly to support coaches who don't feel themselves qualified either as psychologists or as entrepreneurial experts.

■ *Leadership.* Tough times need ever more nimble leaders, but the avalanche of information and demands means leaders are often having to make crucial judgements with imperfect, unclear or conflicting information. The fascinating Leadership Judgement Indicator (LJI) (see www.hogrefe.co.uk) was developed to test how wise leaders' decisions are. It tests them in a number of different business scenarios and is able to determine, for example, not just how they normally behave but whether they have the mental dexterity and complexity of self-concept sufficient to judge even *against* their preferred style when the decision or context require.

And in practice?

Given this wealth of resources to draw upon, what do coaches actually use in practice? A couple of trends are apparent.

Up front *v.* emergent

I notice a difference between approaches on either side of the Atlantic. Of course the practice of individual coaches, coaching organisations, internal leaders and HR/L&D teams varies, but very broadly the US approach is to use a 'battery of tests' upfront, while the European approach is, as I describe it, more 'emergent' – i.e. tests are used in response to a specific need arising in the coaching. An excellent example of perhaps the extreme end of the former approach is in the case study described by Keil and colleagues.[6] In their model, when coaching a CEO, two coaches work together, one a clinical psychologist, the other an organisational development specialist. The first stage of their approach is 'fact-gathering':

> 'The consultants interview the client in considerable depth about work life, personal history, and current personal life, and the client completes a battery of Psychological tests, which may include such elements as the Adjective Checklist (ACL), FIRO-B, Myers–Briggs Type Inventory (MBTI), Minnesota Multiphasic Personality Inventory (MMPI) and a team management instrument. [plus] … the client prepares a list of those individuals who could offer information helpful to the client's development process. Up to 20 work colleagues and significant persons in the client's individual life are individually interviewed by the team following a structured data-collection format.

> The second phase of the programme begins with a 2- to 3-day [offsite] "insight session" during which the consulting team presents all of the collected information to the client to create a comprehensive portrait. This picture pinpoints strengths and shortfalls and offers perceptions of the client's motivation, use of power and influence, decision making, expectations, handling of conflict, integrity, emotional competence, and other dimensions of personal and professional effectiveness. The consultants work with the client to consolidate the information and target areas for development, including the leveraging of identified strengths. Both parties collaborate to produce a document that integrates the collected data and use that information as the basis for a development plan that details specific and measurable goals and action steps.' (p. 69)

By contrast, a respected senior UK leader who read this case as part of his own coaching training was incredulous that any CEO on his side of 'the pond' would have the time or interest for this quantum of introspection – and, with a slight raise of one eyebrow, what must it *cost*!

Balanced approach

The Keil example was from before the current period of austerity. Coaches of The Alliance (www.alliancecoaching.co.uk, see Chapter 2) even in the current climate still use a broad range of approaches to deal with individual difference. Many are expert in applying Positive Psychology: one was in the original cohort of coaches trained by Martin Seligman himself, and several are trained in Realise2. But they also range across the middle of the spectrum, using MBTI and FIRO-B – and go right to the other edge of it, with several also trained on the Hogan Dark Side. Additionally, they take care to see their coaching in its context, through a series of initial interviews (though more like half a dozen than 20), and are through another of their members attuned to the psychodynamic aspects of the client's role and relationships. This *balanced* approach is becoming the norm. Not everyone can be trained or expert in everything, so the desire to build this more balanced offering might be part of a modest trend in the market towards coaches working together rather than individually.

We started this chapter by saying that Big Five coaching on its own isn't enough; it needs to be supplemented by an awareness of how to flex to work with individual difference. In the next chapter we add the final crucial element that all coaching must take account of: the *context*.

8

Advanced coaching: from individuals to groups

In 1961 hundreds of ordinary, normal, pleasant people came into Stanley Milgram's laboratory at Yale University, took off their hats and coats, sat down – and electrocuted the man next door.

It was part of a research study on 'learning'. The 'learner' was strapped into a chair with electrodes. The people who had volunteered to take part came in one at a time. They were instructed by a man in a white coat to read a list of questions, and every time the learner in the next room got one wrong, to flick a switch on a scientific-looking machine, which allegedly delivered him an electric shock. The first switch was marked '15 volts', each switch was stronger, and the last was marked '450 volts, Danger extreme shock XXX'. What percentage of the nice ordinary people who took part, do you think would be prepared to go right along the panel of switches, inflicting increasing levels of shocks – despite first yelps, then cries, then screams of pain, and finally after 330 volts, ominous silence, coming from the other room?

63%.

63% of ordinary decent people were prepared to inflict fatal electric shocks on another human being because a man in a white coat told them to. (In fact of course, the 'learner' was an actor, the screams were a recording and the machine was a fake – but the individuals didn't know that.)[1]

Ah, well, you say, that was decades ago, a more restricted society, we're individualists now, we think for ourselves, we wouldn't do it – wrong. Milgram experiments have long since been banned by psychology Ethics

Committees, but that doesn't stop reality TV: when entertainer Derren Brown[2] and others replicated the study in the 1990s and 2000s, they found almost identical results.

The original studies caused an uproar. Especially as Milgram had carefully repeated them many times: in a sleazy dockside office in case people had been overly influenced by being at Yale; with women-only groups; and with groups composed only of pillars of society such as lawyers, teachers and judges. The numbers varied slightly, but in all cases around half of the participants went right through to the end, inflicting 'Danger XXX 450 volt' shocks despite the man next door screaming in pain and crying out for them to stop. They sweated and squirmed, and clearly hated doing it, but they did it.

The great classic experiments in 20th-century psychology, such as Milgam's, the Zimbardo 'prison experiment' and many many more, proved absolutely conclusively that we are much more affected by our *context* – by roles, stereotypes, group dynamics, others' expectations, etc., than we believe. These were not wicked people, they were good ordinary folk – *us*! But it feels almost unthinkable that we, or our colleagues, neighbours and friends, would have done it.

Underlying all this, particularly in the individualistic West, is our tendency to make the *Fundamental Attribution Error* (FAE). The FAE is the illusion that we (and our clients) as individuals are more masters of our own destiny than we actually are. It *is* an illusion: the evidence is categorically clear that our context has a far more important impact on us than we like to think.

Of all the domains of psychology, this is the one which coaches, and leaders and managers who coach, usually know least about. Coaches use personality insights and tools, as we discussed in the previous chapter, and the GROW model has much good cognitive and behavioural work in it, but the vast field of social psychology (as this area is termed) and in particular the danger of making the FAE, is for many, *terra incognita*. This is despite the existence of literally millions of articles, books, Master's and PhD theses, theories, courses, and therapists specialising in interpersonal, group, team and organisational dynamics. So in this chapter, we just open up the territory, offer some practical suggestions, and hopefully encourage you to sniff the wind and want to explore further.

We consider in particular:

1 how best to *bring the context in*, when coaching an individual
2 what happens when we widen the lens, from coaching just one person to *coaching a group or team*.

1. Bringing the context into individual coaching

In this section, we consider several ways of taking account of the context in individual coaching:

- contracting;
- feedback from the coach;
- 360° feedback;
- hypothesis;
- psychometrics.

Contracting

In fact, we have already laid the foundations of avoiding the FAE, when in Chapter 5 we paid careful attention to *contracting*. A good business coach, or a colleague coaching well, trusts and respects the person they are coaching – but that person is not their sole source of information; they take care to 'triangulate' it by getting good initial briefings and information from a variety of sources. This begins with hearing from all interested parties when defining the work to be done. The initial contracting will often also make provision for gathering '360° feedback,' which we talk about more below, and/or some other data-collection process. Contracting, as ever, is key.

Feedback from the coach

The coaching relationship offers a unique opportunity for a client to receive from their coach that rare thing, direct and honest feedback, (relatively) free from the influence of hierarchy, politics, history and expectations. Good feedback is powerful and rarely given, particularly to those most senior in organisations.

Feedback is distinct from hypothesis, which we consider more below, and which interprets what has been observed. Keeping the two separate can be a challenge.

Imagine a coaching situation where the client is sitting leaning back in her chair, with her hands on her lap, talking. When she begins talking about her relationship with her boss, she leans forward in the chair, takes in her left hand a piece of paper from the table and crushes it into a ball. As the coach you may be tempted to make assumptions (e.g. she is nervous or angry or upset) and to form an instant hypothesis (e.g. this is a difficult or challenging relationship). However, these are not facts – there may be other reasons for the changes you see. Offering to describe what you observe and then being specific, with no interpretation (as in the description above), may be helpful; though not always the way you anticipate, and not always for the client – the coach might learn they were wrong!

Providing feedback well is dependent on accurate observation and your ability to relate that information simply and without interpretation.

If you have established a relationship of openness and trust with your client, you may want to take the feedback one stage further. Your *emotional response* to what the client did or said may be of value. If you as the coach are experiencing something in the coaching session, e.g. believing the client is not listening, and feeling somewhat belittled as a result, others in the organisation may have the same reaction – and be less inclined to share it.

For example:

■ 'When you ... [insert the action or words], I felt ... [insert your response] and I was wondering whether [other team members, colleagues, your manager] might have this reaction too?'

So the rule of thumb for good feedback is to avoid interpretation and confine it to the facts. Second, use only yourself – where you have direct evidence – if some consequences are to be drawn. The formula is hence: 'When you did this ... [insert specific action] I felt this ... [insert actual personal experience].'

That might be all that's appropriate; if more is wonted, the third stage is to 'wonder'* (we have no proof) if others may feel the same way.

---

* A terrific word, borrowed from the therapy world: it signals loud and clear that what follows is not a statement of fact but something offered for consideration.

'360° feedback'

This is the most direct, common and powerful way of getting a quantity of information from the context to your client. (But sadly, unless handled exceptionally well, also one of the most problematic.) There are several alternative ways of doing it:

- interviews;
- using an off-the-shelf 360° instrument;
- using a bespoke instrument, designed specifically for that organisational context.

Interviews by the coach

The coach interviews people in the client's context. This approach is probably best, as the coach thereby hears directly from key people in the client's world. If someone says something puzzling, or drops a hint, the coach is there to pick it up and carefully enquire further.

Six interviews are usually more than sufficient. They need only be quite brief, and although one might think they would need to be conducted in person, in fact telephone interviews also work well if the coach is experienced enough to pick up the nuances. (And importantly for the busy businesspeople being interviewed, they're much quicker.) This process is set up by the client nominating people to be interviewed, ideally those above and below them, internally and externally (e.g. clients if possible) and those who like them plus those who don't. They then advise the interviewees that the coach will be in touch.

The standard interview framework is to ask just three questions:

- What should this person do more of?
- What should they do less?
- What should they keep doing, or stay the same?

Experienced business coach Alice Perkins, (see www.jcagroup.net/AliceP and www.meylercampbell.com/OurPeople), has a nice little improvement on these questions, asking instead:

- What does this person need to do to be successful in this role?
- Against that background, what are they doing really well?
- What could they do better (less of/more of)?

Signalling in advance that only three questions will be asked, and detailing them, gives reassurance that the process will be contained, dignified and respectful – and still gives the interviewees plenty of scope to say whatever they've been saving up! The feedback process then aggregates the input and delivers it back to the client under those three simple headings, with individual comments anonymised.

Bear in mind that no matter how sophisticated the coachee, and how positive the feedback for them, it is still at best an unnerving experience, and possibly a shocking and deeply unpleasant one: each of us has a cherished internal picture of ourselves which is to some extent at odds with how the world sees us, and having that disrupted can be a challenge to our whole ego identity. You should *never give 360° feedback without having received it yourself* in order to appreciate this point fully. (Sometimes participants on training courses swap collecting and delivering feedback on each other: this has the double benefit that they experience the process personally before doing it with clients and can also practise first with more forgiving peers.)

The drawback of this approach is it is expensive in terms of the coach's time. This is however usually still cheaper than the hidden opportunity cost of a dozen senior people within the organisation filling in forms for the computer-based 360° systems (see below) which seem on the surface to be more efficient. One manager of a team of 12 found himself with 144 e-reports to complete every reporting cycle. He took this seriously, but said to me ruefully it felt sometimes as if he had 'no time for the day job'.

Questionnaires

These come in two forms, off-the-shelf and bespoke. *Off-the-shelf* instruments are relatively cheap, appear to have a scientific underpinning, as they show scores against a comparable 'norm group', and have professionally presented reports. In fact however, the sample sizes of such tools are often small and it is important to check they are from the same cultural context and up to date. (A tool developed in the US in the 1980s, for example, is unlikely to be appropriate in Central/Eastern Europe in the 2010s, and vice versa.)

Bespoke instruments can be more appropriate, as these are based on current research within the organisation, with the scores shown compared against the management population your client is actually competing with, and usually in categories (or 'competencies') and language relevant to the organisation. However for these to have value, they need to be based on bespoke research for the organisation which is expensive and time-consuming.

Whatever the source, research has made clear that the feedback from such document/computer-based instruments can be seriously flawed by a number of hidden biases. Raters score people very differently for example: person A will never give anyone 10/10 on principle; person B does so as often as possible, so as to be encouraging. (This can, in turn, be got around by training the raters first: see the British Psychological Society's 360° Degree Feedback: Guidelines for Best Practice at www.bps.org.uk. But senior people with a high opportunity cost to their time, particularly in professional services firms where every six minutes must be billed to meet targets, are disinclined to attend such training.) There can be more serious problems: I know of two separate occasions, in different organisations, where unwilling recipients have formed feedback 'cabals': individuals get together, nominate each other as the feedback givers and generate false but believable reports for each other, to get around a system they despised (in one case) or just thought a pointless bore (in the other). So written 360° documents should be taken with a substantial pinch of salt – used as a possibly valuable basis for discussion but not seen as 'the truth'.

Hypothesis

Based on their observations of clients, experienced coaches often make connections and form theories or hypotheses about their clients. Very judiciously used, these can make a valuable addition to the client's awareness of their context. However such hypotheses are not the truth, and may be incorrect; they are for the client to accept or reject.

In other words, we are using the scientific approach to hypothesis: using our *observations* to develop a *theory to be investigated*.

Because it is not the truth, the key to success is to float your thought as no more than something to be tested. But once you have built a relationship of trust with your client, they are likely to take what you say very seriously – as a fact, or the truth. So to use this technique successfully, you almost have to overemphasise the point that it is just a hypothesis. For example, 'I've just had a thought, it might be completely wrong, but can I just check it out with you ...', or whatever phrasing is authentic for you.

It is generally advisable to present your hypothesis quickly, as the longer you hold on to your theory, the more likely you are to observe those things that support it and to ignore those that contradict it. (Coaches can be a source of corruption of data, too!)

Psychometrics

In the previous chapter we looked at psychometrics such as MBTI and FIRO-B. Where everyone in a team completes one or both of these – and they often are done in groups, so individuals can get to know their fellow team members better – then the data on others represents potentially very valuable information from the context. In larger organisations, even more data might be available if output from 'team climate surveys' or staff attitude surveys, etc. can be accessed.

One very large organisation I knew had annual staff attitude surveys, which included detailed questioning on morale, and also on the leadership, management and developmental/coaching capability of their immediate leaders. The organisation was large enough to break the resulting data down by division, without compromising confidentiality. So there was, to use the research jargon, an annual infusion of both between-subjects and within-subjects data. In other words, you could compare the morale levels of *different* divisions at a single point in time, and you could also compare the results a single leader got in the years *before and after* they received coaching or were trained to coach. It was enormously valuable.

All of these methods – and many more that may also occur to you – bring the *context* into coaching more regularly and reliably than would happen just by chance. If both coach and coachee are opened up to channels of data from the world around them, they are less likely to make the Fundamental Attribution Error. Improving the flow of data from the context improves all the stages of GROW: the Topics and G are broadened if the input of others is carefully sought at the contracting stage on what is truly required; the R is richer, there are potentially more Os, and perhaps most directly of all, the W is significantly enhanced, because the action planning will take much more careful account of all the potential contextual resources and push-backs.

2. Team coaching

When we open up the lens more widely, from coaching one person to coaching several at once, the level of complexity increases (and the adrenalin – which is why some coaches enjoy this more than anything else!). But many of the tools remain the same – and so too, as we shall see below, does the potential for attribution or thinking error, with the consequent need for even more robust coaching.

Team coaching is a huge subject, and is at the stage one-to-one coaching was 15 or 20 years ago, with very little direct research undertaken and not much yet published. There is nevertheless already a great deal we can draw upon from related areas and we mention some of it below – but before we rush to new tools, it's also useful to stop and recall that a good deal we have already talked about is relevant.

In this section we consider:

- Big Five team coaching;
- getting the issues out;
- Kline's Time to Think approach;
- Appreciative Inquiry;
- Katzenbach on teams;
- collective thinking errors.

Big Five team coaching

Big Five coaching is squarely at the heart of team coaching too. Reading Big Five across to the team context, some points to trigger your thinking might include:

- *Contracting.* Working with an individual, you need to contract in advance with those concerned on the business aspects of working together, and with the individual on the psychological contract. This is the case whether you will be working together for six months, or a couple of minutes (for brief 'coffee machine' coaching, the key contracting question is often, 'How long have you got?'), and it's exactly the same with a team. On the psychological contracting, the obvious point to agree with the group is precisely how confidentiality will be handled. The Chatham House Rule (www.chathamhouse.org.uk) is one excellent guideline; an American client uses the more colourful but equally determined, 'what plays in Vegas, stays in Vegas!'.

    In addition, whenever a group of people comes together, Myles Downey's useful rubric is that whatever else is on the table, they want to know 'who are we and what are we here for'.* A few minutes spent on this at the outset, however well the individuals may already know each other, pays dividends. If, for example they know each other well, it is still worth making quick introductions around the table, with a specific focus such as what they bring to the subject, or want from the discussion, followed by someone (the Chair; the coach) firmly stating the business purpose.

---

* Personal communication; his chapter on team coaching in *Effective Coaching* is a very good entry point into the subject: Downey, M. (1999) *Effective Coaching* London: Orion, pp. 100–119. The 'team topics' tool (see p. 134) is adapted from Myles!

■ *GROW*. Getting a goal is exponentially more difficult with a team, but for that very reason, incredibly valuable. Only a coach, with their ability to be comfortable with silence, or confusion, is likely to have the skill to 'hang out' for as long as it takes for a disparate group of people to come to true agreement on a common Goal. I once coached a senior management team at a one-day offsite. The task was to come up by the end of the day with an urgent new marketing strategy to meet a sudden change in the market. After initial contracting on confidentiality, their roles with regard to this issue, and what the overall business task was, I explained the GROW model to them and they agreed to use it. It then took well over two hours of very productive and robust discussion for them to agree the G, after which the R, O and W were tackled in sub-groups and plenary, with flipcharts and walks outside and discussion. The R, O and W took longer, as they worked through the detail of analysis and implementation, but the G was the hardest work of the day, and the breakthrough.

■ *Listening and questioning.* Working with a team, the acuity of both listening and questioning needs to be turned up higher; one of the very best ways I know to do this, is Nancy Kline's Time to Think approach, discussed on page 135.

■ *Non-directive.* It's the same rule as with individuals: the coach manages the process and the clients the content; but as you would guess, when there are more people the visible management and signalling of the process needs to be clearer, more overt, and often more robust.

Getting the issues out

There is a simple pen-and-paper approach which very quickly brings out the issues that are 'top of mind' when a group of people come together. It has great value at the start of life as a team, but can also be used for troubleshooting. The detailed instructions are in the box on the next page.

This is a very fast way of getting out the core issues in a team – or at least, the first crop which they are prepared to discuss! Effectively it generates for you a series of topics on which you can then coach the team.

It has two variants: the less confrontational one is to get them to share their ratings of the current team anonymously (e.g. post their scores on the flip chart, but without initials). If you want to raise the stakes, they can be asked to initial their ratings – this is a high-risk strategy, best undertaken with a team you know well, and where trust between you and them, and between them, is already high.

Team topics exercise

1   Ask team members to cast their mind back and think of the best team experience they have ever had, in a *really* high-performing team (sadly, some people may have no such work experiences, in which case non-work is fine).

2   Ask them to reflect and write down, individually and without consultation, the three qualities that made it such a great experience/team (usually people write honesty, fun, mutual respect, shared responsibility. etc.).

3   On a flip chart, collect and list *all* the characteristics everyone has written, then eliminate duplicates and collapse similar words into a single one if necessary: you want to get to about 8–10 characteristics. (If you still have too many, ask everyone to vote for their top eight or ten.)

4   Then ask individuals to reflect and rate the performance of their *current* team against each characteristic on this list on a scale of 0–10 (with 10 as excellent).

5   Create a table (another flip chart?) with the characteristics listed in the first column, then enough columns alongside for each team member to enter their complete set of scores beside each characteristic.

6   Ask each team to come up and post their individual ratings.

7   Sum the rows and the columns.

8   You now have rich material to coach from – columns showing how some people feel very differently from others, highs and lows in rows showing which characteristics are strengths and weaknesses, etc.

9   From here on it's coaching – what does the team want to work on, etc.

A simpler version using the Post-it notes so beloved of people working with teams, is also very effective in getting out, for example, what are the most pressing tasks to be tackled next in the business. In this version, you simply issue everyone with some Post-its, and ask them to think for a moment, then write on three separate Notes what they think are the three most important and urgent issues needing to be addressed (for example, it could be products to be developed, priority markets, SWOT (Strengths, Weaknesses, Opportunities, Threats), etc.). When they have finished writing their Post-its, ask them to place them on flip charts. Then everyone mills around, moving the individual postings as needed so all the similar ones are grouped together. (Which also nicely breaks the ice, if there is any, and gets the noise and energy levels up in the room.) Finally, when everyone is satisfied the right Post-its are clustered together, ask the group to label each cluster. *Voilà*, the issues.

This is non-directive team coaching, or a beginning to it at least: the coach has run a simple process, but the issues are coming out from the group, and they are also naming and labelling them. Thereafter, you could do worse than just following GROW.

Psychometric team profiling

We have already discussed these in Chapter 6; training courses for each instrument, particularly MBTI and FIRO-B, devote considerable time and effort to equipping attendees with tools, exercises, tips and extensive background materials for using the psychometrics in team settings. It's what they want you to do: sell more tests! But it does mean there is a wealth of predeveloped resource available.

Kline's 'Thinking Environment'

Over the last 30 years Nancy Kline has developed the 'Thinking Environment' approach, designed to ensure groups of people break their usual patterns (BlackBerries, interruptions, inattention, domination by a few) and *listen* to each other so well that *thinking* is greatly enhanced. I have mentioned it earlier, as it is invaluable in individual coaching, but I personally think its true power is only fully unleashed in groups.

Nancy describes applying this process to 'meetings', in Chapter 15 of her first book and Chapter 48 of her second,[3] but I think any meeting run as she describes must transcend normal time-wasting and tedium to become not just a meeting but a highly productive coaching space. I know of several organisations where members are trained in the Time to Think approach, and use it not just with clients in team coaching but as part of their own normal business process, to great effect. There are ten behaviours in the process, summarised in the box overleaf: they might sound impossible, listed baldly like that, but it does work, as is compellingly described in the books.

Katzenbach on teams

Jon Katzenbach's work on forging teams is based on organisational behaviour research and vast experience with forging business teams in his 35 years at McKinsey & Company, and latterly Booz & Company in New York. Though not officially written for the business coaching context, it offers us much of great value. For a start, his excellent definition of a true team:

> '**A team is a small number of people with complementary skills who are committed to a common purpose, performance goals, and approach for which they hold themselves mutually accountable**'. (p. 45)[4]

Every section of that definition repays close scrutiny.

Ten components of a Thinking Environment

1 **Attention**: listening with respect, interest and fascination.

2 **Incisive questions**: removing untrue assumptions that limit ideas.

3 **Equality**: regarding each other as thinking peers
   – giving equal turns and attention
   – keeping agreements and boundaries.

4 **Appreciation**: practising a five-to-one ratio of appreciation to criticism.

5 **Ease**: offering freedom from rush or urgency.

6 **Encouragement**: going to the unexplored edge of thinking by moving beyond competition.

7 **Feelings**: allowing sufficient emotional release to restore thinking.

8 **Information**: providing a full and accurate picture of reality; dismantling denial.

9 **Place**: creating a physical environment that says to people, 'you matter'.

10 **Diversity**; encouraging divergent thinking; ensuring diverse group identities.

Source: Kline, N. (1999) *Time to Think: Listening to Ignite the Human Mind*, London: Ward Lock/Cassell, p. 35. and *More Time To Think: A way of Being in the World*, Pool-in-Wharfedale: Fisher King, pp. 33–95. Reproduced with permission.

Katzenbach has a great deal else to offer coaches working with teams: their ideal size, what they must go through on the journey from disparate group to high-performing team, and much else, but for me there is one absolutely crucial lesson in it above all others: *team forms around task*. In other words, a team forms where there is a genuine need for one, and not before. Teambuilding exercises for the pointless sake of it are likely to cease anyway in a tough economic climate, but anyone still contemplating such things should recall his salutary words. If by contrast there *is* a real business need for a team to form, then his Chapter 3, distilling his wise advice into practical guidelines for people forming or coaching teams, is indispensable.

Appreciative Inquiry

Founded in 1987 by Cooperrider and Srivastva, Appreciative Inquiry (AI) seeks to create positive change in organisations. Like Katzenbach's work, it was not designed for team coaching, but it has much to say to it. (It is also not formally a part of the Positive Psychology movement, though it is very congruent with it.) AI consultancy in organisations seeks not to find out what's wrong in order to fix it but to assist the organisational members to find out what's right and build from there.

It might hence be viewed as the strengths approach at organisational level. There is a great deal more to it than that (see for example The Appreciative Inquiry Commons at www.appreciativeinquiry.case.edu), but it is mentioned here, not just to pique your interest, but also as another salutary reminder that, as with individuals, when coaching a team it is very easy to be drawn down into everything that's *wrong* with the team, the individual members, their interpersonal relations, the organisation, the world. But equally we know from authoritative research that there is equal power in attending to what is *right* and building therefrom.

Tackling collective thinking errors

One of the reasons coaching is so powerful is it improves the quality of individuals' thinking; even the simple discipline of GROW serves to combat habitual thinking errors. (Looking at it in MBTI terms, for example, one might say that R and O cause Js, who are typically at risk of rushing to judgement, to stop and consider the facts and alternative options, while G and W causes Ps, who are typically at risk of keeping things open too long, to set a clear objective and come to completion, and so on.)

If in the 20th century economics had the upper hand in business and political thinking, I believe the 21st will be the century of psychology. It got off to a flying start: the first psychologist to win the Nobel prize was Professor Daniel Kahneman in 2002. (Strictly, he was the first person with a PhD in psychology to win; others with connections with psychology but whose original training was in zoology, etc., had won in the past, but Kahneman was the first 'clear' psychologist.) There isn't a prize for Psychology, so he won it for Economics, for his work on economic decision-making. It was a brave decision by the Nobel committee, as Kahneman's work flies in the face of the consensus which has gripped economics throughout the post-war period – namely that man is a rational decision-maker. Kahneman demonstrated categorically that he is not. (And she isn't either.) He went further: not only do ordinary mortals mix large doses of the non-rational into their decision-making but, crucially for business coaches and boards, the world's leading professional decision-makers are fallible, too. (We knew it; he proved it.)

Kahneman and his colleague Amos Tversky explicitly tested the decision-making powers of groups of expert decision-makers in many fields, including over 40 of the world's leading analysts of a particular type of cancer tissue slides, another group of the world's leading trial court judges, and many others.[5] They found that while each individual believed they rated many complex factors simultaneously, in fact they are no more exempt from basic biology than the rest of us: as Chapter 11 will note, we can process only 'seven plus or minus two' bits of information at once in the 'working memory' part of the brain. The experts (we do the same) cope with this by developing heuristics, or habitual patterns of thinking or shortcuts, enabling them to process the enormous amounts of information needed to get through each day. Their heuristics may be world-class in their expert focus, but they're still shortcuts, and they lead to a percentage of thinking error.

Kahneman's Nobel prize was an early straw blowing in a new wind for economics. With the advent of 'behavioural economics', the 'dismal science'[6] is belatedly catching up with what psychologists had categorically demonstrated for decades: the fact that we are social animals. Even the most introverted and/or strong-minded of us can, as Milgram so graphically showed, be swayed in our decision-making processes by factors in our context – and to a far greater extent than we would have believed possible. Kahneman showed that for a variety of reasons to do with both brain and context, even the individuals who are most highly valued by society for their thinking powers, make errors too.

You would expect therefore that when individuals, even talented ones, then come together in groups, they would bring, as well as their gifts, all their individual capacity for decision flaws, and indeed they do. But research has fascinatingly discovered that when people form groups or teams, the capacity for error is *more* than the sum of its parts: whole new types of error appear!

We began this chapter talking about Milgram and one of the great classic experiments in 20th-century psychology. Let us end it by considering equally disturbing research with regard to the decision-making capability of *groups* – and how business coaching might mitigate some of that risk.

Psychologists have pinned down many of the quirks of non-rationality once multiple people are involved. They've shown the old view of 'safety in numbers' isn't necessarily right. Groups can and often do come up with better solutions than the individuals would have alone – we don't have to abandon trial by jury yet! But phenomena such as 'risky shift', 'group polarisation'* and 'groupthink' have been identified which beyond all

---

* risky shift and group polarisation: groups which are particularly prone to it, can when together make worse (because more extreme or ill-balanced) decisions than each individual would make alone. See Myers, op. cit., p. 680.

doubt exist and represent serious risks to accurate and reliable decision-making.[7] We consider here just one of these: groupthink.

Research identifying groupthink arose directly out of one of the most dangerous periods in recent world history – when the US's Kennedy administration got to the brink of nuclear warfare with the Soviet Union. Aghast that such a gifted 'Camelot' administration, including the most brilliant minds of its generation, could go so horribly wrong in its decision-making, the US Government poured money into research to understand why, and how it could be prevented in future (see below). The first famous study was by Irving Janis, and he and others have since examined other examples of this dangerous phenomenon including the Chernobyl nuclear accident, the explosion of the US space shuttle *Challenger* and the Iraq WMD (so-called Weapons of Mass Destruction) crisis. Already by 2004 the bipartisan US Senate Intelligence Committee was saying WMD

> '... demonstrated several aspects of groupthink: examining few alternatives, selective gathering of information, pressure to conform within the group or withhold criticism, and collective rationalization [which led analysts to]... interpret ambiguous evidence as conclusively indicative of a WMD program as well as ignore or minimize evidence that Iraq did not have [WMD] programs.'[8]

In the Cuban crisis disaster was averted; in Iraq it was not. Groupthink matters.

One of the preconditions of groupthink is an over-cohesive group. The essence of prevention is to break the carapace that then forms by setting up systems to ensure channels of information from the outside, including disconfirming evidence, continue to flow. Military strategists know this, and when major decisions are being made often deliberately task a senior and respected officer from a different area with the specific role of 'Devil's Advocate'.

In civilian life, I believe that a sufficiently strong business coach, either a director additionally trained to coach, or a trusted outsider, supported by a clear and unequivocal anti-groupthink brief, could perform this task in corporate boardrooms.

We have many clear guidelines to help prevent groupthink, and I am struck by how good coaching goes straight to the heart of many of them. Some of the key recommendations from across the research spectrum are summarised in the box.

Keys to averting Groupthink

1 State the problem clearly, indicating its significance.

2 Break a complex problem into separate parts, and make decisions on each part.

3 Encourage each member of the group to evaluate their own and others' ideas openly and critically.

4 Be suspicious of unanimity, especially arrived at quickly.

5 Ask influential members to adopt an external or critical/'Devil's Advocate' stance, or leave the group for periods.

6 Discuss plans with objective outsiders to get reactions.

7 Use expert advisers to design the decision-making process.

8 Avoid wide differences in status among members, or if present, adopt means to minimise them.

9 Develop agreed procedures in advance to deal with crisis or emergency situations

10 Consider external reactions to the decision, and explore several possible alternative scenarios for these.

11 Use sub-groups (committees) to develop alternative solutions.

12 Admit shortcomings (when groupthink occurs, members feel very confident; admitting some flaws in argument might open them to new ideas).

13 Ensure those entrusted with implementation understand exactly what they are to do.

14 Encourage the group to evaluate the skills within it, and find ways of improving them.

15 Have a last-chance meeting, allowing people to voice any concerns before implementation.

Adapted from: Janis, 1972; Baron and Greenberg 1990 and 1996; Zander 1982, as quoted in Furnham, A. (1998) *The Psychology of Behaviour in Organisations*, London: Psychology Press, pp. 500–503.

We're moving into advanced coaching here, drawing on the crucial insights from social psychology, which have been hitherto largely untapped by business leaders and coaches. This leads us nicely into other exciting new domains of the business coaching of the future. In the next two chapters, we consider two more emerging specialist areas. First, in the next chapter, is career coaching for the new world.

9

Advanced coaching: coaching and career transitions

Charles Glass* and Anne Scoular

Freud said only two things really matter – love and work.

When he wrote that, about 100 years ago, average life expectancy was around 50,[1] meaning a working life of perhaps 35 years. Now, with average life expectancy approaching 90, we might be at work for six decades.

It will seem even longer for those who are miserable. Or just unfulfilled, or bored. But by contrast there really are people who love their work, who would do it even if they weren't paid, who are lit up with pleasure when talking about it. These are the people studied by Herminia Ibarra and described in her book *Working Identity*[2]. Many people in the unfulfilled camp would love to get into that tiny high-satisfaction, high-achieving minority. The new field of career coaching, still in its infancy, is the most powerful tool to deliver that change.

This chapter is in two sections:

1 In *'The changing context'* Anne describes the forces ripping old-fashioned careers apart. And outlines a new type of career coaching, combining traditional careers advice but adding in the turbo-charge of Big Five coaching.

2 In *'Career coaching tools'* Charles shares tips and techniques for the three main types of career coaching:

---

* Charles Glass is a Founding Director of the Professional Career Partnership (PCP), a firm of business and career coaches working across Europe who are widely regarded as authoritative on the subject of career change.

(a) career management

(b) career transition

(c) 'third phase' careers.

1. The changing context

An ancestor of mine (i.e. Anne's) was, in successive Victorian censuses, an apprentice silver polisher, Secretary to Singing School, hotel proprietor and Of No Occupation. In between he briefly managed Charles Dickens' North American tour – before Dickens fired him for incompetence. So having to pick yourself up and start again and/or reinvent yourself every decade isn't new – it's just feels rough when it happens to *us*.

But even taking the long view of history, I still think it is true that our own times are making more career demands than ever before. New things we have to navigate include:

- working in cross-border teams, with deep cultural differences but no time to explain them;
- 'matrix' management: the boss is in Hong Kong, the team across five time zones, and you meet in person just once a quarter – but have to deliver;
- rapid production shifts to ever-cheaper sites around the world;
- savage media scrutiny 24/7;
- transnational complexity from EU accession, globalisation, etc.;
- the recession: budget cuts, renewed union militancy, popular protest …;
- introverted technocrats make it to senior management – but find in our media-savvy world, 'everything that got me here isn't going to get me there';
- a career in the public sector is no longer 'safe', with identical pressures as above but much lower individual remuneration to buffer the impact;
- plus local and sectoral issues:
  - in the UK, the legal sector faces its own Big Bang as the Clementi reforms bring to an end lawyers' '80-year bull run';[3]
  - and re-regulation is about to hit the banks worldwide.

It's a wild ride, and even the most capable person sometimes needs help to navigate the rapids.

Of course, there are many new positives to balance the new challenges: really good videoconferencing, flexible working, absurdly high financial reward for a few, etc. But some of the things that keep people going aren't healthy: alcohol, excess of testosterone, cocaine. I once asked in wonderment, when hearing of working round the clock, how *do* people do it? My interlocutor gave me a sharp look, and I realised.

And there's another thing. We're living longer – *much* longer.

The new longevity

Some neuroscientists think the person who will live 1,000 years has already been born.[4]

Professor Tom Kirkwood, who delivered the authoritative BBC Reith Lecture 2001, *The End of Age*, (www.bbc.co.uk/radio4/reith2001/lecture1. shtml) isn't one of them, but he did point out that, contrary to popular belief, ageing is not inevitable: the human body is *not* programmed to die (yes, you read that right); and as a result we are entering nothing less than an entirely new period of human history. This was graphically illustrated in the Meyler Campbell Annual Lecture 2009* by Cambridge neuroscientist Professor Felicia Huppert – see Figure 9.1.

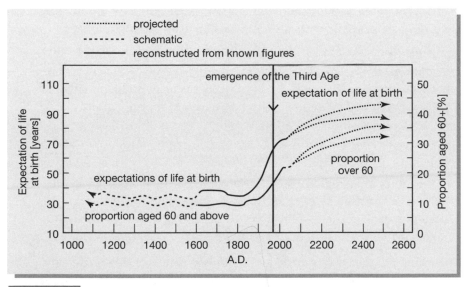

Figure 9.1 The secular shift in ageing in England, 1000–2500 AD

Reproduced with permission from Laslett, P. (1997) 'Interpreting the Demographic Changes', in *Philosophical Transactions of the Royal Society B*, London: The Royal Society, pp. 1805–1809

---

* For summary see Annual Lecture section on www.meylercampbell.com; for more on Professor Felicia Huppert's extraordinary work see www.cambridgewellbeing.org.

In other words for most of human history our ancestors lived to around 35. But Jeanne Calment died in France aged 122, HM Queen Elizabeth the Queen Mother aged 101, and several of my friends' parents are healthy and active in their 90s. They are no longer exceptional: the UK Office for National Statistics shows UK female average life expectancy at age 65 is now 86.6[5] – and 'average' life expectancy of course means that half live *longer*!

The funding gap

So we're living longer than ever before in human history: good.

But we can't afford it: not good. There is a vast gulf currently opening up between what it will cost us to pay for those many more years, and what we have saved. This 'funding gap' is caused by many things, including pensions being mauled by politicians, and battered by economic crises and human malfeasance, but also by social change. Current drivers of the funding gap, and its career consequences, include the following:

- Experts say the 2008 market crash alone means we need to work six years longer to recoup pension fund losses.[6]
- Even before the various crashes, 9 million people in the UK already had inadequate pension provision – approaching half the workforce.[7]
- Defined benefit (DB) pensions are vanishing, switching the risk from employers to individuals.
- Serial marriage and/or later childbearing means many will have children still at home, and education to fund, in their 60s, while longevity means some are at the same time caring for still-living very elderly parents.
- Two-career families can increase earning power, but also increases the intensity of time pressures and juggling.
- Generation Y has the 'triple whammy' of the baby boomer generation ahead of them over-consuming assets and leaving behind systemic debt; carrying (student) debt from the beginning of their working life; yet demanding greater work–life balance.

There are only four ways to tackle the funding gap: save more, consume less, work longer, die sooner. Given that choice, the zeitgeist is going for 'work longer'.*

So pulling all this together:

- work can be a pretty challenging place;

---

* Though the planet would doubtless prefer we tackled it by consuming less.

■ but tempting though it may be to run away, we'll actually need to do it *more* rather than less;

■ (haaalp!).

There is a powerful 'pull' factor from the market: a need for help to navigate the tricky stages in working life and over a longer haul. This strong 'pull' factor of swelling unmet demand from the market is matched by a 'push' factor from business coaches: large numbers of trained people looking for coaching work which genuinely makes a difference. Should be a great match.

But it's not happening – yet. Career coaching is at a much earlier stage than mainstream business coaching: demand is there, supply is appearing, but it hasn't yet taken off: the business and commercial case hasn't been made. We return to this briefly at the end of the chapter, but first, let's dig deeper into career coaching itself.

The new career coaching

Right now, the market doesn't have 'career coaching' in mind as a possible solution; the concept remains to be sold. What they do have is the nasty taste it left last time they tried it. 'I was given some tests at 13 and told I should be a hairdresser,' said one investment banker, still resentful 30 years later. A minority of adults have experienced 'outplacement', where they receive some career assistance as part of a redundancy package, but the majority go it alone. In early 2010 the UK government's *own* report into its official careers advice service recommended, astonishingly, that it be shut down in its entirety because the Inquiry 'barely heard a good word to say for it'.[8]

But the need is there, and will become increasingly urgent. The solution is simple: pull out the useful bits from traditional career advice, add the power of Big Five coaching, and stir. Charles Glass, who generously shares his experience in the next part of this chapter, believes the optimal mix, the powerful blend that makes up the 'new career coaching', is 80% Big Five coaching and 20% careers advice.* This inverts the traditional model,

---

* The ratio shifts over time. Early in people's careers, it may be higher on telling: I could certainly have used a bit more useful advice at the outset about how invisible office politics worked, for example. But business coaches and leaders typically meet with people who are beyond those first few years and hence are at the stage where the optimal 80/20 kicks in.

which didn't work well because the adviser typically spent most of their time telling. However after 20 years helping thousands of businesspeople across Europe with successful career transitions, Charles is also convinced that switching to pure Big Five coaching would also be a mistake, as there are some things people *do* benefit from knowing: how best to work with head-hunters and prepare for interviews, for example. The key to success is to maintain the 80/20 ratio, mostly coaching but keeping a judicious eye out for the other things Charles outlines below.

In the next part of this chapter, Charles assumes you already know about the 80%, i.e. Big Five coaching (see Chapter 5), and concentrates on the *remaining 20%:* the additional skill and content knowledge specific to great career coaching.

2. Career coaching tools

(This is Charles writing) We presume you, or the coach you're bringing in, can 'Big Five' coach, and well. And as always in coaching you need to be yourself: executives don't want a cipher, they want to spark and engage with a real human. As we have said, that's 80% of career coaching, but you also need a little more. The remaining 20% is information people need about how the world of work operates, from large-scale structures right down to the impact of something as seemingly irrelevant as the seasons of the year.

First, let's clear up a distinction between two separate terms. They're often bandied about interchangeably, but there is an important difference. *Career management* is where you have a choice; in *career transitions*, you don't.

In the first case, clients are asking, 'what do I want to do when I grow up', or musing whether they should go off and do something completely different. They're wondering, but there's no driver for immediate change. In the second, they've been fired. Or made redundant, or their partner's job is being moved to another country – whatever the reason, there's no longer any musing, change is forced upon them.

In this section we consider both in turn, then later in the chapter discuss coaching for the new 'third stage' career. All three aspects of career coaching are integrated in Figure 9.2 on page 155.

a) Career management

In career management, there's no rush. The client wants to think about their career, but they're currently employed; there is no 'burning platform' to make them jump – but they're restless enough to go and talk to a careers coach.

They come with different angles on the question. Some say, 'I never really decided to be [in finance, law, etc.], I just got into it and here I am 20 years later...' There is a niggle at the back of their mind that they never *really* made a choice – is now the time to take 'control'? Others are successful, maybe in their mid-40s or 50s, and want another big job – but in a completely fresh sector, and don't know how to switch across. Still others hanker after finding out once and for all 'what I want to do when I grow up'.

Particularly with the last group, the first piece of the 20% can be to disabuse clients of some common misconceptions. Some think the ideal career for them is out there, waiting, and their task is to find it. We can tell them that they're not looking for the one, the ideal, career – there are many ways to skin the careers cat. You might even have two jobs on the go at once, or sequentially, each fulfilling different aspects of your financial and other needs. Similarly, a lot of people think *they* haven't worked out what they should do, but everyone else has – but actually only about 20% of people do have this clarity of direction, and it can change even for them. Another common misconception is that the coach has the answer; as in general coaching, we don't, they do. So in a sense we're again here starting with *contracting* – in this case gently challenging where necessary, and opening up the possibilities of what the task and process might be.

The next is *goalsetting*: what does this particular person want to achieve from the career management conversation? And so on, applying the GROW model, listening, questioning, and working non-directively.

Beyond that, there are eight specific elements to good career management coaching. They are:

- tools for information gathering;
- career frameworks and paths;
- brainstorming;
- resolving dilemmas;
- experience and wisdom;
- environments;

- learning styles;
- conversations with a purpose.

We consider each in turn below. This doesn't mean this is a neatly sequenced process, it often isn't. But if at some point in the coaching you bring in these eight elements, you will be helping your client build a surer footing for their career explorations.

Tools

First, the diagnostic phase, where we help the client identify their motivations, strengths, values and interests.

The aim here is not to get to an absolute truth, but to something clients can use as a basis for their thinking on their career. My own starting point is a question framework developed by our organisation, PCP (The Professional Career Partnership – www.thepcp.com), and we'll often spend the entire first two sessions working through it. It covers not just the obvious material such as their achievements, but also, importantly, what they have *enjoyed* – even if one has to go back to childhood to find examples. (Many people have sadly got into a deeply ingrained habit of not enjoying work and finding their pleasures outside it – or just working harder.) The objective here is to dig out the 6–7 things that are most important to them.

You might wonder why we don't begin with general strengths instruments such as the VIA, or personality psychometrics. While these are often useful in general business coaching, what we are looking for here is the utterly unique way the genetic/personality/ability hand you were dealt, has come together over your life to date. For example, Extravert A's drama teacher in the sixth form made a big impact and they have developed terrific public speaking ability, whereas Extravert B had a critical parent who was a research scientist, so they have a deeply ingrained habit of getting their facts right before they speak. In other words, there has been a constant interplay between person and their context, and the career coach needs to understand the key things that have fused in that crucible.

Career coaches who do want to use psychometrics, find a surprising dearth of them. Schein's Career Anchors, developed by the famous MIT Professor Edgar Schein has an impeccable provenance (see http://mitsloan.mit/edu/faculty). His Career Anchor concept is the very last thing you would give up in your work: if you had to let everything else go, what is the last thing you would cling determinedly on to? For some it is autonomy, for others, pure challenge, or security, or lifestyle (what we would today call work–life balance.) Unlike most quality psychometrics, the questionnaire and scoring are freely available to all and at minimal cost: no training course and/or accreditation is required. Plus the original group studied were high-achieving Yale graduates, so appropriate for our business audience, and the research was, most unusually, longitudinal – i.e. it studied them over the 40-year course of their working lives. But that original research was almost 40 years ago, the cohort was all male, and working patterns have since changed beyond recognition. (Women, for example!) Nevertheless, it can play a modest part in the initial fact-gathering – though in fact it is often more useful in the later stage of resolving dilemmas (see below.) An alternative that gives more specific career guidance input is the Strong interest inventory (see www.opp.eu.com), which is particularly useful for people considering early career change.

Personality psychometrics are, perhaps surprisingly, of less assistance; good businesspeople are usually already well equipped with insight into themselves and others from 360° and structured feedback over the years, and are familiar with MBTI or one or more of the trait instruments such as 16PF, NEO and FIRO. (If not, plugging that gap can of course be an early 'win' in the career coaching process.)

One other instrument that is worth considering is SIMA, a structured personal narrative process which helps identify an individual's motivated abilities and which can feed into career choice. The process is thorough, with an established methodology, and like the personality instruments above, training and accreditation is required to use it (see www.sima.co.uk).

Career frameworks and paths

Career coaches need to know how particular careers work. You don't need to be an expert – indeed part of the art of career coaching lies in knowing a little about a lot! – but some quick advice can save clients from losing valuable time in their job exploration. Professional careers such as medicine need qualifications gained at the outset, and it is difficult – though not absolutely impossible – to enter them later in life. Other qualifications, in personnel and marketing for example, can be picked up while you're working, which is important for those who can't afford years off to retrain. People often get stuck in career changes because they are simply lacking information – they just don't know what other career possibilities are out there.

So different occupations have different entry mechanisms and structures. So, too, do the individual experiences of work which we call a 'career'.

For example, people now on average have three careers. Knowing this is handy: it removes some of the heavy weight of the present decision and alerts people to the need for flexibility; skills might end up being applied in a completely different context. This is a clarion call particularly for lawyers, who almost uniquely these days, have often been in the same sector their whole working life.

A recent development is the *portfolio career*, where instead of working in a job with a single employer, one puts together a variety of ways of earning a living – a 'portfolio' of work. (Business coaches themselves are a good example of this: they often have a contract for one or two days per week with a previous employer; see business coaching clients; and also do consultancy on their specialist field, perhaps strategy, finance or talent management.)

If people are considering portfolio working as an option, coaches can make two useful contributions: to get them to consider whether they are psychologically *suited* to working this way, and to encourage them to think about building a sustainable *mix* into the portfolio.

On whether they are suited, psychometrics such as the MBTI can help (as can Tristart, also mentioned in Chapter 7, though it includes both personality assessment and evaluation of the business plan – no bad thing to have to think of the latter as well though!), or you can ask them questions such as:

■ How much can you cope with uncertainty, not just of income, but of corporate buying processes taking a long time, requiring sudden changes, etc.?

■ Do you need people around you, or can you cope on your own?

■ Do you prefer structure and order, or can you thrive on the challenge of having to figure it out for yourself?

These questions may not come as a surprise to people, but the other aspect, of getting the mix of portfolio activities right, is often more unexpected. The point is that different types of potential portfolio work have broadly three different *paces*. There is:

■ *short notice, intensive, and well paid* – for example, consultancy projects, or designing and implementing a training course;

■ *steady* – for example, bookkeeping for a healthy business – they will need you to work for x days per month, every month, indefinitely;

■ *work you can pick up and put down* – for example, writing a specialist book or web material.

Ideally, clients need a mix of all three for a reasonable balance of life and consistent income. The intensive high-paid work is lucrative, but while projects are on, they're all-consuming. Steady work pays less, but enables the client to sleep at night knowing at least the mortgage is covered each month, and work you can pick up and put down is invaluable for making proper use of the time between the intensive high-paid bursts. (Note from Anne: one great example of this was a shop I knew by a railway footbridge in Primrose Hill, London. It had a high passing footfall, in a good area. It sold antiques in the large industrial space at the back, and flowers at the front. The florist part of the business was low margin but regular, the antiques sales were more unpredictable, but when a high-value, high-margin piece sold, it added the jam. The antiques on their own couldn't have been relied upon to cover the monthly outgoings, and the flowers on their own didn't have the margin to cope with the area's high rents, but together, it worked perfectly – until they closed the railway bridge...)

Brainstorming

Career coaches need to have a way of brainstorming with clients. It's very rare that people end up doing something without there being a clue to it in the past – but for some, reconnecting with that something can be hard work.

Different coaches find different ways to do this: the key is to find a way to help people remove limitations in their thinking. For example, in their current job, lawyers focus intently on words, so we might ask them to work instead with the visual part of their brain by drawing. Another tip is to spend significant time discussing hobbies and interests at the school and university stage: this is often helpful in bringing forgotten themes to the surface.

Resolving dilemmas

If the issue was simple, the client wouldn't have needed to come to you. So there is almost always a dilemma at the heart of career coaching. Typically in financial centres it's being unhappy in an existing job, but knowing the more fulfilling roles elsewhere pay less. Or wanting to go right to the top, but knowing it could mean violating core values. Or having young children who need their parents, but at precisely the stage when career demands are also greatest.

Clients find myriad different solutions, each right for their unique needs and circumstances, but after many years of watching I have seen some patterns emerge. One can for example solve a dilemma sequentially over time

– I do this now, and that then; or by slicing a week: four days in the current job, one day studying for the new one. (And as we noted above, the Schein Career Anchors tool can help here by pointing towards what might matter most to each individual.)

Experience and wisdom

To be a good career coach I firmly believe you need to have *lived* quite a bit, and to have reflected upon that experience. Though you are not being directive ('if I were you I would...' is as unhelpful here as in all other domains of coaching!) you do need to have things that come to mind to offer as 'paper tigers' to clients, or to challenge or stimulate their thinking. Having a wider context of life and work is helpful in negotiating the cul-de-sacs, limitations and preconceptions that clients have often fallen into.

Environments

Sometimes the solution is actually simpler than people think: they may be in the right *career*, but in the wrong sector of it – so the wrong *environment*. You could be a lawyer in the financial district of the City of London, or in the Civil Service in Whitehall. The latter is only a few miles down the river Thames, and the job has the same title, but the atmosphere is quite different. Having worked with hundreds of lawyers across the two locations, Anne has found distinct personality differences: only 5–10% of City lawyers report an MBTI 'F' preference, but about 40% of Civil Service lawyers – those working in public policy on justice, home affairs, etc. – do; the different environment has attracted different types of people. Working 'in-house' as a lawyer in a large public company is a different environment again. Of course people are vaguely aware that there must be some differences, but most don't understand in any detail the specific qualities of the other possible environments. They can find it an eye-opener to go and investigate properly. I (Charles) have found about 30% of the time, switching to a different environment within the same career is all it takes for them to be much happier.

Learning styles

There are stages to career change, and different learning styles incline people to prefer different stages. The best career change involves sitting in a room and talking about it; then going out and hunting, then coming back and digesting the information, then out again. It is sadly the case that extraverts *do* fall into jobs more, as they're naturally inclined to get out where the jobs are; introverts might need to be encouraged to move from reflection to action.

Writers in the field concentrate on particular stages, too. The best-selling Richard Bolles' *What Colour Is Your Parachute?*[9] focuses on analysis. Herminia Ibarra's *Working Identity* by contrast encourages exploration.[10] In reality, every career process needs both. Coaches need to keep an eye on whether clients are skimping on less preferred but critical parts of the process.

'Conversations with a purpose'

This is networking, but I prefer the term 'conversations with a purpose' as that's what they are. Most people know this is important, but they feel embarrassed about it and also do it badly, i.e. without clear planning as to its purpose. Yet the more senior the career being managed, the more crucial this core skill is. A light touch on the rudder is often all that's needed: when people see this as a business task rather than asking someone for a job, they apply to it the standard methods they already know from their business life: clarifying their business proposition, listing targets, developing question lists, sequencing the action plan, etc. Once they understand that other people enjoy being asked for advice and that it is a mark of respect, they normally find the process surprisingly effective and even enjoyable. In some sectors, social media networking is also becoming an important tool; John Reed's book is excellent on this.[11]

b) Career transitions

In career transitions, everything we've said about career management remains true, but in addition there is a sense of *urgency*. They've been made redundant, their company has gone under – whatever has happened, their situation has changed abruptly. Even if they saw it coming, now it's different: it has actually happened.

That abruptness, that urgency, mean the coaching carries an additional load it didn't have in career management. The client may have taken a knock to their confidence and need to rebuild it. If it has been a 'clean' redundancy, with perhaps an entire division closed down, so nothing personal, then this may not be so, but if the job has gone wrong, and over a long time as they usually do, then the client's confidence may well have been eroded (in which case see Chapter 6 for Carol Kauffman's indispensable '4 steps to confidence' technique). Career transition work also tends to be more about the whole life agenda. They're in a jam, you are offered to them – if they really decide to work with you, clients often then take a 'boots and all' approach and open up about their whole life situation, in ways ordinary executive coaching and even career management coaching clients don't.

Yet paradoxically, it's actually easier to work with clients in career transition – they *have* to do something. In my experience, less than 40% of career management clients who are currently successful, do actually move. Career transition clients don't have the luxury of that decision – they've already moved, even if it wasn't their idea. This is why a clear majority of people who have been made redundant will tell you, two years later, 'It was the best thing that ever happened to me.' They were forced to take their life into their own hands. Recent examples include the corporate law partner who became a handyman to older people in his local village, a lawyer who set up her own art gallery, a trader who became a driving instructor and now trains examiners, and a junior professional who became an international development consultant – it was just what they needed, though it didn't seem so at the time.

In career transition coaching, the largest part of the work is still mainstream business coaching. Plus the additional career management tasks discussed above. But because people now don't have a job, there is another layer. The essence is to help them rebuild for themselves the structure and containment they have suddenly lost. They don't have to get up and travel to work; they're accountable to no one; a chunk of their social network has vanished; and they probably feel to some degree a failure. Hence much of the task is to help them self-manage, replacing the exoskeleton they have lost.

So, in addition to the core 80% of Big Five coaching, and the issues in career management outlined above, there are six further elements to career transition:

- structure;
- rhythms and seasons;
- managing oneself: emotions and confidence;
- practical job-hunting skills;
- momentum, energy and pacing;
- relationship management;
- benchmarking.

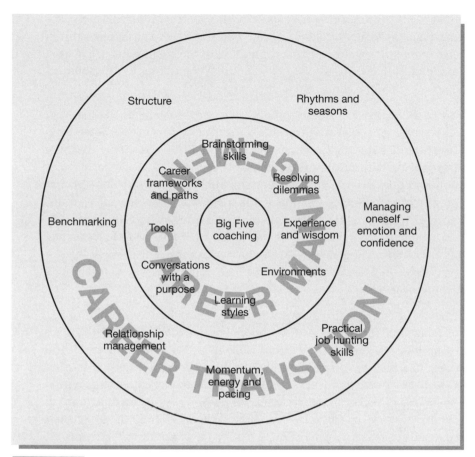

Figure 9.2   The three levels of career coaching

Structure

There actually *is* one piece of structure: the time by which they need to get a job, before the money runs out. (If there happened to be no financial pressure, then it would in effect be back to being a career management conversation – 'what do I want to do with the rest of my life?' So by definition, in career transition coaching the money is going to run out at some point. They may be able to survive for a month, or six months, or a year, but there is still hanging over the conversation the additional pressure of 'I need a job'.) The coach needs to help them add some more, and more helpful, landmarks. I tell people that no one can job-search for more than two days a week, or at most, three. That gives shape to their week straight away: 2–3 days on the main task. Next question, how are they going to fill the remaining time usefully? It may feel indulgent, but if, for example, they finally tackle the research project they've always been interested in, or write, or make that contribution to the community, then apart from anything else, it gives them something interesting to talk about in interview when the conversation strays to chat.

Part of this early task is also to help them let out some of the emotion – the very presence of that end marker can cause panic, or at least anxiety. There will also almost always be emotional baggage arising from the disengagement from the previous job. That needs to be processed, not swallowed down, or it will come back and bite. This is mostly done by that core coaching technique – just listening. For those where the emotion lingers, and risks becoming entrenched into bitterness, I find the solution is forgiveness. If, having had the chance to air their feelings, whatever they are – frustration, anger, fear – they can get to the point of forgiving the company or individual(s) involved, they are well on the way to regaining a healthy balance.

Structure also applies to managing money. If people have enough to last six months if they spend a little on themselves, or seven if they deny themselves altogether, they're more likely to get a job if they do the former. It's hard to convince people of this, particularly if they're in early high-anxiety mode, but it is true. Funnily enough, it then becomes a little benchmark of success. If they come into a session, smile ruefully and say they have signed up for the woodworking course after all, it shows their anxiety has been managed down, and they have started to take the kind of action that will sustain them through a long haul, if that's what it turns out to be. (And then, of course, it hopefully won't be.)

Rhythms and seasons

The toughest time to be given a career transition client is November to January (in the northern hemisphere; April in the southern). When we are in work, inside buildings, dashing to and fro, we notice the seasons less, but when that is taken away we suddenly become much more aware of the dark and cold of the approach of winter. And Christmas is coming up, other people are partying and buying presents, but the client is not sure how much they can afford to spend. By February it's getting lighter, and in spring career coaches see a noticeable change in their clients – the sap rises, and their energy with it. We also have ingrained from education and childhood, memories of September and January being points when we start afresh, and they too can give a fillip – but coach and client need to be aware of the winter dip, plan strategies to combat it, so far as possible, and know that it exists and it too, will pass.

Dealing with lulls in the job-hunting process is another kind of rhythm to be aware of and plan ahead for. Preparing for the summer and Christmas lulls by increasing the activity levels in the run-up to them, then actively using the lulls for other purposes, keeps people fresh and positive for when the interview activity picks up again.

Managing oneself: emotions and confidence

Coaches may wonder how they can help do this on a sustained basis – but this is where Carol Kauffman's work is an invaluable resource for us. We have already discussed building confidence in Chapter 6. For helping people to manage their emotional state positively, so as to get to and stay at peak performance despite all that is happening (or not happening), see the section on 'F', Feelings, in her Editorial on PERFECT in *Coaching: An International Journal of Research, Theory and Practice*.[12]

Practical job-hunting skills

Clients think this is what they are coming for, but in fact it's the least of the work of the career coach – mobilising the client's *own* resources is always the key. But there are skills to be taught, if the client doesn't already have them: how to use agencies, how to prepare for interviews, how to work best with headhunters. This is one of the areas where traditional career advice approaches are useful, and where the good new career coaching companies are able to brief their coaches thoroughly: many develop handouts or web materials for both employees and clients covering all this detailed information – and update them regularly.

Momentum, energy and pacing

The coach may need to help clients build and maintain their energy – career transition is tough, personal, hard work, so what energises them so they can keep going? The starting point is simply to ask: many people are well aware of what works best for them to get to and stay at their peak.

If they need something to trigger their thinking, then you already know of two very useful tools: Csikszentmihalyi's Flow, and Kauffman's 'PERFECT' models (see Chapter 6). You'll recall the crucial first four steps to get to the 'Flow' or peak performance state are:

- balance between challenge and skill;
- clear goals every step of the way;
- boundaries;
- feedback.

– are any of these missing?

Turning to Carol Kauffman's PERFECT model, the crucial point here is the first one: 'Physical'. I have already noted above that you can only do so much job hunting in a week. In the rest of the time I advise clients to go and learn something/contribute somewhere/do something creative. These are all valuable antidotes to depression. It is also *vitally* important that they put physical activity into the mix – being in shape makes a big difference. For some people, this can be one of the great 'pluses' of the enforced time off: it's finally that chance to get fit again. Or even, very fit indeed: fit enough to climb Mt Kilimanjaro, cycle from Lands End to John O'Groats, run the New York, Berlin and London marathons, or sail across the Atlantic – all of which our clients have actually done.

For the exercise-phobes such prospects might be very unappealing indeed, but I'm afraid they need to do something. It is absolutely crucial, to ward off depression and maintain their energy at the level they will need, to build in more regular exercise that they probably managed in the stressful lead-up to their transition. For the erstwhile sloths, the proper advice is of course always that they should see their doctor, or a trained exercise specialist, to plan a safe programme. Building the regular exercise sessions in can then have the added benefit of adding some of that important structure!

Relationship management

If all this talk of exercise has made you feel faint, let us move on! Another task clients need to prepare for is relationship management: it's not easy to be asked for the fourth time in a day how it's going. Just as people are taught the need for an 'elevator pitch' on sales training courses, so in career transition people need to work up a phrase for the inevitable moment when someone turns to them and asks, 'And what do *you* do?'

The greatest pressure will come from those closest to them. Family and friends are going to be concerned, perhaps anxious, and can intentionally or not put pressure on the client. Managing this is obviously a matter of much more than developing an 'elevator pitch' equivalent, but it is readily tackled with normal coaching: 'what are going to be the issues here do you think? And how could you best tackle them?'

Benchmarking

People want to know they're doing alright. You could always do more job hunting – and if that's their only criterion they will always be depressed. Often people are too hard on themselves and then they don't interview properly.

This is classic '20%' territory. I tell clients, as you've already seen, that you can't job hunt more than three days a week, and that 2–3 job-hunt activities a week (or more, or less, depending on their particular sector, context or circumstances) is a solid achievement. In other words, I give them a benchmark.

Then, as ever, it's back to the 80%: what other benchmarks can we develop together, in both the career transition part of their week and in the essential other parts? One might be physical: jogging the perimeter of the park in under 40 minutes (or the mightier feats mentioned above), or it might be getting the children through their forthcoming big exams, or being elected a School Governor, or onto the Board of that charity they've always wanted to help.

c) 'Third Stage' career coaching

For years career management and career transition were it. Now there's a third tranche of work, so new it doesn't even have a name yet – we've called it 'third stage careers' but a catchier term will doubtless be along soon!

It refers to the Baby Boomers, living longer but facing the pensions funding gap. The basic choices are as you'll recall, save more, consume less, work longer or die sooner. So there has been a sudden shift in the zeitgeist. Where ten years ago people were talking about wanting to retire at 50, now the talk is of 'having to work longer'. But there are also many who continue working not because they have to, but because they want to: they are able people, still at their intellectual, social and physical peak. They don't want to go 'cold turkey' from work to golf, but instead switch to a 'portfolio life' of working for perhaps shorter hours, but still at the same level of intellectual challenge and reward. But this time there are no well-trodden paths to follow: how do they go about it?

We can help.

First, you'll observe it's actually the same split as in the earlier stage of working life: some people will want career management (how can I make this the most fulfilling stage of my life?) and others will be in enforced career transition (I need to work longer to fund my pension gap). So the principles above still apply: for the career management people, it's structuring their exploration and for those who have to find work, it's all the career management processes plus the additional techniques of career transition.

And underlying them both is again, the Big Five: coaching works, and it works particularly well with a group such as this entering uncharted territory.

But perhaps the needle needs to shift: the right ratio for mainstream career work is we believe, 80:20, in other words, 80% coaching topped up by a little judicious nudging from our professional expertise. There are no rules yet for 'third phase' career coaching; we are the generation who will need to develop them. But we think it's probably closer to 90:10. You can't *tell* an intelligent resourceful 55 year old, with all those years of experience, hidden interests and personal connections, what they should do with the remaining decades of their working life, but you can *coach* out of them their own hopes, fears, gifts, strategies and plans.

What is the remaining 10%? There are at least four parts to it:

- what people want from work;
- pace in the 'third phase' career;
- risk and reward;
- practical input.

What people want from work

Or indeed need. Salary matters, but it is in some senses the least important. Time and again the things people say they are looking for in this stage of their working life are:

- meaning, purpose, making a difference;
- belonging;
- identity;
- a framework to life.

So the first step is to help people work out what really matters to them. It may be that they are actively involved in a large extended family, or Church, or community of hobbyists, so their need to belong is amply met outside work. Conversely people who have thrown everything into a successful career might find it gave them, without their realising it, framework *and* identity *and* purpose *and* the place they belonged – but all four have now vanished. So for them, much of their 'third phase' will need to be built afresh. Eventually that could be exciting, but right now it probably feels very strange and unfamiliar, and they may well relish some good, strong non-directive coaching, which structures the *process* of some of their thinking and exploration while drawing the *content* very much out of them.

With regard to identity, one practical question is how are they going to describe themselves? It's the answer to that question at parties again – but whereas the recently redundant person needs to come up with something quickly, for someone embarking on the 'third phase', developing this answer is part of the fun, and they may like to try several on for size for a while. An interim phrase to say to other people may be useful to provide 'cover' while the exploring is going on (perhaps for years!) but otherwise the exploration shouldn't be cut off too quickly.

Pace in 'third phase' career

This is similar to constructing a portfolio career as we discussed above, but the scope of decisions now is broader. Clients will of course have many thoughts already on what they want to do, but to give them food for thought we ask, do they want work which:

- is controllable; or
- involves a certain number of days per week; or
- where they work hard in bursts, with gaps between projects?

People typically start by thinking in terms of X number of days per week, but in fact intensive bursts, such as are needed in major consultancy projects, or interim management roles, may suit them better. These can then be balanced with the third element, regular work which is able to be moved around during bursts, is not time-linked and is usually controllable by the individual, to fill in the gaps.

Risk and reward

There's a big difference here between retirement and 'third phase' careers. If you retire, and were an accountant, people suddenly expect you to do the accounts for the local cricket club, or whatever you're involved with, and 'of course,' pro bono. 'Third phase' careerists aren't having any of that – they're still working, though differently, they have been earning well to date and see no reason why that should change. Even if they don't need to earn, proper remuneration is, as one competitive client said to me, 'a way of keeping score'.

The risk in 'third phase' careers is of a different kind. It is important not to do the wrong thing, as there is often quite a high level of moral invest-ment in commitments people make at this point. Once in, it's therefore hard to extricate oneself, so even if there is a funding gap and a need to keep earning, the coach can usefully deploy the O of the GROW model, working with the client to explore other options, checking each one out thoroughly for not just its upsides, but its potential risks.

Practical input

At this stage it's generally unlikely that people will get work through con-ventional channels such as advertising, so networking will be absolutely crucial. Many people don't know how to do it effectively, and you may have to help them by referring them to the social media book we men-tioned above, for example.[13] For others, it's just coaching out of them the skills they actually have, but hadn't hitherto thought to apply to this con-text or stage of life.

They can also use briefing on particular routes to 'third phase' work. In the UK, for example, the Public Appointments Office of the Cabinet Office is the starting point for around 18,500 (pre-austerity!) appointments to boards and committees of an extraordinary variety of local and national bodies. The particular process varies from country to country, and securing posts in international organisations is even more arcane. In most coun-tries the pressure is on to make such appointments more transparent and accessible, so you could in theory equip yourself with the correct and up-to-date information from websites and published guidelines in order to brief your clients – but in practice, it's usually far more efficient to ally yourself with a well-informed local specialist in this area.

Another area where specialist advice is important is whether or not to take on non-executive directorships. Requirements for this vary from country to country, and in some jurisdictions it can involve individual personal legal liability, so specialist legal advice should be obtained if this is under consideration.

Next steps

By now you might be thinking, how on earth do I as a leader in organisations, or a prospective or actual coach interested in doing this work, equip
myself with all this specialist content knowledge? First, bear in mind what
we said at the beginning – at least 80% of this work, more in many cases,
is mainstream Big Five coaching.

Beyond that, as career *coaching* is so new, there are so far as we aware,
no formal trainings in the field yet available. There are places to train in
career *counselling* – the MSc in Career Counselling at Birkbeck University
in London is one possibility. But for most people the most viable option
at present is to join, or ally with, one of the emerging organisations in
the field, and benefit from their in-house staff training. The content of
the 20% can be gained surprisingly quickly – and then, as with Big Five, it
takes at least a couple of years of sustained practice, supervision, CPD etc.
to consolidate it and to get to fluency.

What of the issue that, as we said at the outset, though the need for
career coaching is emerging fast, and the supply of coaches with at least
the 80% is ready and able, the market hasn't yet been built? We have
no ready answers, except the suggestions in Chapter 12 on how to build
your individual business as a coach. And that indeed is doubtless how it
will happen: career coaching is where mainstream business coaching was
10–15 years ago and it will grow as its parent did: by countless individual
coaches, and coaching organisations, winning business, doing excellent
work for clients and winning repeat business. In the process they built not
only their own reputations, but that of the field.

Plenty to be going on with! But what of the client where you pour in all of
the above, but, frustratingly, they don't *do* anything?! It seems to fall on
deaf ears, or they shuffle their feet in the next coaching session, having
done not very much … . Or the cynical, the unenergised: the demotivated.
This is a crucial issue in all coaching, and we turn to it in the next chapter.

10

Advanced coaching: motivation and change

They *can* do it – but *will* they?!

Sooner or later every leader, HR whizz, coach (parent!) despairs: people who are perfectly capable of doing something, know exactly what needs to be done, say yes yes yes they're going to do it – and they don't.

Business development, for example: we know the simplest, most powerful thing to do is just pick up the phone and make that call, but instead we 'circle the desk'.

And that's just one phone call. Then there's bigger structural change: breaking a lifelong habit, switching jobs, introducing new HR practices, leading your whole company into a merger, changing the political structure of a nation.

These are vast topics; here we just scratch the surface. We don't dive into what academics, philosophers, writers, poets or pop songs have had to say on the subject; the objective of this chapter is rather to give you an initial taste, through *two great tools* to use in coaching and managing your teams, one for motivation, one for behaviour change. Some coaches already use the change tool, but few are aware of the motivation one. Both deserve much greater prominence.

Motivation

Understanding motivation has been the object of study for thousands of years, with a particular depth of enquiry triggered by the horrors and

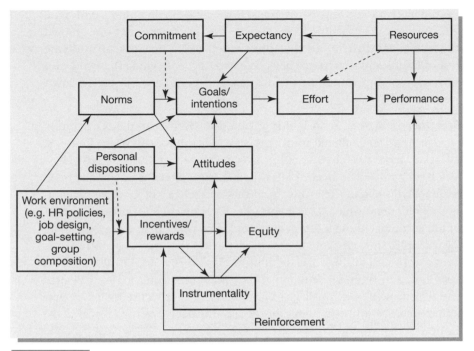

Figure 10.1 | Integrative model of motivation

Source: Taken from Furnham (2001), p. 283. *Source*: Katzell, R. and Thompson, D. (1990) 'An Integrative Model of Work Attitudes, Motivations and Performance', *Human Performance*, 3, pp. 65–85. © Copyright Lawrence Erlbaum Associated, Inc. Reprinted with permission.

miracles of the 20th century. Brilliant minds around the world have come up with many lessons: needs, value, fairness, equity, reinforcement, all play a role in motivation.[1] The scientists have probably cracked it – it's even been pulled together into a single conceptual framework, with the answers all in there: see Figure 10.1.

But you see the problem. You're standing at the podium, facing 2,000 anxious pairs of eyes, about to deliver a crucial speech. You need to persuade them to let go of the past, rouse them to action, inspire, motivate. Your palms are sweating slightly. The 'integrative model' probably *has* got all the answers, but in that moment it's not going to help. Too complicated.

If that weren't bad enough, a further twist is the huge variation between individuals. One is profoundly motivated by service to humanity; another will do anything for chocolate. Sometimes you know your client well, and/or have had the opportunity to do extensive psychometrics, and/or it has been appropriate to do extensive coaching to draw out their unique motivations. But many times, if a manager is helping a colleague with 'one-minute coaching,' for example, we don't have that fine-grained knowledge. And there are the times when we're needing to motivate groups, teams and conference halls. We need a simple guide that works for most people. Something like the diagram in Figure 10.1, but boiled down even further.

Great news: there *is* such a thing! Like the GROW model it is simple enough to be remembered under pressure, yet it has deep scientific roots. It doesn't have a catchy name but was developed by the eminent scientists Ryan and Deci so I call it after them.[2] Their model is one of the most profoundly important first fruits from the hard science of 'positive psychology' (for more on which, see Chapter 11. Their research is fascinating and I would encourage those interested, to read it for other points of great value: for example, they cite research demonstrating that moving motivations from extrinsic to intrinsic has, in addition to the obvious business benefits described, an even more important outcome – it is good for your health. The achievement of extrinsic goals doesn't significantly raise wellbeing, but achievement of intrinsic ones does (Ryan and Deci, op.cit.p.75). So make money, be happy!)

How do we motivate people? Ryan and Deci start with the simple fact, known from both scientific research and common sense, that we can't – it's an internal state in a person and there isn't a magic question or word or pill that can cause it to be raised from the outside – yet.

Then they untangle the different types of motivation and arrange them along a spectrum, from totally external, or *extrinsic*, at one extreme, to profoundly inner, or *intrinsic* at the other (see Figure 10.2). An extreme example of extrinsic motivation on the hard left of the spectrum might be, 'I have a gun, do it or I shoot.' At the other most intrinsic end, perhaps a parent's love for their child such that they would leap to save them from harm, with no thought to their own safety. Between the two there are many intermediate steps along the way.

When we put it that way, we see instantly that a core task in business is to help employees, customers, sales prospects, etc. move along the spectrum from left to right, from extrinsic to intrinsic: from, 'do I *have* to ...?' to 'WOW I *so* want to!' Especially where the tasks might seem at first glance to be wholly of the outer world – increasing shareholder value, cleaning up that major oil spill, making the quarterly sales target, dealing with the pension fund liability – management would love to know how to have team members seize them as their own, unleashing the full-on dedication and energy of intrinsic motivation!

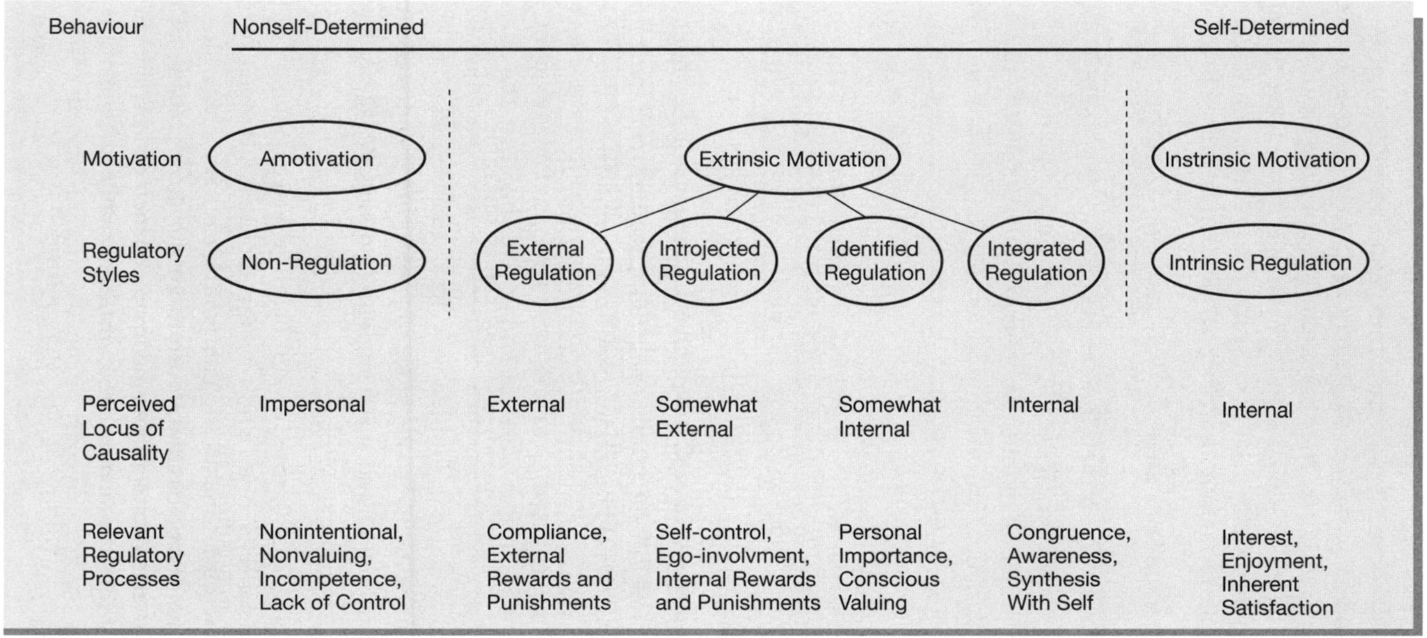

Behaviour	Nonself-Determined					Self-Determined
Motivation	Amotivation	Extrinsic Motivation				Intrinsic Motivation
Regulatory Styles	Non-Regulation	External Regulation	Introjected Regulation	Identified Regulation	Integrated Regulation	Intrinsic Regulation
Perceived Locus of Causality	Impersonal	External	Somewhat External	Somewhat Internal	Internal	Internal
Relevant Regulatory Processes	Nonintentional, Nonvaluing, Incompetence, Lack of Control	Compliance, External Rewards and Punishments	Self-control, Ego-involvment, Internal Rewards and Punishments	Personal Importance, Conscious Valuing	Congruence, Awareness, Synthesis With Self	Interest, Enjoyment, Inherent Satisfaction

Figure 10.2 The Ryan and Deci Continuum

APA, reprinted with permission. From, Ryan, R.M. and Deci, E.L. (2000), Self-determination Theory and the Facilitation of Intrinsic Motivation, Social Development and Well-being, *American Psychologist*, 55 pp. 68–78

And how is this Holy Grail of management achieved? Ryan and Deci, as I said, are clear that we can't (yet) beam it into people's minds. What we can do though, is *create the conditions* where it is likely to happen – or remove the conditions preventing it. They argue that if these core conditions are present, people are much more likely to make that move along the spectrum and absorb the goal as their own. (Particularly if they are supported by coaching, as found in Daniel Burke's 2007 research, discussed below.)

According to Ryan and Deci, there are three such core conditions:

- **autonomy**: do I have a choice about doing this?
- **competence**: do I know how to do it?
- **relatedness**: is there social support in my context for doing it?

Let's consider each in turn.

Autonomy

Straight away of course we hit a problem: clients will protest they have no choice at all. Salespeople need to meet their targets or else. The management consultant's board presentation tomorrow must be a) finished, b) perfect, even if she has to work through the night to do it.

If other pressures pile on as well – a partner made redundant, school fees to pay, a boss who's allergic to saying thank you, people can indeed feel demotivated – or as one put it, 'trapped like a rat in a hole'. Coaching can haul clients out of that mental hole by reconnecting them with the fact that they *do* have a choice: they are not bodyslaves, somewhere along the way they decided to do this work, and they can undecide. They can at least revisit the original basis for their decision and see if it is still valid or if things need to be adjusted in some way. This usually needs to be done in two parts: first, giving them safe space to let out their feelings and frustrations, and only then to unblock them with O of GROW questions (see Chapter 5).

As ever in coaching, this intersects with the individual personality of the client. I coached someone once who was fine as long as I listened sympathetically to the terrible demands his glamorous life made on him, but who would get enraged when I ventured into the next part, of raising awareness that he had made choices and could revisit them. He was very high on Neuroticism (see Chapter 7) and it was clearly too unbearably painful for him to admit he had played a part in constructing the situation and that he had made, and actually was continuing to make, a choice. The coaching went nowhere and was eventually terminated. But for most people, airing the issues brings relief. They may remain in the same situation, or they may make some adjustments, but reconnecting with the fact they have ultimate freedom to act removes that particular block to their motivation.

Competence

This is I believe the huge dark secret of modern business (and indeed political) life. Many people simply do not know how to do their job well. For reasons which are often beyond their control: screamingly fast technological innovation, rapid job churn, career changes, training gaps, big promotional leaps, etc., they do not have at their fingertips the procedures, best practice, explicit and tacit knowledge that a seasoned practitioner would. The seasoned practitioners have gone (fired in the last round of 'stripping out unnecessary layers of management') and the new people do the best they can.

The starkest example of this is lawyers. Highly intelligent people are trained thoroughly and updated regularly on the law, but in their first 10–15 years most have scarcely a day of training in management.* Then they are appointed to a senior role and are suddenly responsible for a budget of tens even hundreds of millions, and hundreds, maybe thousands, of people. (The even darker part of the joke in some firms is they are expected to do this in about 20% of their time, while continuing to make their 80% billable hours target. Without dedicated support. You can't argue with the financial results – law firms' earnings are high – but coaches (and families) see the toll taken on some people.) They might be sent for a week to Harvard or Cambridge, and the enlightened firms are now trying to equip their high fliers with the skills they will need, but many still enter their new role having received less training than the average trainee accountant. No wonder they turn to coaching – but in fact coaching is not enough of the answer: there are often simple skill gaps which need to be plugged for intrinsic motivation to grow.

The case of lawyers is particularly stark, as their training is almost unique in remaining so largely technically focused, but it is also a general problem of seniority. Until recently incoming British Cabinet Ministers received no training at all for the vast responsibility they were about to assume; the same applies to some non-executive directors of major businesses.

---

* This trend is beginning to change as competitive advantage becomes marked by better knowledge of clients' business and industry sectors, with one firm (Simmons & Simmons) now giving their junior staff an MBA programme – but this is still the exception rather than the norm.

(The Institute of Directors' courses, right up to its Chartered Director programme, are not a mandatory requirement to be a UK company director.) Above a certain level of august seniority, no one dares suggest training, neither do the incumbents dare admit to wanting or needing it. Coaches *must* dare. Many times I have punctured a client's ballooning anxiety by asking outright what precisely they needed to know to tackle the issue at hand. Once clarified, the solution is rarely for the individual to go off and do a PhD on the subject themselves but rather to ensure someone in their team can cover it. I have for example, seen senior lawyers bridge the gap very effectively, and fast, by working closely with specialists in business development, finance and personnel.

Relatedness

This is self-explanatory: humans have been herd animals for millions of years, and even the introverts among us feel more at ease if others are doing something similar, and/or if we are being supported and encouraged by our colleagues. Or put the other way, it's not easy to fight a lonely battle. Again, coaching can help by simply raising this legitimate human need and seeing what can be put in place. A newly appointed division head, for example, may find a mentor helpful.

How do I use Ryan and Deci's mantra of 'Autonomy, Competence and Relatedness' in everyday business coaching? Usually, simply: if a client is experiencing personal demotivation, or a leader has to plan how to motivate their team, I outline the model, and we work through each of its parts. Are there any A, C or R factors missing in the environment, and if so what has to be done to build it in? Or is something blocking one of the three?; if so, how could it be removed, or minimised? For example, making that sales call is much more likely if the team gets refresher training on how exactly it should be handled (C); sets aside time to have a sales blitz together (R); and some element of choice is acknowledged (A). ('I know this isn't really your scene Joe, but would you like to join us?')

Of course, the Ryan and Deci tool isn't going to solve everything: we must avoid the Fundamental Attribution Error and remember all the forces in the context which are at play too. Plus the other research from Positive Psychology about the motivating value of playing to strengths, and what Charles in Chapter 9 and Carol in Chapter 6 call respectively, meaning and purpose, and transcendence. But the Ryan and Deci three points I find in practice to be a very useful start.

And fascinatingly, there is emerging research to support the view that Big Five coaching of *itself* may raise levels of intrinsic motivation. The research, by Daniel Burke and Alex Linley, was interesting for a number of reasons: it involved coaching senior executives, it measured the complex links between goals and motivation, and most importantly of all, as we shall see in the next chapter, it yielded results which were statistically significant.[3] We can expect to see more research looking at Big Five coaching and intrinsic motivation in the future.

Advanced demotivation – 'I quit!'

There is a special problem if things have gotten so bad that demotivation has reached the point where clients want to quit. Or when it's really bad, to leave the industry altogether and go off and grow carrots. In theory, this seems like a difficult ethical challenge for the coach: we can't take the organisational client's money in order to help a key individual leave the firm.

In reality, I find it is rarely a problem. First, sensible corporate buyers know this is always a potential risk, and sensible coaches explicitly cover it when contracting. Second, if it does come up, decent clients know themselves they're straying near a boundary. I state my rules clearly: I can't of course help them leave, but what I do think is valid and indeed useful to do is to give them some space to air the issue. They may get to the point where they do want to explore external options further, and at that stage the coaching must obviously cease. But in the vast majority of cases, I find they take a deep breath, spill it all out, and then having got it off their chest, after a while reconnect with the original choice they made to be there.

Change

I was aware of the Ryan and Deci tool, and had been using it happily for years, but the change one is a more recent discovery. I was talking with my coaching Supervisor about a piece of work that wasn't going as well as I thought it should, when she asked, not entirely innocently, 'Hmm, I wonder what stage of change he is in?' In a single flash I got it – there could be *different* stages of change! And presumably different readiness for action, and hence the coach would have different expectations, and ask different questions ...

This was my introduction to the work by Prochaska *et. al*, a group of scientists working for the last two decades on the tough task of helping people give up smoking – where all the usual challenges of behaviour change are made worse by physical nicotine addiction.[4] They found successful change is not an off–on switch but a series of *stages* as we build our level of preparedness. And visible 'action' comes pretty late on in the process.

Prochaska sets out five stages of change:

- **Precontemplation**: where change is not yet on the radar.
- **Contemplation:** where there is ambivalence; they may have seen the need for change but equally want things to stay as they are.
- **Preparation:** where they have made the decision to change, but are still uncertain.
- **Action**: where they're actually taking steps to change.
- **Maintenance:** which may need to continue for life (or **Exit**, which is job done!).
- Plus a loop of **Relapse:** which can occur at any point, is normal, and indeed to be expected.

The throws a whole new light on the GROW model. It still works as well as ever – but the coach needs to appreciate that the G and the W might be very different, depending on which stage the client is in. And the questions need to be adjusted, too. For suggestions of helpful coaching questions in each stage, see the box below.

Questions for Stages of Change

Precontemplation

Not intending to act. Questions can only *raise awareness:*

- How could things be better?
- What are the implications of not changing?

Contemplation

Intending to act, but ambivalent. Questions should still *raise awareness,* and *acknowledge the ambivalence* (don't confront the resistance). Can also *gently* test their concerns – using 'R' of GROW.

- So on the one hand, this could be helpful, but on the other you're concerned it might not work?
- I'm hearing a choice here, between… and …. Is that right?
- You said the new strategy is a 'total disaster', would it be helpful to explore that – or not at this point?

Preparation

Intending to act soon. Questions are still *raising awareness*, and *transitioning towards action.*

- So how could you explore this further?
- What might you broadly want to achieve?
- Any thoughts on how you might go about it?

Action

Acting.

Questions are *helping to plan action* and *monitoring results*: O and W of GROW.

■ What specifically could you do? etc. …

■ How did that work out? So how will you adjust the plan?

[if Relapse]

Emphasise this is normal, and as in GROW, go back to whatever was missed and rebuild the process.

Maintenance may need to continue for life; if *Exit* happens, celebrate!

Adapted from: Prochaska, J.O., Norcross, J.C., DiClemente, C.C. (2006) *Changing for Good*, New York: Collins; and Greene, J. and Grant, A.M. (2003) *Solution-focused Coaching*, Harlow: Pearson Education.

The stage concept stops us from leaping to the assumption that a person coming to coaching is ready to act. They may well not be – so we're thrown back into Big Five coaching: listening, probing, checking, without prior expectation, to test out where the client is at. Once that is established, it also gives us some pointers for going forward. You might argue, it is a deepening, or a sub-component, of the 'R' of the GROW model.

So, two simple, but soundly evidence-based tools, for two crucial issues in coaching. (Like everything else in this new field however, while both have been tried and found useful by practising coaches, neither has been tested scientifically for senior executive coaching. The field awaits the results from several generations of masters and PhD projects.) To explore these topics further, see the further reading suggested overleaf.

In the final two chapters, we switch to totally different topics. Coming up next, why coaching works: you may not care, but if like me you take pleasure in finding out *why* things work – of no practical value at all, but oh so fascinating! – then you may enjoy Chapter 11. If on the other hand your remaining query is how to earn a living through coaching, you may prefer to turn to Chapter 12.

Further reading

Furnham, A. (2001) *The Psychology of Behaviour at Work,* Hove: Psychology Press/Taylor and Francis.
Chapter 6: 'Work motivation and satisfaction'.

Greene, J. and Grant, A. (2003) *Solution-focused Coaching,* Harlow: Pearson Education.
Chapter 4: 'Models of change', for a little more on coaching using Prochaska, plus two others: Bridges' Transition model and Lewin's force-field analysis.

Prochaska, J.O., Norcross, J.C., DiClemente, C.C. (2006) *Changing for Good,* New York: Collins.
Written for the general public.

Ryan, R. M. and Deci, E. L. (2000) 'Self-determination Theory and the Facilitation of Intrinsic Motivation, Social Development, and Well-being', *American Psychologist,* Special Issue on Happiness, Excellence, and Optimal Human Functioning, January, Vol 55, No 1.
The original academic source.

11

Why it works

What use is it to know why and how coaching works? You may not care. Some have no idea what happens under the bonnet of their car, they just want to turn it on and go. You may feel the same about coaching. On the other hand you may be curious, for several reasons: innate curiosity about most things, or a desire to know in order to do it better or faster, or to know how to fix it when it goes wrong. If you're in the 'just turn it on and go' camp, then you might like to skip this chapter.

Still here? Great!

This chapter considers:

1 simple practical reasons why coaching works;
2 reasons from scientific research;
3 the research basis of Big Five coaching;
4 contributions from allied fields.

1. Simple practical reasons

At one level, I believe coaching works for basic common-sense reasons.

Pause

It's that nice Mr Edison's fault. Before the lightbulb, wax candles were expensive, tallow smelly, rushlights dim, so unless there was some special need to struggle on peering through faint light, the vast majority of workers stopped at sundown. In the last 100 years, average working hours have gone up and average hours of sleep down. *The Oxford English Dictionary* says the phrase 24/7 appeared in 1983 (in the US; 1997 in the UK) and with it, ever-on communications, food delivered to desks and sleeping cells in firms' basements.

Fifty years ago senior businesspeople were mostly men, with wives to ensure there were clean shirts and nourishing meals. Fifty years before that there were staff. Now we all work, and cram the other things in somehow. Our families are in another city, or country, and friends are busy too, so if you want support you need to pay for it – and organise it – more to think about. And technology, of course. (When I started proper work in 1977, a letter was posted and you could rely on at least a week's grace before the reply was posted back to bother you again.)

In sum, most normal people in business have an enormous amount on their minds. On good days, it's fun and exhilarating, but it doesn't take much to push it over into stress.

Coaching works because for an hour, or two hours, or even just a minute waiting at the lift, it presses the pause button. Sometimes it's enough for a client just to have a space which is calm, quiet and where silence can be constructive. It's no coincidence that the rightly famous coach Nancy Kline, and indeed many great business dynasties, are Quaker.

Clearing your head

I have a client with huge responsibilities. Most sessions he arrives late, stressed, papers bulging out of his briefcase, and his head in a similar state. Whatever work we do together, the main value to him is almost aways that by the end of the session he has sorted through everything he has on, realised some things must be delegated/declined/pushed back, and reconnected with the key things to focus upon. He arrives stressed, sometimes almost overwhelmed by all that has to be done, and often disaffected. He leaves 90 minutes later with a clear head, and hence re-energised and remotivated.

Venting

There's a lot in business to fear, hate and be anxious about – or even excited and joyful. Yet senior executives often need to play their cards close to their chest. No one can know, yet, that the finances are so close to the brink, or the breakthrough research discovery is about to pay off. One of the formative experiences all new business coaches go through is when a client comes to the session and instead of working obediently through the GROW model, or coming up with fiendishly clever strategies, they spend the time pouring out their anxiety, or fear, or anger, or excitement. Nowhere else is safe for them to do it. If it's minor, they'll get it off their chest and move on to 'proper' coaching; if it's major it's the coaching topic itself.

Time

We all know we should, but in practice few of us actually block out time in the diary to think. Instead we rush from one project to the next, constantly feeling overloaded and behind the game; the urgent pushes aside the important, we fight fires instead of focusing on what really matters.

So the coach helps simply by showing up – time is blocked out in the diary, the secretary holds calls, people don't put their head in the door because 'someone's in there', and the executive has an hour or hour and a half of quality thinking time. I sometimes say to clients, you could replace me with a decent sheet of wallpaper – just block out the same length of time, look at the wall, and think: it's cheaper. (The difference between me and wallpaper is I fight back; if they get to the point where the wallpaper does too, coaching isn't the answer.)

Many clients say the single biggest value from coaching is 'it gives me space to think'. When we pull back briefly, we see priorities more clearly. Just space to think means clients pick up a lot of the 'low-hanging fruit' in coaching – the simple idea or improvement that's been brewing for a while but never had space to pop out: the 'oh God, now I stop and think it's just so blindingly obvious ...'.

Sounding board

Executives often say the great value for them in coaching is to have a 'sounding board'. Particularly if they're really senior. The issue may be *about* the board, so they can't share it with them, and they have to look confident with the next layer down. They've been working so hard they've lost touch with the old friends; the long-suffering first spouse has heard it all too many times before, or has gone, and the hot younger number gazes incomprehendingly. Lawyers, financiers, advisers, all have a stake in the decision. You see why an intelligent sparring partner whose discretion can be utterly trusted, who will challenge fearlessly, yet who is 100% on your side, is precious. I've been through three bad recessions now, and senior executives don't let go of their coaching if they can possibly help it: the tougher it gets, the greater the need, and the more fiercely they protect that space.

Speaking truth to power

As noted above, the difference between me and a sheet of wallpaper is I fight back. This role has a long history – rival nobles daren't tell the King the truth, but the Court Jester could, as long as he was made to seem harmless with the cap and bells. Modern business coaches find their own ways of getting the message across in a way it will be heard.

2. Reasons from scientific research

Why does this matter?

According to the old joke an economist is someone who looks at what's working in practice and asks if it would work in theory. I used to laugh at that, now I am that economist/business coach: I believe it's not enough to know in practice that coaching works, or to guess at some common-sense explanations for its effectiveness. We also need to be able to demonstrate *scientifically* that it works, and why. There are at least three reasons for this:

- Professional bodies can be expected to get ever tougher, with complaints procedures against coaches developed and sanctions enforced. Tests in such cases include what a reasonable person could be expected to have done and/or whether the coach abided by best practice. A coach who can demonstrate they are trained in, and use, only methods grounded in reliable evidence-based science should be safe – but first we need to know what those methods are.

- In tough economic times, the demand is for higher-quality services, delivered ever faster and more cheaply. If we don't know why and precisely how coaching works, then we can't strip it down to the essentials and rebuild it to meet evolving demands.

- Consider a different field. In his classic text on architecture, Sir John Summerson says the period 1753 to 1768 was crucial in British architecture because

  'from this period we can date the real existence of an architectural *profession*, a profession to which young men [sic] are trained up and not merely one whose members have all graduated from a trade or have adopted through a combination of circumstance and predilection, often late in life.'[1]

Coaching is currently going through the same 15-year transition. To become a full profession we require a theoretically valid, empirically based and rigorously tested body of knowledge which is widely agreed upon and subject to constant further development, evaluation and review. This in turn will enable us to make our work, and its impact on people, teams and organisations, explicit, measurable and verifiable.

What is scientific research?

Proper scientific research differs from the business research with which we are more familiar. The objective of business research is often to provide the sort of information which enables organisations to take more informed decisions, usually by *describing* what is happening. Do customers prefer green ones or purple ones? What are competitors up to? Scientific research by contrast may also seek to describe, but at heart it has a more challenging objective: to *explain* what is going on.

The philosopher J.S. Mill articulated one set of requirements to be met before one can actually claim to have explained anything. Before *A* can be said to have caused *B* – for example, before you can say that coaching causes increased performance – he says the following conditions must be met:

■ A must precede B;

■ B must covary with A (i.e. if A pushes, B moves); and

■ All other explanations must be ruled out.

Clearly it is difficult to satisfy such rigorous criteria when dealing with complex, mutable scientific subjects like humans. Though not impossible: psychology, for example, is full of ingenious experiments where precisely these conditions have been met and aspects of human behaviour illuminated.

Furthermore, good scientific work usually develops from an established theoretical base, investigates in the light of that theoretical paradigm and builds up therefrom a body of tested evidence. (Hence the phrase 'evidence-based'.) Science also prefers explanations which are 'parsimonious' that is, the very simplest and clearest explanation is the best. (Which is why those who could fathom it, got so excited about $E=MC^2$.) Experiments must be conducted according to tight rules of procedure and ethics, and in general the results must meet the standard of being statistically likely to the magic level of 0.05%: in other words, the chances of the outcome of the experiment happening by chance, are less than 5%.

How can you tell if coaching 'research' passes these tests? There is one shortcut. If ever you find yourself at a Nobel cocktail party and are at a loss for small talk, mutter quietly, 'of course, in the reviewed journals ...' and bask in the respectful silence. The 'peer-reviewed' journals are a benchmark for scientific rigour and respectability. All sorts of procedures exist to try and make sure that if something ends up being published in these famous journals, the science in them is sound.*

Like everything else in life, there is a hierarchy. Atop the pecking order is the journal *Science*; if ever an approving article on business coaching appears there, then we've arrived. Coaching being a relative newcomer in the research world, our peer-reviewed journals are currently rather lower down the pecking order, but they do exist. Currently there are three and a half of them: *Coaching: an International Journal of Theory, Research and Practice*, the *International Coaching Psychology Review (ICPR)* and the *Annual Review of High Performance Coaching and Consulting (ARHPCC)*. The 'half' is the *Consulting Psychology Journal*, which is not officially dedicated to coaching (it's the journal of Division 13 of the American Psychological Association), but US scientist-practitioner executive coaches have semi-colonised it, and it frequently has good to excellent Special Issues on top-level coaching.[2]

The scientific research on coaching

So how much parsimonious, theoretically sound, accurate to 0.05% coaching research is there?

Very little, but it's about to start appearing in greater quantity. Harvard's Institute of Coaching, for example (www.instituteofcoaching.org), is ploughing significant funding into coaching research grants.

That's good, as there's a lot to be done. For a full 'shopping list' see the 2004 chapter on this by Carol Kauffman and myself in Alex Linley's *Positive Psychology in Practice*.[3] In brief, we don't yet have, and need, documention of the theoretical sources of coaching; published statements linking the theoretical sources and how the interventions are operationalised; agreed standard procedure(s); and testing of coaching's efficacy, in individuals, teams and organisations.

Work has already begun and the pace is picking up fast. In 2001 Dr Anthony Grant, the head of the world's first university-based Coaching

---

* Nothing in life is of course perfect, the reviewed journals very much included, particularly these days when the stakes in scientific reputation and hard cash are so high.

Psychology Unit, at Sydney University (www.psychcoach.org), surveyed the reviewed journals in psychology (which is, of course, only one of the source fields for coaching, as well as sport, counselling, psychotherapy, business/management/strategic studies, etc.) and found 93 substantial references.[4] Of these however, only 17 represented actual scientific studies of coaching interventions with adult normal people. There were also at that time 25 published PhD or Masters dissertations, indicating further research would be coming through the journals' pipeline. Since then there has been exponential growth: see Figure 11.1. Updating his work in 2005, Dr Grant found 231 studies in the 'scholarly business literature' alone – not including the many thousands more in psychology, medicine and education.[5]

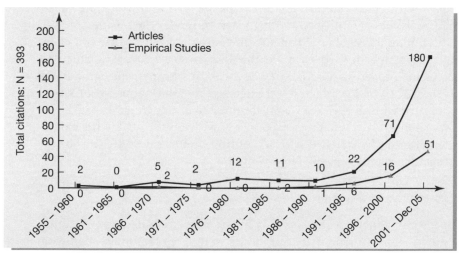

Figure 11.1 Articles compared with Empirical studies in the scholarly business literature 1955–2005

Grant, A. M. (2006) A Bibliography from the Scholarly Business Literature, in D. R. Stober and A. M. Grant (eds) *Evidence-Based Coaching Handbook*, John Wiley & Sons: Hoboken, NJ, p. 369.

Examples of studies published so far, from the old but still useful, to the much newer, include:

Olivero, Bane and Kopelman: Combining coaching and training improves productivity[6]

This pioneering 'action research' found training alone increased productivity by 22.4%, but training combined with follow-up coaching increased productivity by 88%. The authors noted that as the study was live research done 'in the field', i.e. in a real business context with all its complexities, there must be many caveats on their findings, but the magnitude of the results was such that they had some confidence in ascribing the astonishing performance outcome to the coaching. They further broke down the coaching into seven key elements, of which they thought two, goal-setting and having to make a public presentation of the results of the coaching (a feature of that particular project; in a way, a compulsory 'W' of GROW), were the two most important.

Real estate salespeople: coaching improves sales performance[7]

A coaching programme explicitly based in cognitive behavioural psychology was introduced for real estate salespeople in a firm which previously had poor sales performance and high staff turnover. The subsequent evaluation found a number of benefits, including increased sales, and client and staff satisfaction. For example, the time for a new sales associate to get their first property listing fell to 3.53 weeks (compared with an industry average of 10 weeks), which represented first month commission of $2,430 compared with an average of $871 for those who did not participate in the programme. (This is another aspect of good scientific work – the experimental group is matched with a 'control' group, who differ in no way other than the experimental intervention.)

Coaching in teams[8]

In a study which looked *inter alia* at the role coaching plays in teams, Ruth Wageman found that team basics were more important than team coaching. In other words, having the right team members who were properly resourced, well trained, etc. had more impact than good coaching. However, in teams which were well constructed and managed, good coaching had a powerful impact. Here again we see (as in the Olivero *et al* study on training and coaching) the additive effect of coaching: allied to existing good management practices it makes the latter's impact more powerful.

3. The research basis of Big Five coaching

Let's look at this from another perspective. In Chapter 5, I outlined the basic foundations of coaching:

- Contracting.
- GROW, including goal-setting.

▨ Listening.

▨ Questioning.

▨ Non-directive.

How much of this is tested to scientific standards?

As a combination, none: this book is the first time the bedrock of business coaching has been articulated in this particular way. But many of the component parts have been, namely:

Contracting

You may recall from Chapter 6, Mihaly Csikszentmihalyi's Flow model. Flow is securely based on exhaustive research, spanning most of the world's cultural contexts, genders and age ranges.[9] One of the first four of Csikszentmihalyi's '9 conditions of Flow', i.e. the crucial preconditions of peak performance that coaches work with, is *boundaries*. It may seem odd to some in our modern free-wheeling world that humans perform best where there are rules and limits (though the traditional English nanny always knew it) and here's a reason: boundaries make people feel safe, and build trust. Comprehensive contracting establishes those safe boundaries.

Therapists have long recognised this, and use many techniques to contract and hence create safe boundaries. One example is the sanctity in some therapeutic approaches of the 50-minute hour: no matter how bad it gets, even if you are sobbing, you know that, without fail, a few minutes before ten to the hour, the therapist will pass across a particularly large handful of tissues and say, 'well, we need to be bringing this to a close ...'.

So contracting has in some senses been tested to high scientific standards, and it's also based on long-established practice in a different field; more research is needed on how it can be optimised in business coaching.

GROW and goal-setting

Here too some key component parts have been tested, but not the whole.

GROW has not been subjected in its entirety to scientific research. But its arguably single most important element, goalsetting, certainly has been.[10] In mainstream psychology, already by 1975 Latham and Yukl were reporting 27 separate studies, under laboratory conditions or in the workplace, many with hard outcome measures such as 'net weight of truck loads' or 'dollars collected'. One of these early studies was by Kolb and Boyatzis (1971), who found positive behaviour change was greater in goal-setting than in non-goal conditions in personal development work.

A vast amount of work has been done in this area since: the keywords 'goal setting' in the psychology database *Psycinfo* listed 2,456 studies in the period 1975–2003, in widely varied fields. Recent examples include, in sport, Weinberg (1995), who summarised 30 years of research in kinesiology and athletic performance; from cognitive science, Berry and West (1993) who looked at cognition, self-efficacy and goal-setting across the lifespan; and Ilgen *et. al* (1987), who considered the research with regard to increasing the efficacy of group/team work. In 1991 Latham and Locke published a further major review of the field, noting that continued research over the almost 20 years since had supported and broadened the original proposition across a wide variety of organisational and national/cultural contexts.

The original proposition still holds: in essence, the more crisp and clear the goal at the outset, the higher the performance at the end, but four decades of research have shown us infinite permutations of this, including some conditions where it doesn't hold, and many where more subtle and nuanced understanding and application of goals is needed. For an excellent and searching further exploration, see Tony Grant's chapter on goal-setting in *Evidence-Based Coaching*.[11]

Listening, questioning and non-directive

We have seen for almost five decades that this works, and powerfully, in the client-centred approach of humanistic psychology, whose leading thinkers included Abraham Maslow and Carl Rogers. But though this has become the basis of much of modern counselling, humanistic/client-centred approaches have been criticised for not sufficiently subjecting their approach to empirical testing.

Positive Psychology (PP) – described by one of its founders, Martin Seligman, not entirely tongue in cheek, as 'Maslow plus science' – is putting that to rights. Seligman alone has raised over $30 million for research, much of it directly relevant to coaching, which he has designated as one of the core delivery mechanisms for Positive Psychology. Already there is a rich outpouring of quality research relevant to coaching: by far the best and most comprehensive current description is by Carol Kauffman in *Evidence-based Coaching*[12], but more research arrives by the hour.

A sub-field applying all this to business has sprung up: see *Positive Organisational Scholarship*,[13] which has all the big names, including (the sadly late) Donald Clifton on strengths at work; Barbara Fredrickson on the business impact of positive emotion; David Cooperrider on Appreciative Inquiry; and Fred Luthans and Bruce Avolio on authentic leadership development. But not, you will note, anyone on the utter basics of listening, questioning and non-directive. This is the way of science, which often (game-changing Newtons and Einsteins apart) begins with myriad small studies and monographs, and is only then able to develop the super-perspective needed for synthesis of the core components. But as quality PP research is now thudding down upon us like hail in a thunderstorm, it won't be long.

4. Reasons from scientific research: allied fields

While we are waiting, many allied fields have long-established, reputable work which we can draw upon – indeed we already are. We can't yet definitively claim that coaching works because it is securely grounded in this research, because it isn't: we have borrowed it, and are using it in practice to good effect, but for our field to be fully robust, each borrowing needs to be rigorously tested in *our* specific business coaching context. We see in practice that the borrowings work: we need to use that to form good theoretical hypotheses, and test those out, in order to deepen our understanding and make more secure the foundations of our practice.

If we peer over our neighbours' fences, some of what we see, which has been scientifically tested over there, but not yet over here, includes:

- from *psychotherapy*: the 'common factors';
- from *cognitive psychology*: cognitive load/limit to working memory;
- from *organisational psychology*: cross-cultural coaching;
- from *Positive Psychology*: lots;
- from *neuroscience*: why it works, at brain level.

Psychotherapy and the 'common factors'

Pushed in part by spiralling medical costs, there has been considerable research over the last 40 years in the field of psychotherapy on whether 'talking therapies' work, and if so why. The consensus is they do work and there are four reasons why.[14] To the fury of the warring factions, which specific therapy is applied accounts for little of the difference.

Instead, four 'common factors' (Hubble and Miller, 2004) are said to be shared by all effective therapies. These are not definitively established and tested but are instead conceptualisations to enable future research investigation to be more focused, but they are interesting nevertheless.

The four are:

1 The *client/extratherapeutic factors*, which account for 40% of the estimated contribution to treatment outcome. These include factors such as the client's strengths, supportive elements in the environment (e.g. a kind grandmother) or even chance events such as a good day at the races.

2 *Relationship factors*, which account for an estimated 30% of the treatment outcome. These include 'caring, empathy, warmth, acceptance, mutual affirmation, and encouragement of risk-taking and mastery, to name but a few'. (Hubble, op.cit. p.341.)

3 *Placebo, hope and expectancy*: estimated contribution to treatment outcome, 15%. This derives from 'clients' knowledge of being treated and assessment of the credibility of the therapy's rationale and related techniques ... [i.e.] the positive and hopeful expectations that accompany the use and implementation of the method'.*

4 *Model/technique factors*, accounting for only 15% of treatment outcomes.

The above may cause you to raise an eyebrow, but remember this is about therapy, not coaching. Therapy works with ill people seeking personal healing. Business coaching works with healthy people, teams and organisations seeking business outcomes, so all sorts of different factors are at play.

Second, the common factors view is controversial even in therapy (but has some heavyweights behind it.)

Third, even if it has something to say to us as business coaches, the organisational setting, and particularly the tough worlds most senior coaches operate in, will doubtless skew the percentages – though I'm not sure which way.

Client and client context factors are estimated to account for 40% in therapy. Our clients are not ill but well, and not just healthy but more intelligent, more driven and more pathological** than the general population – so does a more dominant client mean that number is in fact higher in coaching? Alternatively, organisational settings are full of other people just

* Hubble, op.cit. pp 341–2. Don't knock a good placebo effect: medicine uses it all the time.

** More intelligent: at least one standard deviation above the norm, i.e. an IQ of 115 or above is required to succeed in management levels and up according to Professor Adrian Furnham (Closing Address to participants in the Meyler Campbell Psychology for Coaches course 2008); more driven, look around you; more pathological, see Babiak, *Snakes in Suits*.

as determined as our clients, plus tough legislative constraints, powerful role stereotypes and expectations (e.g. what a first-rate chairman/CEO should do), etc. – does this mean it's less?

In other words, it might be that since our worlds, and the work we are contracting to do, are both so different, that the 'common factors' debate raging in therapy may be irrelevant to us. We won't know until significant research on this is done in our own business coaching context. (You may well have your appetite whetted to read more of Hubble's and Miller's chapter, and I do indeed recommend both that and the entire Linley and Joseph book.[15] It's a full-on dense academic tome, but a brilliant one – my own copy has pencilled scribbles, underscorings and exclamation marks down the margin of almost every paragraph. Apart from the one (Kauffman, 2004) chapter already mentioned, it's nominally not about coaching, but the greater part of the book is in a deeper sense directly relevant.)

In the meantime, if even part of it is right, then to me it reinforces the importance of Big Five coaching: *contracting* in the business context starts by taking careful account of the client and what Hubble and Miller call 'extratherapeutic' factors – we would say, the business context – and anchoring the coaching accurately for that unique organisation and client; *GROW* provides the necessary model framework and established expectation on both sides of success; and *listening, questioning and non-directive* provide the conditions for relationship factors, and client resources, to flourish. (In fact, I sometimes think GROW operates as 'trainer wheels' for high-achieving businesspeople learning to coach: it keeps them occupied and stops them doing what they would otherwise have done (telling clients what to do, etc.), thereby allowing client thoughts, client solutions, etc. airtime. Great coaches can transcend GROW, but coaches in training need to go through strict adherence to it in order to get to that point. Another Myles Downey-ism is, 'In coaching, there are no rules, and you have to know them'.)[16]

Cognitive psychology: cognitive load and the limits to 'working memory'

Do you know your blood type? If you are like me an O blood group, then I'm afraid to tell you our blood is Neanderthal. If on the other hand you are from the A/B blood groups, then you have a new type which developed only 10,000 years ago, when humans moved from nomadic existence to settled agriculture. And that, I have been told, is the last major innovation in the human body.

Which means our brains are coping with the 24/7 life described above, with a brain which has many accretions, but is at its core, Stone Age.

Yet today with all the noisy visual clamour of our modern advertising-blitzed, communications-dense overcrowded age, it has been estimated that in any nanosecond, there are coming in upon us 300,000 bits (in the computer sense) of information. Cognitive psychologists however say our 'working memory', the essential 'desktop' of the brain where we process current information, can handle only 'seven plus or minus two' bits of information at any one time. That is, we can all, on average, hold only about seven things in our conscious mind at once – which is why for example, telephone numbers in every country in the world are broken up into manageable chunks as soon as they get longer than about seven digits.

If we're being blitzed with 300,000 bits of information each split second (noise, sights, barometric pressure, gravity, sensation, etc.) yet can only process seven, how on *earth* do we cope? Partly by habits (I drink my tea black – saves having to think about it), heuristics, patterns, routines. But we still often feel – and are – overloaded.

Cognitive psychologists haven't so far as I know researched how coaching helps with that, but I hypothesise it is in two ways, through *downloading* and *organising*. In coaching sessions clients download a lot of current material, not just to the coach but also onto paper or a computer – action plans, etc. – taking a load off current memory and attention. And coaching often causes clients to organise, delegate or deal with the incoming data stream and existing backlog. But these are just hypotheses and remain to be tested. The sharp contrast between what working memory can cope with, and the deluge of information is however an established fact.

Organisational psychology: cross-cultural leadership

One huge piece of research from organisational psychology points to why on occasion coaching *doesn't* work – and how we need to adjust so it does. Part of the enormous GLOBE project, Felix Brodbeck and others have looked at differing leadership paradigms in each of 22 European countries.[17] Anyone coaching in Europe will probably want to see the full data (which is unfortunately buried in particularly inaccessible psychologist-ese) but it is helpfully summarised in the report's Table 3, reproduced here as Table 11.1.

In essence, the report's finding is that, despite the external similarities of briefcases, business suits, cappuccinos and PowerPoint, there are deep and significant cultural differences in what an effective leader does across

Table 11.1 Leadership attributes in 22 European countries/country clusters

| | North/West European region | | | | | South/East European region | | | | |
| | Anglo | Nordic | Germanic | | | Latin | Near East | Central | | |
Leadership prototypically	(GB, IRL)	(SWE, NL, FIN, DEN)	(CH, GER/w, GER/e, AUS)	(CSR)	(FRA)	(ITA, SPA, POR, HUN)	(TUR, GRE)	(POL, SLO)	(RUS)	(GEO)
High positive (facilitates outstanding leadership)	Performance Inspirational Visionary Team Integrator Integrity Decisive Participative	Integrity Inspirational Visionary Team Integrator Performance Decisive Non-autocratic Participative	Integrity Inspirational Performance Non-autocratic Visionary Decisive Participative Administrative Team Integrator	Integrity Performance Administrative Inspirational Non-autocratic Visionary Participative Self Sacrificial Team Integrator Diplomatic	Participative Non-autocratic	Team Integrator Performance Inspirational Integrity Visionary Decisive Administrative Diplomatic Collaborative	Team Integrator Decisive Visionary Integrity Inspirational Administrative Diplomatic Collaborative Performance	Team Integrator Visionary Administrative Diplomatic Decisive Integrity Performance Inspirational	Visionary Administrative Performance Inspirational Decisive Integrity Team Integrator	Administrative Decisive Performance Visionary Integrity Team Integrator Humane Diplomatic Collaborative Modesty
Low positive (slightly facilitates)	Non-autocratic Administrative Diplomatic Collaborative Modesty Self Sacrificial Humane Conflict Avoider	Collaborative Diplomatic Administrative Conflict Avoider Self Sacrificial Humane Modesty	Diplomatic Collaborative Self Sacrificial Modesty Humane Conflict Avoider Autonomous	Collaborative Decisive Modesty Autonomous Humane	Inspirational Integrity Team Integrator Performance Visionary Decisive Diplomatic Collaborative Conflict Avoider Administrative Modesty	Non-autocratic Participative Self Sacrificial Modesty Humane Status Conscious Conflict Avoider	Participative Non-autocratic Self Sacrificial Modesty Humane Status Conscious Conflict Avoider	Collaborative Participative Non-autocratic Modesty Self Sacrificial Status Conscious Autonomous Humane Procedural	Participative Collaborative Diplomatic Status Conscious Self Sacrificial Modesty Conflict Avoider Autonomous	Inspirational Non-autocratic Self Sacrificial Status Conscious Autonomous Participative Procedural
Low negative (slightly impedes)	Autonomous Status Conscious Procedural	Autonomous Status Conscious Procedural	Status Conscious Procedural	Status Conscious Procedural	Self Sacrificial Status Conscious Autonomous Humane Procedural	Procedural Autonomous	Autonomous Procedural Face Saver	Conflict Avoider Face Saver	Humane Non-autocratic Procedural Face Saver	Conflict Avoider Face Saver Self Centred
High negative (impedes)	Face Saver Self Centred Malevolent	Face Saver Self Centred Malevolent	Face Saver Self Centred Malevolent	Status Conscious Self Centred Malevolent	Face Saver Malevolent Self Centred	Face Saver Self Centred Malevolent	Self Centred Malevolent	Self Centred Malevolent	Self Centred Malevolent	Malevolent

Key, AUS = Austria, CH = Switzerland, CSR = Czech Republic, DEN = Denmark, FIN = Finland, FRA = France, GB = Great Britain, GER/w = Germany, GER/e = former East Germany, GEO = Georgia, GRE = Greece, HUN = Hungary, ITA = Italy, IRL = Ireland, NL = Netherlands, POL = Poland, POR = Portugal, RUS = Russia, SLO = Slovenia, SPA = Spain, SWE = Sweden, TUR = Turkey

Brodbeck, F.C. et al (2000), Cultural variation of leadership prototypes across 22 European countries, *Journal of Occupational and Organisational Psychology*, **73**, pp. 1–29.

Europe. The real richness for business coaches is the detailed breakdown of the ideal leadership paradigm for each country (outlined in Table 11.1). For example, a French coach working in the Czech Republic (or vice versa) should note carefully that being 'self-sacrificial' is an essential element for outstanding leadership in the Czech Republic; in France by contrast it is seen as an impediment. Mining this data – and the comparable data sets which have been published since for 62 countries round the world[18] – should be an essential part of the well-briefed business coach's toolkit if they coach at senior levels in any of the reported cultures.

Positive Psychology

I won't say too much more about this here, as there has already been much about Positive Psychology and the underpinning science of why it works in this book. In particular, we saw Carol Kauffman's '4 steps to confidence' tool and PERFECT toolkit in Chapter 6, and several approaches to Strengths in Chapter 7. There is a vast further wealth of riches for business coaches to draw upon, but this has been comprehensively described by Carol in her book chapter already cited.[19]

But, there is just one further crucial insight from PP that I would like to flag: the Fredrickson/Losada Ratio.

Our starting point is that the brain is hard-wired to negativity. This makes Darwinian sense – for almost the entire length of human history it was a matter of life and death to be alert to the negative in our surroundings – the fire is about to go out and we will all die/watch out that dinosaur is about to eat you. (Having used this example for years, a 13 year old recently gently informed me that dinosaurs and humans didn't in fact co-exist – pity, it made such a great story.) Noticing those things enabled the body to flick into 'fight or flight' response, and as a result, the human race survived. Now, however, the fact that the old parts of our brains and nervous systems constantly fire under threat is no longer helpful: trigger-noises or events happen all the time, and we end up with high blood pressure. Conversely, perhaps for equally sound Darwinian reasons, (there were times when this too was useful, though fewer of them) Barbara Fredrickson has found that *positive* emotions have beneficial effects on our brains and bodies – the 'broaden and build' effect. If we are in positive mind frame, we are able to generate more creative solutions, think more expansively, and perform better at the sort of complex tasks that are better suited to today's more cerebral world; though remembering the hard-wiring to negativity, it takes conscious effort and practice to 'reverse the focus' to what's right about things.

At different times and in different combinations, Fredrickson, Losada and Heaphy have done a number of studies[20] of high-performance individuals and teams to explore how those conflicting forces, i.e. our natural predisposition to negativity, and the positive benefits of positive emotion, play out in the real world of business. In detailed analysis of team interactions, they found that the highest performing teams were those where the optimal ratio of positive to negative feedback was, in varying contexts, from 6:1 to 3:1, i.e. three positives for every negative. Not, as people assume, the teams where the ratio was only 1:1, that's *not* enough for peak performance (it doesn't counteract the hard-wired bias: people seem to need to hear 3:1 or above to experience it as evenly balanced), and also interestingly, not in a team they found where it was 13:1 (who *were* those people?!). Leading-edge organisations are already building the 3:1 ratio not just into their coaching but into performance appraisal systems and training programmes.

Neuroscience: how the brain changes through coaching – maybe!

If you can read just one further book this year, or in the next many years, my humble suggestion would be Norman Doidge's game-changer, *The Brain that Changes Itself*.[21] The blurb on the dust jacket says the methods described result in 'blind people who learn to see; learning disorders cured; IQs raised; ageing brains rejuvenated; stroke patients recovering their faculties; entrenched depression and anxiety disappearing; and lifelong character traits changed'. Yet astonishing as it seems, this is reputable work, world-class even, and deeply rooted in sober science.

In essence the research described overturns traditional notions that the brain peaks at about 16 and it's downhill, and fixed, all the way thereafter. Instead, high-precision modern neuro-imaging techniques have found instead that the brain rewires constantly – hence the 'neuroplasticity revolution'.

One specific technique described is 'focused attention' which is central to the transformations described. The neuroscience of this is Nobel prize-winning work on nerve growth factors, including one called brain-derived neurotrophic factor, or BDNF. Under conditions of focused attention BDNF consolidates the connections between neurons; promotes the growth of the thin coating of fatty myelin around them; which in turn speeds up the transmission of electrical signals. Altogether these add up to a 'magical epoch of effortless learning' which characterises childhood, and is activitated thereafter only when something important, surprising or novel occurs – *or* when both clinician and patient are paying close attention to a task set up for the treatment.

So this could explain the brain process underlying much of what we have learned in this book: the need for deep listening, highly disciplined and targeted questions, and the crucial importance of tightly focusing goal-setting. Focused attention changes the brain. (So having to pay close attention is brain-enhancing for the coach as well!)

Most interestingly of all, the changed brain chemistry and increased plastic rewiring ability generalises *beyond* the immediate task: BDNF puts not just the part of the brain required, but the entire brain, in an 'extremely plastic state'. Over time the more this happens, the more completely unrelated parts of the brain are also roused into higher performance. So that pattern you may have noticed, where people who have practised with deep attention for years at one thing (playing the piano for example, or maritime law) also seem to become unfairly good at many other things – sport, deep connection with friends and family, writing poetry. A good hard consistent workout for one part of the brain seems to exercise and energise the whole system.

There is however a dark side to the above. Focused attention on good things builds the brain – but the reverse is also true: scattered attention on rubbish degrades it.

> 'Television watching, one of the signature activities of our culture, correlates with brain problems. A recent study of more than twenty-six hundred toddlers shows that early exposure to television between the ages of one and three correlates with problems paying attention and controlling impulses later in childhood. For every hour of TV the toddlers watched each day, their chances of developing serious attentional difficulties at age seven increased by 10%'. (p. 307)[22]

I have always said, not entirely in jest, that one reason for the rise in coaching is because children are no longer taught the classics. I presumed the extraordinary ability of well-educated 19th-century public schoolboys to survive and flourish in all the remote and inhospitable corners of the Empire to which they were sent, was because the classical syllabus drummed into them taught them to think with exceptional clarity. And so it unquestionably did – but it may also be generalised BDNF at work again. Classics students at Cambridge in the 1830s for example worked for years at an almost unrelenting peak of focused attention, combining the most rigorous training of their minds with demanding physical exercise every day.[23] Did that give them exceptional brain density and neuroplasticity?

And if watching television rewires children's brains what about the adults listening to 'the news'?

We are aghast in history lessons on the Middle Ages when we learn that raw sewage ran down open drains in the streets, and people emptied bedpans out of windows onto the heads of passers-by. Knowing the Fredrickson/Losada ratio, will future generations look back with equal horror on our constant diet of completely unbalanced bad news, seeing this as the equivalent of medieval raw sewage pouring through our minds?

But I digress. The next and final chapter is about how to build your business as a coach.

12

Building a freelance coaching business

Now what was that thing we were talking about in Chapter 5? Ah yes – the GROW model!

This chapter seeks to help you build your business as a freelance coach. But it's a jungle out there: conflicting advice, facts and rumours, some indispensable tips and guidelines, but some things you could trip over and others that bite. So we use the trusty GROW model to hack a pathway through it all.

The chapter therefore contains, as you could doubtless chant by now, four sections:

1 **Goal:** what is yours?
2 **Reality:** what are the facts?
3 **Options:** what could you do? (There's lots here!)
4 **Will:** how do you feel after absorbing all this, and when you recover, what will you do?!

Right, pith helmets adjusted, machete to hand? Off we go.

1. The Goal

Your goals in fact. Before we plunge into marketing and selling (two very different things as we shall see below) let's do this properly and start with your Goal.

In a way, this sends you back to reconsider much of the rest of the book. Chapter 2 described many different ways others do it: which of these appeals to you, which fits your personal circumstances best, and your personality?

And maybe it even means revisiting Chapter 1: is your interest and your gift, in mentoring or coaching, life or business coaching, directive or non-directive, business, personal or leadership coaching?

This might prepare your thinking for when we go into detail below, asking which market sector or niche makes sense for you.

To be very practical about it, you may be best to start with the opportunities closest at hand. To vary the jungle metaphor, I often say to our graduates, when helping them build their business, it's like Tarzan swinging from vine to vine through the jungle: you start with the vine nearest you. So if you are in financial services you might know several people there who need coaching. Do a good job with them, and you could end up not just with their colleagues in the same sector, but with their friend the architect, and his contact the track manager at Silverstone, and so on… . One of our graduates was in insurance, and presumed he would be coaching there for a while. He did indeed start by contacting fellow insurance executives: but over the months contacts referred him on to contacts, and his first pieces of actual coaching work were with the manager of a scuba-diving operation in southern Spain, and someone expanding their Pilates studio businesses. So you start with the vine close by and never know where the vine several swings along will take you! But you need to start somewhere.

You may also want to think about your Goal in very concrete terms. What little information is available on potential earnings I share in the next 'Reality' section. But before we get into what others do, what do *you* want? Do you have or need explicit income or other targets for your first year, or first 2–3 years? One person I was working with went through a process something like: 'I doubt I could see more than two clients a day from a pure psychic energy perspective. Given that typically means four hours a day and assuming a theoretical maximum of 220 working days, it gives 880 hours. Put in a target income (gross) of say 220,000 [sterling, euros, beads …] then the theoretical hourly rate is 250. BUT you also need to factor in overheads such as office rent, bookkeeping, etc.' and so he went on through his thinking.

Other people see their Goal differently: one coach I know just set the principle that they charged their client, what their client charged others. So if the client is an accountant charging out at £270 an hour, the coach would bill them £270 an hour. The objective was to get to that position and stay there. A variation on the same theme, but coming from a very different place, is wanting to be respected. So another coach's reasoning was, if they charged low fees, they could get more work, but if they billed at a higher rate – and could carry it off – they would be taken more seriously. It's what they called the 'Harrods principle': if it's expensive, it must be good. (They also knew they had to avoid overshooting, which might engender disrespect, even disbelief!)

Others have very different kinds of goal: personal fulfilment, stepping back from the golden treadmill to create enough space in their life to find love, being able to support their children through an expensive education. Or, these days, their parents in retirement.

It needs, as always, to begin with a Goal. Or goals.

2. Reality

In this section, I first nail the two big myths that are out there, that a) all is wonderful and b) all is doom. Then I give you the facts from the research and my observation over decades on the four key questions I am asked daily:

- How much can I earn?
- How long does it take?
- How recession-proof is coaching? And
- What is the difference between those who make it, and those who don't?

I am in contact with hundreds, maybe in a busy year for conferences even a thousand, coaches a year. On the topic of building their businesses, I hear two totally different stories. Some people speak (or email) disapprovingly: the market is tough, even impossible, most coaches don't in fact make it, and anyone who says to the contrary (looking at me meaningfully) is a menace, raising false expectations which are doomed to disappointment. The others report cheerily they have had their best months/quarter/year ever, and contact me for help with finding more good coaches to handle their fast-growing business. (Perhaps there's a silent majority in the middle just getting on with it and muddling through, but they remain silent.)

So who's right? For many years we were frustratingly buffeted from one anecdote to another, with no objective facts to turn to. Hence in 2008 Meyler Campbell commissioned the first of our 'Business of Coaching' surveys, to plug the gap. The surveys are certainly not to be relied upon too heavily: only just over 100 people replied in 2008, 500 in 2009, and pure scientists would sniff at our 'convenience' sample (i.e. going through networks we knew). But that's the way of real-world research, the information it yielded is better than none, and we will keep seeking to improve it. The full reports are available on the website, www.meylercampbell.com. Here I just highlight a few of the key findings.

a) How much can I earn?

From Figures 12.1–12.3, you see that 22.9% of respondents earned less than £5,000 per annum. Elsewhere in the survey it was reported that 29% were less than two years post-qualification, so we assumed that there was at least some overlap between these two groups, i.e. those still in training or just out, were not yet earning much. Modal average earnings for those who were up and running then fell in the £30,000–50,000 category, but with an upward tail: 9.4% earned £50,000–£75,000, 5.9% £75,000–£100,000 and 3.7% £100,000–£200,000. Add in from elsewhere in the survey that coaching typically represents on average only 34.3% of respondents' *total* earnings, and one begins to understand the sector's continued growth. Serious, high-calibre people are attracted as they can do work they feel passionate about *and* pay the bills.* Of course, one can't draw any definite conclusions from these two surveys, but they do confirm what I see in my daily contact with people in the business: the answer to the question, 'what can one reasonably expect?', is that it is possible to earn a tolerable living. Of course you can't add the two data points together – the high-earning coaches may be devoting much more than 34% of their time to it – but broadly some business coaches earn a decent living.

People who earned *really* large amounts in their previous lives need to be aware there is not, barring rare exceptions, the same scope for that in coaching, but most people transitioning to freelance careers are usually well aware of that. The usual trade-off is to earn less, but have more of one's life back.

---

* People love this work: 87% of survey respondents in the 2008 survey (*Coaching at Work* magazine, September 2008 issue) reported that their objectives for coaching as a career were met.

From the list below, please allocate your approximate
annual income percentage split.

Area of income	%	Area of income	%
Coaching	34.3	Mentoring	1.4
Training, development or facilitation	23.8	I am a Non-Executive Director	1.1
Consulting	19.6	Work in interim roles	1
Employed part time	3.7	Research services	0.3
Work in an academic institution	1.9	Other income activities	12.9

Respondents	330
Responses	992
Multi response	Yes

Key Others
- Investments/Property
- Employment (internal coach)
- Retired
- Author
- Psychotherapist
- Psychometric profiling/recruitment assessment
- Coach supervision

Figure 12.1   Meyler Campbell Business of Coaching Survey 2009: Slide 32

b) How long does it take?

The data on this is less clear, but the indications are it takes at least two years post-qualification for people to get up to speed, i.e. charging full commercial rates. Business coaches tend to be an ethical group, and are often reluctant to charge anything like full fees immediately upon graduation, despite being officially qualified to do so at that point. They transition their fees up only as they become convinced from client feedback and results, that they are delivering real value. (It frequently even takes an external challenge, e.g. colleagues, friends, former tutor, even clients, saying, 'you really are undercharging for this, you know', before they finally move to proper market levels.)

We noted in Chapter 4 that it's important for reasons of professional development to keep up ongoing learning, support systems and supervision. Going to things like Coaching Fishbowls (where leading coaches coach live and for real, in front of a small audience, and discuss it afterwards with the audience), conferences or networking events also help 'normalise' the up-and-down process of learning the craft and building the business. There are setbacks – not all coaching sessions will always have a breakthrough or great result – but talking to and watching others helps you know what to expect in the first few years. Quite apart from professional learning, and hearing others' stories, attending events also gives great opportunities to research the market.

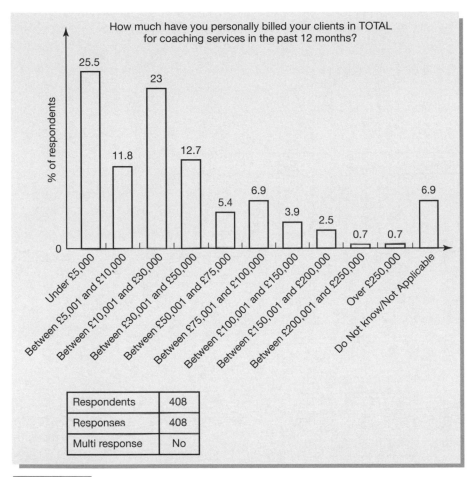

Figure 12.2   Meyler Campbell Business of Coaching Survey 2009: Slide 35

c) How recession-proof is coaching?

The truth seems to be, surprise surprise, part-way between the optimists and the pessimists – but tending, and this *is* a surprise, given the difficult economic circumstances, towards the optimists. When in mid-2009 people were asked to compare their earnings with the previous year, the response was as shown in Figure 12.4.

In other words, some coaches' earnings significantly increased, others significantly decreased, and a third group stayed the same. Overall this averages out to 'the same or slightly better' but in fact for any particular individual, this is misleading: the vast majority did either a lot worse, or a lot better, so the individual experiences were on the whole more extreme than an 'average' implies.

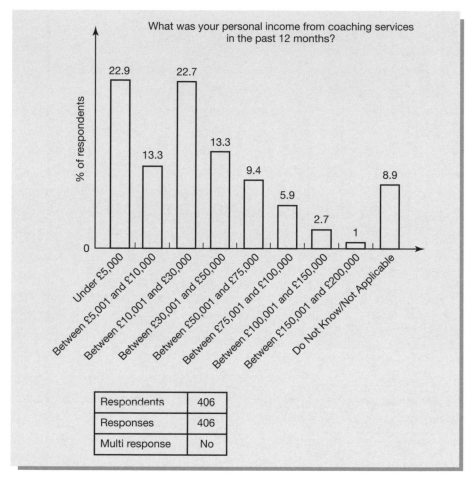

Figure 12.3 Meyler Campbell Business of Coaching Survey 2009: Slide 36

d) What is the difference between those who succeed, and those who don't?

So some thrive, others don't: the difference seems from the data to boil down to two things: *longevity* and *activity*. The first makes sense; people who have been building their businesses for ten or more years are naturally likely to be more successful than new entrants, if only because those who didn't succeed have gone elsewhere. Those who remain can reach the useful stage of critical mass, where satisfied clients refer other clients and business snowballs.

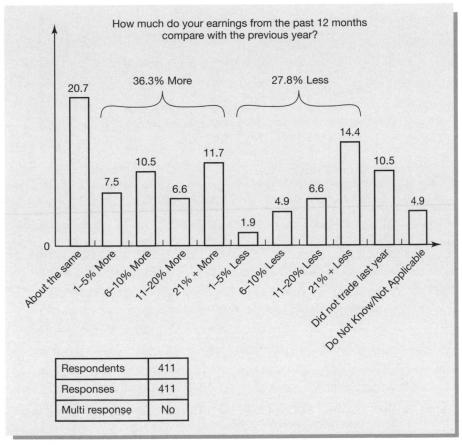

Figure 12.4 Meyler Campbell Business of Coaching Survey 2009: Slide 37

It's the *activity* finding that's particularly important for those starting out. This is exactly what I have observed many times: the difference between real success, and bumping along, has less to do with innate coaching skill and more to do with straightforward hard business graft. Indeed, for some coaches, having it too easy at the beginning is something of a trap: gifted initial work by virtue of a previous role, or contacts, they dive into the coaching, doing little or no marketing. Then one by one their contacts/ grateful clients retire or move elsewhere, and eventually the stream of business dries up. (The rule of thumb is you need to bring in at least 10 per cent new clients a year, just to replace 'natural wastage'; some say even 20 or 30 per cent.)

What does a higher earner look like?

They have been coaching for longer

They are more likely to have been self employed prior to becoming a coach

More of their time is spent coaching

They are more likely to be a member of an accredited body

They have a wider range of methods to secure clients. In particular they over-index on coaching clients approaching them directly

They are more likely to have a coaching supervisor

Their fee rates will be higher

They see more emerging trends in coaching

They have a wider array of activities to keep their skills up to date. In particular:

- Supervision
- Reading

Figure 12.5   Meyler Campbell Business of Coaching Survey 2009: Slide 'what does a higher earner look like?'

By contrast those who start with fewer advantages often work harder to compensate. One of our graduates had spent 22 years in the same firm. The thought of going out on her own after so long in a safe context was exciting, but terrifying. She said it was the fear that drove her: long before she left her role, she spent nights and weekends developing a plan, then took a deep breath and set to work, looking up contacts, defining and making her offer, following up, delivering good work and keeping in touch. She exceeded her targets in her first year and I will never forget the sheer pleasure on her face as she told me that, adding, 'And Anne, I've had a *ball*!'

Others do it with sheer discipline. Another of our graduates has a very simple rule: every day, he does three marketing activities. It may be making a phone call, or revising a document, and often it just takes a few minutes, out on the road between meetings, but he does three things a day without fail. This simple method alone, combined with hard work delivering the business that comes in, and sustaining his consistently high standards, yields an income some financiers would envy.

So the difference between the coaches who thrive is not necessarily their coaching, but their *marketing/selling* activity.

Hence that's what we focus on in the rest of this chapter. But before we move on to that, there is obviously a lot more than marketing to building a new business. Most of it you doubtless know, as someone already in business, but for a great refresher (and for those who don't, a comprehensive primer) the indispensable *FT Guide to Business Start-up* covers everything: from the initial nervous dipping your toe in the water right through to stock market listing, it's all in there, and it's updated annually.[1]

3. Options

So what *could* you do to build a business?

There are two basic ways to approach this: either by planning to the hilt and executing that plan, adapting it as necessary, or, by Herminia Ibarra's iterative, exploratory mode that we outlined in Chapter 6. (Or perhaps, like most people, working hard on a plan, then in reality operating on a combination of that and serendipity!)

But before we get into that, there's something very important to do first.

How's your coaching?

The essential first step may not appear to be a marketing one, in the conventional sense at least. It is instead to get your coaching to the point of inner confidence. We always have more to learn, but there comes a point in one's training or experience or development, where you can look a prospective client in the eye, and know in your heart that you can do a good job. You may not have all the fancy extras you will add later, but you *know* you can deliver good straightforward coaching.

Buyers can tell: they can 'smell' uncertainty and hesitancy. Nervousness is another matter, but they can spot the difference between someone who is initially nervous, but who once they get going lights up when talking about their coaching, from someone who just hasn't got on top of the subject yet. So the first task is to build your coaching hours until you have that inner core of confidence. It needn't take long: it's months, rather than years, in a good coach training. (And if despite decent training, more practice and good feedback from clients, colleagues and your Supervisor, confidence is still an issue, it might be worth revisiting Carol Kauffman's '4 steps to confidence' tool in Chapter 6.)

Right, having got that out of the way (or under way!), now we need to enter the bit of the jungle where it gets *really* dense. To guide us through this part, where there are tangles and vines and alarming low growls from the undergrowth, let's pull out another key tool for orientation, the MBTI, discussed at length in Chapter 6.

That is to say, I have broken down all the potential tips and pieces of advice or options into two different sub-sections: perhaps with tongue slightly in cheek, they are the 'N' one and the 'S' one.

So there are first, some big-picture general comments on the options for sales and marketing of your business. And then, the biggest box in this entire book, the 'Marketing Checklist' into which I have stuffed as many detailed points as could possibly be crammed into one chapter!

Options for building a freelance coaching business: general comments

Some general tips gleaned from over a decade's experience of watching and helping our graduates build their business include:

■ Do *something*. If you undertake marketing activities A and B and C, then work comes in – but often, puzzlingly, from areas X and Y and Z, not apparently connected to the marketing you did at all. But if you don't do A, B and C, it doesn't happen. I have no scientific explanation for this (I think of it as 'kicking up dust in the Universe') but have observed it to be the case many, many times.

■ Do *more than you think*. When I was starting out, I asked a wise older coach which of the several possibilities were the most effective – networking, running seminars, writing articles, etc. She smiled slightly and said I should do them all, and that you have to do more than you think. She's right.

■ Do *the things that make most impact*. Coaching is a service delivered by people to people; hence the marketing methods that work are those that get you in front of the right buyers, so they can assess your suitability for their current business needs. Or, as an early client of mine once memorably put it, so they can 'sniff your air'. So face-to-face contact is the objective. The best way to get there is *networking*, i.e. politely but effectively letting people know precisely what you can do for their organisation and/or themselves. If you dislike or fear it, join the club, so do most people, but there is no escape.

■ *Apply The Golden Rule of Networking*. If you read the last bullet point with a sinking heart, then may I offer my Golden Rule of Networking. It's just one word: *give*. Think constantly – and ask aloud, or in emails, as often as you can – how can I help? Do I know someone who would be interested that this person can coach in Italian? Is there a terrific book reference they might enjoy on the subject they've just been talking about? Like everything else, this gets better with practice. It also only works when it's mostly true generosity; people can detect insincere manipulation. Sainthood isn't required – my own constant sharing of tools I've found useful, etc. is about 85% altruism, 15% awareness that something might come back one day. I know that, they know that – but the balance still seems to work. How does this count as networking? Because as the saying goes, 'what goes round, comes round'. People remember you when possibilities crop up, and send them your way. Often not the same people – it's the ABC–XYZ rule again. For more on networking, see Les Garnas' classic book,[2] and we will come back to it again below.

■ *Pick up the phone; pound the streets.* As someone put it rather crudely, it's a numbers game: the more connections you make, the more work you should expect to pick up. Coaches who keep at it, rain or shine, are the ones who are so busy they are turning business away. What exactly you do will vary; one great rainmaker for a coaching business I know genuinely delights in others' company at lunch or dinner, and keeps in close and real contact that way. Others thoughtfully send clients press clippings or articles relevant to them. Speak at conferences; write a blog. Do what feels natural for you, play to your Strengths (see Chapter 7) – but it's also true that one needs to refresh the approach every now and then by doing something different as well. (Sorry!)

■ *But also say 'No'.* One of our graduates, Emeritus Professor John Stopford of London University, CEO coach and one of the world's leading thinkers on strategy, says one of the most-forgotten keys to business success is what you say 'no' to. This has long-term impact, as good clients send good clients, and bad clients send bad clients. Listen to your instincts and decline a client when that little alarm bell is ringing; tough to do when starting out, but one learns.

■ *Headhunting not recruiting?* In the next section, we discuss detailed full-scale marketing activity to build a coaching practice. But for some people, this is not what they should be doing at all. Exceptionally senior businesspeople, or those with outstanding contacts, or who have a great deal of other work already in their portfolio, should be thinking of their marketing not in terms of 'recruiting' clients but of 'headhunting' them.

Many of the graduates of our own programme fall into this category: they start talking about business development, but when I ask how much time they will *actually* have available each year, and hence how many clients they can realistically fit in, there is often a brief contemplative silence, or the raising of an eyebrow. If the answer is that they only need or want, say, five clients a year, then my next challenge is to ask them, by name or possibly by position, who precisely they want those individuals to be. Given 'six degrees of separation', if the optimal mix is, say, four CEOs in the pharmaceutical sector, two of whom they already know + one rising star in a charity where they would offer their time pro bono, the marketing planning is already done, and they just need to pick up the phone. They may or may not win coaching contracts with their exact initial targets, but the opportunity cost of their time is so great, and the likelihood of a deluge of unwanted interest so high if they went public, that they must proceed discreetly, like a headhunter.

Options for building a coaching business: the detailed checklist

OK, lace up your boots tightly, we're about to plunge into the densest part of the forest!

According to PSF marketing expert Kevin Wheeler (kevin.wheeler@wheelrassociates.co.uk), there are *seven core components* in successful services marketing:

1 Understanding the market

2 Marketing planning

3 Managing existing clients

4 Winning new business

5 Building the brand

6 Internal marketing

7 Measuring results

The Marketing Checklist (see box) takes you through each of these, with specific regard to building a business coaching practice. Some of the points are briefly elaborated, but for more in-depth coverage there is a list of references at the end of the chapter.

Marketing Checklist

1. Understanding the market

'Time spent in reconnaissance is never wasted'

Checklist

■ How are you going to keep in touch with what's happening in the coaching market?   ☐

One simple step is to subscribe to the magazine *Coaching at Work* (see www.coaching-at-work.com). Each issue has an astonishing amount of information on who's doing what, what's new and increasingly global coverage.

■ And in the sector(s) you'd like to work: the web, subscribing to their journals, **asking!**   ☐

■ And in possible clients: the above sources plus their websites, annual reports, their in-house/staff journals (get on the mailing list?), **asking**!   ☐

■ Who are your competitors? Keep an eye out at conferences; track their websites.   ☐

2. Marketing Planning

2.1 Where are you going?

Those who are energised by proper planning will want:

■ a **plan** pulling together the following: ☐

– a clear *life mission*. Where does work fit in? What are other priorities? (This doesn't normally feature in business planning, but it is often what prompted the move to freelance.)

– a clear **business mission**. For example, Praesta's is to offer globally 'executive coaching at its best'; CAPP's is to be 'the world leader in strengths development and building strengths-based organisations'

– clear **business goals**: the **BIHAG** (Big Hairy Audacious Goal)[3]; timed objectives: the 200-year, five-year, three-year, one-year goals as appropriate (or long, medium, short-term, however you define them): and goals that are **SMART** – you know about good goal-setting! What are your success measures and milestones along the way?

■ or, **the non-planners' plan:**   ☐

A less apparently business-like approach, but one which may sit better with some people and hence be more likely to work, is to have clear 'lines in the sand'/principles/articulated values – whichever phrase or concept appeals, it's helpful to have *something* as your anchor. For some with families to support, the crucial thing is paying the bills. (How much, precisely, do you need to cover?) For others moving to a portfolio career is about getting back some work–life balance, or finally adding in service to the community or a cause (which particularly?), or having fun (how exactly?), It helps to have that clearly articulated so it doesn't get lost in the rush.

2.2 Who do you want to see?

▨ Which target industry/sector(s)/organisations?

☐

To identify your optimal target sectors/clients, a quote from Aristotle might help:

'where the needs of the world, and your own passions, meet, therein lies your vocation'[4]

So who has a need for coaching, and within those possibilities, which sectors/clients/types of issues do you find most fascinating? Remember intrinsic motivation (Chapter 10) is the most powerful – who do you *really* want to work with?

▨ Exactly which person? (who buys, who takes the decision?)

☐

▨ What problem/need do they have that you are going to meet?

☐

Many people say 'but what I/we do is relevant to everyone'. Yes, but I talk about the 'funnel' below: you have to offer something quite precise to get in the door. Plus if you look unfocused and/or piteously grateful for anything, you'll attract the wrong sorts of clients. If by contrast you set out to get sales meetings with, say, health and safety managers in the transportation industry, a) you may find them, or someone similarly relevant, and b) you'll look focused and impressive, so paradoxically will be attractive to others as well.

▨ Then cut it in half: everything takes longer than you think, other things will crop up: if you tackled only half what you originally planned, which are most crucial/rewarding?

☐

2.3 What do you want to say?

▨ What is your '**elevator pitch**', i.e. preprepared single-phrase answers to two questions:

☐

a) 'what do you do?' and

b) 'what could you do for my company?'

Get a friend to be coach/devil's advocate, asking simple and/or irritating questions until this is crystal clear. Polish and refine and practise it, so you can blurt it out whenever the unexpected opportunity arises.

2.4 What kit do you need?

▨ **Business name**

☐

– a tip: register your web domain name *before* you register your company name: a scam allegedly pounces on new company registrations, registering their web addresses, then asks inflated fees for them.

– logo/design, for business card; stationery, web concept, etc.

▨ **Website** even if just a one-page site giving your contact details so people can find you.

☐

▨ **Bios**: for the website, and to send, for example to an HR contact so they can put you forward to a possible coachee. Useful to have both short (50-ish words) and long (400 words). Might need a friend/coach to dig out the facts you're overly modest about. See www.peerprofessionals.co.uk;

☐

www.meylercoaching.co.uk; www.alliancecoaching.co.uk; www.praesta.com
for examples.

■ Clear, concise **information**: what benefits you offer/problems you solve, why
you're different (i.e. *not* 'what we do'. Think client benefit rather than coach
output!). May include individual pages for descriptions of each product/serv-
ice if needed: press clippings; published articles; case studies; client list (with
their permission), and/or testimonials. (You might think you have no clients to
testify at the outset – but what about those you practised with while training,
pro bono coaching … etc.?)

2.5 Some hard questions

■ What format are you going to work in: company/partnership/sole trader/LLP?

■ If working with others, whether you're a partnership, company or whatever, a
partnership/shareholder agreement is essential, to minimise anguish later.

■ In your planning, have you ensured someone will do all these tasks:

– sales: calls/proposals, etc.

– delivering the work

– managing others

– accounting/bookkeeping

– administration

– checking legalities/compliance: contracts, data protection, health and
safety. etc.?

I.e. how are you going to balance doing the work, keep marketing and running the business? Play to strengths, outsource/trade the rest.

■ **Aptitude**: if the above is beginning to sound all a bit much, it may be a good
time to ask,

– sell, sell and continue to sell – is that you, or can you learn, or find someone
to do it for you?

– are you prepared to flex occasionally for your business, e.g. gritting teeth
and rearranging a holiday?

– psychometric/business readiness testing: if you haven't yet done Tristart
(see Chapter. 7), now you have a prototype plan to test yourself on, it might
be a very good idea.

■ **When won't you coach?**

As we discussed in Chapter 1, there are organisations, and there are people,
where coaching is not the answer. When should you not coach, and when
is coaching not the answer for them? Clearly, when you don't know what
you're doing; coaches in training work under the close scrutiny of experienced people and with carefully selected practice clients. But assuming you
are trained and qualified, there are still times to be wary:

– when you are affected by serious issues in your personal life, such as a
close bereavement, which prevent you from thinking clearly.

– when you know someone else is better qualified to do the work proposed
– not when you *think* this, that might just be natural diffidence, but when
you *know* that another coach has a specialist ability (such as a shared first
language with the client) that you don't have. Refer them on.

3. Managing existing clients

▨ It's allegedly seven times easier to get more business from *existing* clients. And because they know you, they will also entrust you with the new, innovative work which could build your reputation. ☐

▨ So your *first port of call* should be people you have already coached even if just practice coachees from your coach training. If they/their organisations don't need more coaching, can they introduce you to someone who might? ☐

▨ This is important: people often leap straight to seeking out new business, but the research is clear that the most money is to be made, and the most productive work done, with existing clients. Business coaches have an advantage here as their connections are with organisations not just individuals. Within an already-client firm, can you branch out to work with another division, or office, or level of management? ☐

▨ For an entire book on just this topic, see *Managing Key Clients*, by the PACE Partnership team.[5] ☐

4. Winning new business

First, wise guidance from guru David Maister:

> '... [professional services] marketing must be a seduction, not an assault. It must not scream 'hire me!' but must gently suggest 'Here is some concrete evidence as to why you may want to get to know me better.' Marketing is truly about *attracting* clients – doing something that causes them to want to take the next step... Since all clients are skeptical, they need to be given a good reason to [invite you in].'[6]

Precisely which methods you use will depend on your background, experience, sector, cultural context, etc., but the options to consider include:

4.1 Networking

Research shows 80% of new professional services business comes this way.[7] The research doesn't add there's a lot of chance involved (though there is!) but to give Lady Luck a nudge along:

▨ List everyone you know – the objective is 200 names. ☐

You may or may not go on to contact many – but even if you write them down and never use them, it has brought the names into your conscious awareness.

▨ Look at your target segments/people and review the '200' list – who's on-target or may know someone who is? From this prepare a more focused target list. ☐

▨ If appropriate, send out to the focused list an initial communication advising you are 'in business' (using key message(s) as above). ☐

▨ Or if there's a budget, a launch party/event. ☐

▨ Or in manageable groups (3–5 a week?) write an initial letter/email with brief background and saying you're going to telephone, then call a week later to request a meeting. (No wails of 'what will I *say*?'! That's why you've defined your target sectors, and your key message, and researched your individual client, all as above – you know something about what their problems are and how you might help. Talk a little along those lines.) At the meetings, ask questions, listen. They should be talking at least 60% of the time. Use your coaching skills! ☐

■ Use 'six degrees of separation', the theory that because we know A, and A knows B, we are all no more than six degrees of separation from anyone on the planet. I find in my own world of financial/professional services in the City of London, it's actually often only two degrees.

■ Use serendipity – as you move around in life, just mention that you do coaching … you'll be surprised.

4.2 Promotion

There are only two basic options: your warm body appearing at **target client** industry conferences, workshops, etc. (or at live functions you run) or your words/ideas appearing in print. *Not,* to be clear, in your professional field but in your prospective *clients'* media. (Advertising, appearing in directories, etc. just doesn't work. Would *you* get a coach, or lawyer, etc. by answering an ad in the paper? Only as a last resort (and who needs *those* clients!). You'd use word of mouth, and so are your potential clients, out there, right now.)

■ **In person:**

– find out the major *target industry* conferences and attend – preferably as a speaker/running workshops, etc. (3–12 months lead time). At the Dog Biscuit Manufacturers' Annual Convention you'll be the only one talking about something really different (coaching) so could make quite an impact.

– find the smaller-scale local *target industry* network events and attend/speak.

– run events: breakfast briefings, etc. (Having done your research and knowing what clients/potential clients want to hear about right now, of course!)

■ **In print:**

– identify the target industry journals, contact the editors and offer a story on the problem(s) you know from your research their readers (your potential clients) are facing. References to your solutions (and contact details!) should be low-key – they'll get the point and they can find you on the web. Industry journals are much easier to get into than major national newspapers and journals: the editor of *Taxidermists' Weekly* may even be mildly desperate for copy.

– local press ditto, if appropriate.

– or use specialist professional PR help, but pay per project until you're satisfied with their performance. (Avoid retainers.)

– coaching gives us a real advantage here, as a carefully targeted article could go anywhere. For example, the building trade press may be pestered by PR people promoting a new type of steel beam; but an article on what coaching has done for some firms in the sector could be fresh and of interest.

5. Building the brand

■ Again, getting a coach or friend to dig out of you the essence of your brand is a useful beginning: what do you want to be known for? If someone were to describe the essence of your business, what words do you want them to use?

■ Brand also emerges over time, arising from how you actually go about what you do: one becomes well known for crisp reliable client responsiveness,

Checklist

another for being able to bring out creative, innovative solutions. Build on that truth.

Checklist

6. Internal marketing

▨ In a large organisation, it's hard work to get everyone 'singing from the same hymn sheet'; in smaller groups starting out, you may think there isn't any need – but are you *SURE* everyone who knows you has the facts about what you offer exactly right, and also knows precisely how you want the 'spin' to be?

☐

7. Review, measurement of results and quality control

▨ What process will you have to check with clients how they regard your service?

☐

▨ On measuring results, the basic coaching tool of goal-setting is extremely useful here: you more than most will have established a clear baseline from which to measure, and SMART measures of success to check against at the conclusion.

☐

4. Will

Still there?! Told you it was a jungle, thank goodness you had that hat!

But you've made it through the densest part of the jungle, congratulations. Now we're out in a clearing, and having considered many of the possible options, there is space to consider what you will do.

Resource books

It may be that having battered your way through all of the above, you decide there's a lot more to this than meets the eye. You might – absolutely rightly in my view – have decided to delve into it more carefully and find out more than this single chapter can provide. If so, some readable and highly relevant books I would encourage you to consider include:

▨ For UK/European readers, Jenny Rogers' excellent *Developing a Coaching Business*: comprehensive, humane, sensible and far-ranging.[8]

▨ For US readers, Lew Stern's equally indispensable *Executive Coaching: Building and Managing Your Professional Practice*.[9]

Each is written for the particular nuance and practice of their respective markets, but if you have a little extra time, trawl both: they're full of useful content.

▨ For a refresher on professional services marketing – i.e. where the 'product' one is selling is intangible (as opposed to, say, biscuits) – see Harry Beckwith's *Selling the Invisible*.[10] One key point from it is what I call the 'funnel': of course you *could* do most types of coaching, but prospective clients don't buy something vague, they buy to meet a specific immediate requirement. You need to narrow down your offer to get through that buying funnel. Once inside, you will probably get the chance to broaden out again – 'Steve, you were really helpful with Mary Jones, do you think you could take on John Smith?' – but to get through the funnel, you need to identify, and be the solution for, a real, pressing need they have right now.

A coach!

You could doubtless see this coming! Being coached for a session or two might be all it needs to reconnect you with what you do actually know – and also to dig out your 'elevator pitch' and your initial thoughts on, for example, the market sector(s) you wish to target, how you will be differentiated, and so on. Could you perhaps swap coaching sessions on this with a friend or colleague, someone else from your training course for example?

Harking back to Chapter 6 and the PERFECT model, when thinking about your plan you may also want to think about the following:

- Energy: how are you going to preserve yours?
    - aerobic fitness?
    - relaxation/stress management technique?
    - Mindfulness training, meditation, regular time playing with the kids, cycling, gardening?

Growing a business can be exhausting, and you want to be not just coping, but flourishing.

- Intellectual freshness and edge
    - are your professional memberships up to date?
    - training/retraining and keeping a record thereof
    - Supervision, again
    - conferences/seminars/workshops (*your* profession this time!)
    - reading
    - writing
    - fun

And remembering Chapter 8, and the crucial importance of support from your context, and avoiding the FAE, the fallacy that you are doing this all on your own:

■ Support: what support mechanisms have you put in place?
  – professional Supervision
  – shoulder to cry on, to help deal with the inevitable knockbacks
  – collegial support – like-minded souls, colleagues, to bounce ideas around, improve the quality of your work, have a fresh eye to look over key documents
  – mentor – business, your profession, both …
  – and some of the other ideas from earlier chapters: a book club, alumni associations, professional groups, networking communities?

The *very* best of luck! I do hope that in your personal jungle, the vines are just for swinging from, and the lions turn out to be Aslan.

The end

I'm afraid we've come to the end of the book. Doing endings well is a key coaching skill, and I'm absolutely *hopeless* at it. I prefer not to have endings at all. Coaching client relationships I do demurely bring to a close when the business need dictates, but in this book we have been in a much bigger conversation, and one that, as you can see, I find utterly gripping: opening up the possibility of becoming a business coach, and once I'm in *that* conversation with people, I don't want to let go! So if you have comments on how this book could be made better, reactions, observations, debate, dialogue, discussion, do please email me at anne@meylercampbell.com.

In the meantime, may I wish you every success, and profound fulfilment, in whatever part of this wonderful new field you want to make your own.

Further reading

Beckwith, H. (1997) *Selling the Invisible*, New York: Warner Books. Great for stressing the need to be very focused in your offer.

Lewin, M. D. (1995) *The Overnight Consultant*, New York: John Wiley and Sons. Good on all aspects of starting up on your own, very practical.

Maister, D. (1993) *Managing the Professional Service Firm*, New York: The Free Press. Especially the middle section on marketing.

McCormack, M. H. (1996) *Mark H McCormack on Selling*, London: Arrow Business Books.

Rogers, J. (2006) *Developing a Coaching Business*, Maidenhead: Open University Press. Indispensable.

Stern, L. S. (2008) *Executive Coaching: Building and Managing Your Professional Practice*, Hoboken, NJ: John Wiley & Sons Inc.

Williams, S. (2010; but issued annually) *The Financial Times Guide to Business Start Up 2011* Harlow: FT Prentice Hall. Comprehensive and accessible.

Author's acknowledgements

This book have would never been completed without the assistance of McVitie's Digestive biscuits and the Pret à Manger on the corner of Wimpole and Wigmore Streets, London.

And some *wonderful* people.

For Heidi, who first believed – I have waited over ten years to write that phrase! Heidi Adcock coached me long ago, saw the possibility of my writing a book way before I did, and has steadfastly believed I could, ever since. Thank you Heidi, and here it is at last.

The book owes its more immediate existence to that glorious thing, the 'Old Girls' Network': Professor Carol Kauffman several times picked my small piece on executive coaching up off the cutting room floor and ensured it saw the light of day in the January 2009 *Harvard Business Review*, where the editor of my dreams, Liz Gooster, spotted it and contacted me to propose the book. (Promptly disappearing to the Amazon and Antarctica for six months, as one does!) Thank you Carol, for this and so many other blessings, and thank you Liz, I am *so* glad you survived the piranhas and icebergs and came back to egg me on! Most grateful thanks to Helen Savill; you are an editorial wizard.

This book is an upwelling of the fun, the inspiration and the sheer volume of learning brimming over in the Faculty of the Meyler Campbell Business Coach Programme. Daniel Burke, Charles Glass, Sam Humphrey, Henry Marsden, Ann Orton, Alice Perkins, Anna Phillips and Jon Stokes are in my view, and that of many others, among the very best in the world at what they do, and I would like to keep playing with you all, please!

All errors and omissions are mine, but if the book makes any sense at all it is thanks to the tireless contributions of its many 'Book Friends', official and unofficial. First up was Ori Wiener, who practically had to drive a bulldozer through the first rough chapters, but gave the feedback to me so kindly, that it still felt inspiring: thank you Ori! He paved the way for the equally generous, constructively critical yet always kind and encouraging Andrea Adams, Claire Andrews, Geoff Bird, Colleen Boselli; Laurence

Bridot; Catherine Chapman and the team at OPP; Michelle Cummins, Karen Donley, Alison Gill and the team at Getfeedback, Julia Hayhoe, Mary Fenwick, Sarah Fenwick (no relation, but both adventurous), Charles Glass and the team at the Professional Career Partnership; Robin Hindle-Fisher, Adrian Furnham, Anita Hoffman, Sam Humphrey, Felicia Huppert, Jana Jeruma-Grinberga, Richard Jolly, Alex Linley, Karen Lombardo, Lis Long, Sarah Martin, Stephen Mayson, Sarah Mellor, Anne Miller, Liz Mullins, Stephen Newton, Billy Norris, Ann Orton, Alice Perkins, Anna Phillips, Vega Roberts, Fiona Robertson, Julian Roskill, Ruth Sack and The Alliance, Caroline Shore, Nigel Spencer, John Stopford, Jayne Styles, Penny Terndrup, Dick Tyler, Luisa Weinzierl, Ali Willocks, Sally Woodward, and Linda Woolston. Daniel Burke nobly read the entire draft, and gave the feedback with both the acuity, but also the sensitivity and kindness, that all who know him love.

This is a book about business coaching. Without wanting to get too Oscar-speechish about one's entire life, I hope I might therefore be allowed also to thank those most important people, Myles Downey and Jane Meyler, who taught me to coach. I still remember with great clarity the day Jane, observing me stumbling around in a practice coaching session, asked quietly but with her usual laser accuracy, 'Are you listening to respond, or listening to understand?' In that moment, it all suddenly tumbled into place in my brain, and I became a coach.

Many years ago when I was exploring the field, Terry Bates generously gave thoughtful time to a stranger, and advised me to study psychology in order to give my coaching deep roots. The joy that advice has given me I trust shines through the book; that's thanks to you, Terry.

My profound thanks too to the three who got Meyler Campbell off the ground, and shepherded it with such dedication through its first decade: Jane again, who designed the first version of the wonderful Business Coach Programme; the warmly supportive and ever astute Jenny Hough, and our magnificent Chairman, Sue Cox, who has been my steadfast rock. (Can a rock have sparkle as well?!) And to Debbie Sherrell and Claire Maidana, who have so ably taken over the reins, with the added burden in the last year of supporting me as I became a 'book hermit'. The Meyler Campbell office and the community it supports are a very happy ship, and thanks to Claire and Debbie's great efficiency, warmth and kindness, the organisation stayed in great shape while I became increasingly absorbed in The Book.

Everyone in the Meyler Campbell community, that extraordinary group of dazzling, generous and mutually supportive people, has been amusedly tolerant of me this year, and I am most grateful – my heartfelt thanks to you all. In the book I have only written down what we have been saying to each other all these years, and I look forward more than I can say to seeing you all again now the book is done.

This book is dedicated to my parents, and to my husband. But despite having written hundreds of pages, when it comes to articulating what I feel for them, I can't find words. Therefore may this book end, as it began, thanking my Alpha and my Omega:

for my parents,
and
for Daniel.

References and further reading

Chapter 1
1 *The Economist*, 15 November 2003, p. 61.
2 See www.meylercampbell.com; www.sherpacoaching.com; 'What can coaches do for you?', *Harvard Business Review*, January 2009 (Reprint No. R0901H), for the full *HBR* research report underpinning the article see www.carolkauffman.com; EFMD 'Corporate Coaching' special supplement to *Global Focus*, Vol 03 Issue 03 2009; www.frank-bresser-consulting.com.
3 In 1980, 6% of American men in their forties had never married, by 2004 it was 16.5%, *New York Times*, 6 August 2006, www.nytimes.com, accessed June 2010.
4 Putnam, R. (2000) *Bowling Alone. The collapse and revival of American community*, New York: Simon & Schuster.
5 Linley, A. (2007) Lecture 10, 'Positive Psychology', Meyler Campbell *Psychology for Coaches* course, London, 28 November. See also Linley, P. A. and Joseph, S. (2004) *Positive Psychology in Practice*, Hoboken, NJ: John Wiley & Sons, Inc.; Linley, A. (2008) *Average to A+: Realising Strengths in Yourself and Others*, Warwick: CAPP Press; and www. cappeu.com.

Chapter 2
1 Goleman, D. (2000) 'Leadership That Gets Results', *Harvard Business Review*, March–April, posted courtesy of Microsoft and available at http://urgenceleadership.lesaffaires.com/attachments/743_leadership-that-gets-results_Goleman_Daniel.pdf. I wouldn't myself conflate coaching and 'teaching', but his general point holds.
2 Babiak, P. and Hare, R. D. (2006) *Snakes in Suits*, New York: Regan Books/HarperCollins.
3 Ciampa, D. (2005)' Almost Ready – How Leaders Move Up', *Harvard Business Review*, January.
4 Oswald, W. (2002) 'Are you happy at work? Job satisfaction and work–life balance in the US and Europe'. Available at www2.warwick.ac.uk/fac/soc/economics/staff/academic/oswald/finalnywarwickwbseventpapernov2002.pdf, accessed June 2010.

Chapter 3

1   Furnham, A. (2003) *The Incompetent Manager*, London: Whurr. Very useful book.

Chapter 4

1   Ibarra, H. (2004) *Working Identity: Unconventional strategies for reinventing your career*, Boston, MA: Harvard Business School Press.

2   Rogers, J. (2009) *Coaching Skills: A handbook*, 2nd edn, Maidenhead: Open University Press/McGraw-Hill Education, p. 2.

3   Whitmore, J. (1996) *Coaching for Performance*, 2nd edn, London: Nicholas Brealey Publishing.

4   Doidge, N. (2007) *The Brain That Changes Itself*, New York: Penguin.

5   Myers, D. G. (2010) *Psychology*, 9th edn, New York: Worth Publishers.

6   Rogers, *op. cit.*, p. 2.

7   Gladwell, M. (2008) Outliers, London: Allen Lane; Seligman, M. E. P. (2003) *Authentic Happiness*, London: Nicholas Brealey Publishing; Seligman, M. E. P. (1998) *Learned Optimism*, New York: Pocket Books.

8   www.meylercampbell.com/research.

Chapter 5

1   Hardingham, A. (2004) *The Coach's Coach*, London: Chartered Institute of Personnel Development.

2   Downey, M. (2003) *Effective Coaching*, London: Texere.

3   Frankl, V. (1946/1984) *Man's Search for Meaning*, New York: Simon & Schuster.

4   Whitmore, *op. cit.*

5   Kline, N. (1999) *Time to Think*, London: Ward Lock/Cassell. For details on Time to Think training, see www.timetothink.com.

6   Gallwey T. (1975) *The Inner Game of Tennis*, London: Jonathan Cape.

7   Doidge, N. (2007) *The Brain That Changes Itself*, USA: Viking Penguin, p. 68.

8   Doidge, *op. cit.*

Chapter 6

1   Jenkins, S. (2009) 'The Impact of the Inner Game and Sir John Whitmore on Coaching', plus 11 subsequent commentaries', in Jenkins, S. (ed.) *Annual Review of High Performance Coaching and Consulting 2009*, Brentwood: Multiscience Publishing Co. Ltd, pp. 1–72.

2   Brock, V. (2009) 'The Impact of the Inner Game and Sir John
    Whitmore on Coaching: a Commentary', in Jenkins, S., *op. cit.*, p. 57.

3   Jenkins, S., *op. cit.*, pp. 1–72.

4   Jenkins, S. *op. cit.*, p. 12.

5   Jenkins, S., *op. cit.*, p. 13.

6   Gallwey, W. T. (1975) *The Inner Game of Tennis*, London: Jonathan
    Cape Ltd.

7   Hardingham, A. (2004) *The Coach's Coach*, London: CIPD.

8   Jones, G. and Spooner, K. (2006) 'Coaching High Achievers', *Consulting
    Psychology Journal*, Vol 58, No 1, Winter, pp. 40–50.

9   Jones, G., *op. cit.*, p. 45.

10 Lloyd, P. J. and Foster, S. L. (2006) 'Creating Healthy, High-
    performance Workplaces: Strategies from Health and Sports
    Psychology', *Consulting Psychology Journal*, Vol 58, No 1, Winter,
    pp. 23–39.

11 Peltier, B. (2001) *The Psychology of Executive Coaching*, Hove:
    Brunner-Routledge.

12 Personal communication, email to author, 28 July 2010.

13 Prochaska, J. O., Norcross, J. C., DiClemente, C. C. (2006) *Changing for
    Good*, New York: Collins.

14 Ibarra, H. (2004) *Working Identity*, Boston, MA: Harvard Business
    School Press. A good book for giving to clients.

15 Seligman, M. (2003) *Authentic Happiness,* London: Nicholas Brealey
    Publishing; Seligman, M. (1998) *Learned Optimism*, New York: Pocket
    Books/Simon & Schuster.

16 Kauffman, C. (in press) 'The Last Word: How to move from good
    to great coaching by drawing on the full range of what you know'
    (Editorial), *Coaching: an International Journal of Theory Research and
    Practice*.

17 Stober, D. R. and Grant, A. M. (eds.) (2006) *Evidence-Based Coaching
    Handbook*, Hoboken, NJ: John Wiley & Sons Inc.

18 Peltier, B., *op. cit.*

19 Knight, S. (2002) *NLP at Work*, London: Nicholas Brealey.

Chapter 7
1   Luft, J. (1970) *Group Processes: An Introduction to Group Dynamics*, Palo
    Alto, CA: National Press Books.

2   Rogers, J. (2004) *Coaching Skills: A Handbook*, Maidenhead: Open University Press, pp. 102–114.

3   Jung, C.G. (1921/1999) *Psychological Types,* London: Routledge and Kegan Paul.

4   Closing address to Meyler Campbell Psychology for Coaches course, London, 2007.

5   Peterson, C. and Seligman, M. (2004) *Character Strengths and Virtues: A Handbook and Classification*, Oxford: Oxford University Press; Gallup instruments see Buckingham, M. and Clifton, D. (2002) *Now Discover your Strengths,* London: Simon & Schuster; Rath, T. (2007) *StrengthsFinder 2.0*, New York: Gallup Press; Rath T. and Conchie, B. (2009) *Strengths-Based Leadership*, New York: Gallup Press; and Realise2 see Linley, P. A. (2008) *Average to A+: Realising Strengths in Yourself and Others*, Coventry: CAPP Press; Linley, P. A. Willars, J. and Biswas-Diener, R. (2010) *The Strengths Book*, Coventry: CAPP Press.

6   Keil, F., Rimmer, E., Williams, K. and Doyle, M. (1996) 'Coaching at the Top', *Consulting Psychology Journal*, Vol. 48, No 2, Spring, pp. 61–66.

Chapter 8

1   For more on this, one of the greatest experiments in psychology, see Myers, D. G. (2010) *Psychology*, New York: Worth Publishers, pp. 683ff.

2   *The Heist*, UK Channel 4, 2006.

3   Kline, N. (1999) *Time to Think: Listening to Ignite the Human Mind*, London: Ward Lock/Cassell, pp. 102ff; *More Time To Think: A way of Being in the World*, Pool-in-Wharfedale: Fisher King.

4   Katzenbach, J. R. and Smith, D. K. (1998) *The Wisdom of Teams*, London: McGraw-Hill International.

5   Judgement and decision-making', seminar London Guildhall University, June 2003; for more information see Myers, *op. cit.*, pp. 374–5, 520–4, and passim, and for the original, try Kahneman, D. and Tversky, A. (2000) *Choices, Values and Frames*, Cambridge: Cambridge University Press.

6   Carlyle, T. (1849) *Oxford Dictionary of Quotations*, 3rd edn, Oxford: Guild Publishing/Oxford University Press, p. 131.

7   For more on these fascinating topics, see Adrian Furnham's *The Psychology of Behaviour in Organisations*, (1998) London: Psychology Press, Chapter 10 on 'Group Dynamics' and Chapter 11 for human irrationality in decision-making/Groupthink.

8   Myers, D. G., *op. cit.*

Chapter 9

1   Professor Felicia Huppert, Director, Well-being Institute, University of Cambridge, in *Meyer Campbell Annual Lecture 2009*, for report see www.meylercampbell.com/programmes/lecture/2009.

2   Ibarra, H. (2004) *Working Identity*, Boston, MA: Harvard Business School Press.

3   Patrick Raggett, private conversation, 2007.

4   Dr Aubrey de Grey, University of Cambridge, interviewed on the BBC Four programme *It's only a Theory* (7 October 2009).

5   www.statistics.gov.uk/CCI/nugget.asp?id=168.

6   AXA quoted in the *Financial Times*, (23 May 2009).

7   UK Pensions Commission (2004) First report: pensions: *Challenges & Choices* (commonly known as the Turner Report).

8   *The Guardian*, 18 January 2010, Government abandons key proposals in Milburn report on social responsibility.

9   Bolles, R. (2010) *What Colour is Your Parachute?* New York: Ten Speed Press.

10 Ibarra, H., *op, cit.*

11 Reed, J. (2010) *Get Up To Speed with Online Marketing: How to use websites, blogs, social networking and much more*, Harlow: Pearson.

12 Kauffman, C. (2010) 'The Last Word: How to move from good to great coaching by drawing on the full range of what you know' (Editorial) *Coaching: an International Journal of Theory Research and Practice.* 3 (2); pp 87–98.

13 Reed, J., *op. cit.*

Chapter 10

1   Furnham, A. (2001) *The Psychology of Behaviour at Work*, Hove: Psychology Press/Taylor and Francis, Chapter 6, for a thorough description of the academic research on motivation, including each of these key areas.

2   Ryan, R. M. and Deci, E. L. (2000) 'Self-determination Theory and the Facilitation of Intrinsic Motivation, Social Development, and Well-being', *American Psychologist*, Special Issue on Happiness, Excellence, and Optimal Human Functioning, Vol 55, No 1, January.

3   Burke, D. T. and Linley, P.A. (2007) 'Enhancing Goal Self-concordance Through Coaching', *International Coaching Psychology Review*, British Psychological Society Special Interest Group in Coaching Psychology

(BPS/SGCP)/Australian Psychological Society Interest Group in Coaching Psychology, Vol 2, No 1, March, pp. 62–9.

4 Prochaska, J. O., Norcross, J. C. and DiClemente, C. C. (2006) *Changing for Good*, New York: Collins.

Chapter 11

1 Summerson, J. (1993) *Architecture in Britain*, 1530–1830, 9th edn, London: Yale University Press, p. 342.

2 *Coaching* is published in association the Association for Coaching (AC) and is free to AC members, for non-member subscriptions see www.tandf.co.uk/journals; *ICPR* is published jointly by the Australian Psychological Society and British Psychological Society, issued free to coaching sub-groups of both societies, for non-member subscriptions, see www.bps.org.uk; the *ARHPCC*, editor Simon Jenkins of Leeds University, UK, for subscriptions see www.multi-science.co.uk/arhpcc. htm; the *Consulting Psychology Journal* published by Division 13 of the APA, to subscribe see www.apa.org/pubs/journals/cpb.

3 Kauffman, C. and Scoular, A. (2004) 'Towards a Positive Psychology of Executive Coaching', in Linley, P. A. and Joseph, S. (eds.) *Positive Psychology in Practice*, Hoboken, NJ: Wiley.

4 Grant, A., Dr (2001) 'Towards a Psychology of Coaching', presentation to Oxford School of Coaching and Mentoring Conference.

5 Grant, A. M. (2006) 'A Bibliography from the Scholarly Business Literature', in Stober, D. R. and Grant, A. M., *Evidence-Based Coaching Handbook*, Hoboken NJ: John Wiley & Sons.

6 Olivero, D., Bane, K. D. and Kopelman, R. E. (1997) 'Combining Coaching and Training Improves Productivity', *Public Personnel Management*, Vol 26, Issue 4, Winter, p. 461.

7 Quoted in Grant, 2001, *op. cit.*

8 *Ibid.*

9 Csikszentmihalyi, M. (1990) *Flow: the Psychology of Optimal Experience*, New York: Harper Perennial, p. 4.

10 All references in this and the following paragraph may be found in full in Scoular, A. (2004) 'Executive Coaching: An Application of Positive Psychology?', Unpublished MSc Dissertation, London Guildhall University.

11 Grant, A. G. (2006) 'An Integrative Goal-focused Approach to Executive Coaching', in Stober, D. and Grant, A.G. (eds.) *Evidence-based Coaching*, Hoboken, NJ: John Wiley & Sons.

12 Kauffman, C. (2006) 'Positive Psychology: the science at the heart of coaching', in Stober, D. and Grant, A. G. (eds.) *Evidence-based Coaching*, Hoboken, NJ: John Wiley & Sons.

13 Cameron, K. S., Dutton, J. E. and Quinn, R. E. (eds.) (2003) *Positive Organisational Scholarship*, San Francisco, CA: Berrett-Koehler Publishers Inc.

14 Hubble, M. A. and Miller, S. D. (2004) 'The Client: psychotherapy's missing link for promoting a Positive Psychology', in Linley, A. and Joseph, S., *Positive Psychology in Practice*, Hoboken NJ: John Wiley & Sons.

15 Linley, A. and Joseph, S. (2004) *Positive Psychology in Practice*, Hoboken, NJ: John Wiley and Sons.

16 Myles Downey, personal communication

17 Brodbeck, F. *et al* (2000) 'Cultural Variation of Leadership Prototypes across 22 European Countries', *Journal of Occupational and Organisational Psychology*, Vol 73, Part 1, March, British Psychological Society, pp. 1–29.

18 House, R. J. *et al* (2004) *Culture, Leadership and Organisations; the GLOBE study of 62 societies*, Thousand Oaks, CA: Sage Publications.

19 Kauffman, C., (2006) *op. cit.*

20 Kauffman, C., (2006) *op. cit.*, and e-mail from Alex Linley, 29 July 2010.

21 Doidge, N. (2007) *The Brain that Changes Itself*, New York: Viking Penguin/Penguin Group.

22 Ibid, p. 307.

23 Bristed, C. A. (ed.) and Stray, C. (2008) *An American in Victorian Cambridge: Charles Astor Bristed's Five Years in an English University'*, Exeter: University of Exeter Press; Smith, J. and Stray, C. (eds.) (2003) *Cambridge in the 1830s: the Letters of Alexander Chisholm Gooden 1831–1841*, Woodbridge: The Boydell Press/Cambridge University Library.

Chapter 12

1 Williams, S. (2010; but issued annually) *The Financial Times Guide to Business Start-up 2011*, Harlow: FT Prentice Hall.

2   Garnas, L. (1994) *How to Use People to Get What You Want and Still Be a Nice Guy: A guide to networking know-how*, Princeton: Peterson's.

3   Professor Shai Vyakarnam, Centre for Entrepreneurial Learning, Cambridge Judge Business School.

4   Boldt, L. G. (1996) *How to Find the Work You Love*, New York: Arkana/Penguin Group.

5   Walker, K., Denvir, P. and Clifford, D., Dr. (2000) *Managing Key Clients*, privately published by the PACE Partnership, see www.thepacepartners.com/products/books.

6   Maister, D. (1993) *Managing the Professional Services Firm*, New York: The Free Press/Simon & Schuster, p. 122.

7   *Ibid.*

8   Rogers, J. (2006) *Developing a Coaching Business*, Maidenhead: Open University Press.

9   Stern, L. S. (2008) *Executive Coaching: Building and Managing Your Professional Practice*, Hoboken, NJ: John Wiley & Sons Inc.

10 Beckwith, H. (1997) *Selling the Invisible*, New York: Warner Books.

Index